Facundo

LATIN AMERICAN LITERATURE AND CULTURE

General Editor
Roberto González Echevarría
Sterling Professor of Hispanic and Comparative Literatures
Yale University

Facundo

CIVILIZATION AND BARBARISM

The First Complete English Translation

Domingo Faustino Sarmiento

Translated from the Spanish by Kathleen Ross,
with an Introduction by Roberto González Echevarría

UNIVERSITY OF CALIFORNIA PRESS
Berkeley   Los Angeles   London

University of California Press
Berkeley and Los Angeles, California

University of California Press, Ltd.
London, England

© 2003 by the Regents of the University of California

Library of Congress Cataloging-in-Publication Data

Sarmiento, Domingo Faustino, 1811–1888.
  [Facundo. English]
  Facundo : civilization and barbarism : the first complete English
translation / Domingo Faustino Sarmiento ; translated from the Spanish
by Kathleen Ross ; with an introduction by Roberto González Echevarría.
    p.   cm. — (Latin American literature and culture ; 12)
  Includes bibliographical references and index.
  ISBN 0–520-08159-5 (cloth : alk. paper)—ISBN 0–520-23980-6
(pbk. : alk. paper)
    1. Argentina—History—1817–1860.   2. Argentina—Description and
travel.   3. Quiroga, Juan Facundo, 1790–1835.   4. Rosas, Juan Manuel
Jos Domingo Ortiz de, 1793–1877.   I. Ross, Kathleen.   II. Title.
III. Series : Latin American literature and culture (Berkeley, Calif.) ; 12.

  F2846 .S2472 2003
  981'.04—dc21   2003011742

Manufactured in the United States of America

13 12 11 10 09 08 07 06 05 04
10 9 8 7 6 5 4 3 2 1

The paper used in this publication is both acid-free and totally chlorine-
free (TCF). It meets the minimum requirements of ANSI/NISO Z39.48–
1992 (R 1997) (*Permanence of Paper*). ♾

Contents

Facundo: An Introduction

ROBERTO GONZÁLEZ ECHEVARRÍA

Sarmiento's *Facundo,* published in 1845, is the first Latin American classic and the most important book written by a Latin American in any discipline or genre. Fame has granted it the privilege of a one-word title, but the book was originally called, in Sarmiento's idiosyncratic spelling, *Civilización i barbarie: La vida de Juan Facundo Quiroga, i aspecto físico, costumbres, i ábitos de la República Arjentina* (Civilization and barbarism: The life of Juan Facundo Quiroga, and the physical aspect, customs, and practices of the Argentine Republic), and in its first English translation, *Life in the Argentine Republic in the Days of the Tyrants.*[1] For the same reason, tradition bypasses its author's unwieldy names—Domingo Faustino—in favor of his sufficient and resonant surname, Sarmiento. *Facundo* is a work that survives its critics; it seems immune to historical changes, intellectual fashions, and literary movements. It absorbs them into its own discourse and figures. To criticize Sarmiento is easy, even facile, but it is impossible to ignore him. *Facundo* thrives through its stylistic flaws, its cavalier deployment of sources, its errors, and its aura of improvisation. All these contribute to the work's vitality, to the reader's sense that the book is alive, making itself as he or she turns the pages.

---

1. Sarmiento aimed at simplifying Spanish spelling, eliminating the *y*, which represents the same sound as the *i* and has been kept in the language for historical reasons. He did not succeed, but his effort reveals his pedagogical vocation and his willingness to renovate language and tradition. Notice that Facundo Quiroga's whole name is Juan Facundo Quiroga. I will refer to him as Facundo Quiroga, which is how he was generally known, and to the book as *Facundo.*

Among other reasons, *Facundo* is still read because in it Sarmiento created a voice for the modern Latin American author, which is also why Latin American authors struggle with its legacy, rewriting *Facundo* in their works even as they try to untangle themselves from its discourse.

An inventory of *Facundo*'s contributions to Latin American thought and literature is impressive indeed.[2] In proposing the dialectic between civilization and barbarism as the central conflict in Latin American culture it gave shape to a polemic that began in the colonial period and continues to the present day in various guises (the latest being the vapid debate about globalization). In its account of the origins of Juan Manuel de Rosas's tyranny in Argentina, *Facundo* set the bases for the understanding of dictatorship in Latin America and created in the dictator himself one of the most enduring literary figures to emerge from the area. A whole series of "dictator novels," from Miguel Angel Asturias's *El señor presidente* (1946) to Mario Vargas Llosa's *Feast of the Goat* (2000), attests to its continuing vitality. By establishing a determining link between the Argentine landscape and its culture and political development, *Facundo* set the bases for the study of the uniqueness of Latin American culture in terms of its own specific geographical setting. In this regard, *Doña Bárbara* (1929), the classic regionalist novel by the Venezuelan Rómulo Gallegos, can be read as an allegory of *Facundo*. By expressing the grandeur of its landscape and the struggle to represent it, Sarmiento created the voice of the modern Latin American author as a response to an exceptional American reality. The Venezuelan Andrés Bello, the Cuban José María Heredia, and a few others had already provided hints of this, but they were corseted by neoclassical poetics, while Sarmiento, a romantic, wrote, untrammeled by the demands of form, a majestic work that belongs to many genres and to none at the same time—it is essay, biography, autobiography, novel, epic, memoir, confession, political pamphlet, diatribe, scientific treatise, travelogue. But it is mostly Sarmiento's powerful voice, infused by the sublimity of the boundless Pampas, that rings through and true in *Facundo*, a

---

2. By far the best criticism of Sarmiento is contained in the collective volume *Sarmiento: Author of a Nation,* ed. Tulio Halperín Donghi, Iván Jaksić, Gwen Kirkpatrick, and Francine Masiello (Berkeley: University of California Press, 1994). The book covers the entire spectrum of Sarmiento's writings, preceded by an incisive historical précis by Halperín Donghi. More recently, Diana Sorensen Goodrich has provided an intelligent rereading of *Facundo* in the light of current theories on literature and nation-building in her *Facundo and the Construction of Argentine Culture* (Austin: University of Texas Press, 1996).

voice that will be echoed by the major poetic and fictional works by Latin Americans, from Pablo Neruda's *Canto general* (1950) to Gabriel García Márquez's *One Hundred Years of Solitude* (1967). Sarmiento is to Latin American literature what Walt Whitman is to American literature: a voice that in singing about itself sings America's song.

Though a reader of *Facundo* might leave the book thinking that the Pampas comprise all of Argentina, the reality is quite another. Stretching north to south, roughly twenty-three hundred miles and east to west about eight hundred miles at its widest, Argentina covers more than a million square miles.[3] This is an area equivalent to that of the United States east of the Mississippi, with California and one or more midwestern states added—only Brazil is larger in South America. In the south, Cape Horn reaches down to the frigid waters of the Antarctic, and in the north there are subtropical areas at the foot of the Bolivian Andes—the south is cold and the north warm, in what to the reader from the Northern Hemisphere must seem like a world upside down. In between its northern and southern extremes Argentina displays a broad range of climate and terrain: the dry wastelands of Patagonia in the south, the desertlike regions to the west, all the way to the imposing Andes, which separate Argentina from Chile. In the northwest are forests and sugarcane fields that stretch into Bolivia and Paraguay. But the Pampas, 250,000 square miles encircling the capital of Buenos Aires, are indeed the core of the country both materially and in the myths that make up the Argentine nation—*Facundo* contributed to this in no small measure. These immense, fertile plains, rich in pastures that give sustenance to the country's huge cattle population, also produce most of the corn, wheat, and flax.

Its optimistic first explorers named the estuary of the River Plate "Río de la Plata"—river of silver—and the area around it "Argentina," land of silver (from the Latin *argentum*), yet they found neither that metal nor gold in the area. Quick riches, like those yielded by Mexico and Peru, were not available in what became Argentina, so it languished, for most of the colonial period, as a dependency of faraway, tramontane Lima. In fact, the original settlers moved east into the region from Peru and Chile to found the first Argentine cities: Santiago del Estero (1553),

---

3. This elementary sketch of Argentina, intended for the nonspecialized reader, should be supplemented with the work of historians like Halperín Donghi. Facts and statistics—approximations in most cases—are drawn from conventional reference works.

Mendoza (1561), San Juan (1562), Tucumán (1564), and Córdoba (1573). An expedition from inland Asunción founded Buenos Aires in 1580 (the first settlement, in 1536, did not last long). This geopolitical configuration favored the cities in the interior rather than Buenos Aires, which was neglected by the Spanish and left to conduct illegal trade with smugglers. To reach Lima, and from it the rest of the Spanish empire, Buenos Aires goods had to travel west, through the cities of the interior, which levied heavy taxes upon them. It was a long, expensive trek. *Porteños,* or citizens of the port of Buenos Aires, grew to mistrust those in the provinces, and, disconnected from Spain, sought economic progress and cultural inspiration from elsewhere in Europe, mostly England and France. The divide between the interior and the capital, fundamental to Sarmiento's interpretation of Argentine culture, widened as a result.

Because of this fragmentation, Argentina achieved independence in a state of political turbulence, divided against itself. While it was the *porteños* who founded the Republic on May 25, 1810, it was not until July 9, 1816, at the Congress of Tucumán, that the formal break from Spain was declared and the "United Provinces of South America" proclaimed. This was the second misnomer applied to Argentina, for united these provinces certainly were not. Various groups from the interior refused to accept the leadership of Buenos Aires, and *porteños* looked down on the provinces, which seemed backward and out of touch with modern ideas, customs, and fashions. The decades that followed saw the split acquire political shape in the conflict between two parties: the Unitarists, who favored a centralized national government with its seat in Buenos Aires, and the Federalists, who championed the independence of the various provinces or regions. The Unitarists were cultured, European-oriented, and had a vision of the nation as a cohesive political unit derived from the Enlightenment and the founders of U.S. independence. The Federalists, by the very nature of their convictions, were factional even among themselves. They were led by the caudillos, or local bosses, who had emerged during the Wars of Independence from Spain.[4] Originally they were gauchos, whose power and appeal lay in their attachment to the land and to their intimate familiarity with the regions and people they commanded.

---

4. *Caudillo,* from the Latin *capitellum,* the diminutive of *caput,* or "head," means a commander or chief, according to Joan Corominas, *Diccionario crítico etimológico castellano e hispánico* (Madrid: Gredos, 1980), vol. 1, p. 928. *Caudillismo,* or the dictatorship of military leaders like Batista, Somoza, and Castro, is one of the characteristics of Latin American politics and has been extensively studied.

The reader will find in *Facundo* the most compelling description of the gaucho ever written.[5] Suffice it to say here that gauchos were nomadic inhabitants of the Pampas whose culture centered on horsemanship, self-reliance, stoicism, and contentment. The gauchos did not want to be anything else, feeling in fact a mixture of pity and scorn for city folk and their ways. Nature provided plentifully for the gauchos' needs, which were few, and they knew how to defend themselves from its threats—like jaguars and isolation—and from those who would "civilize" them (by conscripting them into the army, for instance). They reveled in their defiant solitude. The limitless plains and fabulously abundant cattle gave them meat and hides to barter or sell, and to make ropes, saddles, and other tools of their trade. Very much like the American cowboy, the gaucho wanted to be left alone. When the Wars of Independence came he fought against the Spanish because he was always spoiling for a fight against any authority, and mostly because he was forcibly conscripted into the army as a vagrant.[6] After independence he followed his regional leaders in the civil wars that followed, against other caudillos and against centralized government. By 1819 the caudillos, with their bands of gauchos, were in control of much of the countryside. Estanislao López ruled in Santa Fe, José Santos Ramírez in Entre Ríos, Martín Güemes in Salta, Bernabé Aráoz in Tucumán, Facundo Quiroga in San Juan and La Rioja, and Rosas in Buenos Aires province. These caudillos were united in their disdain for the city of Buenos Aires and its Unitarists, but were hardly each others' friends. In February 1820, gaucho armies from the provinces of Santa Fe and Entre Ríos overpowered the *porteño* forces, led by José Rondeau, in the Battle of Cepeda. By 1829 the caudillos had installed one of their own in power: Juan Manuel de Rosas, boss of the province of Buenos Aires, became ruler of the whole country. Ironically, he gained power as a Federalist defender of provincial autonomy but was toppled in 1852 because he had forced upon the provinces a centralist rule more unbending than the Unitarists had hoped for. His tyranny, based on a personality cult, absolute fealty displayed in a panoply of icons and symbols to be publicly worshiped,

5. The most compelling and original study of the gaucho in Argentine literature is Josefina Ludmer's *El género gauchesco,* now available in English: *The Gaucho Genre: A Treatise on the Motherland,* trans. Molly Weigel (Durham, N.C.: Duke University Press, 2002). A summary of the book's arguments can be found in "The Gaucho Genre," in *The Cambridge History of Latin American Literature,* ed. Roberto González Echevarría and Enrique Pupo-Walker (Cambridge: Cambridge University Press, 1996), vol. 1, pp. 608–31.

6. Ludmer (in *El género gauchesco*) has brilliantly linked the gaucho's conscription with the appropriation of his "voice" by literature to create a national discourse.

and the merciless persecution of real and perceived dissidents, became the blueprint for Latin American dictatorships, including the whole sorry string of caudillos up to, in the present, Fidel Castro. One of the theories about the murder of Facundo Quiroga in Barranca-Yaco, where he was ambushed and shot, is that Rosas had him killed to eliminate a potential rival. Rosas was a caudillo of caudillos and Sarmiento's foe and foil. In the process, another irony, Sarmiento immortalized him in *Facundo*.

But caudillos and gauchos were by no means the only forces in Argentina. The country's economy, particularly that of Buenos Aires, improved with the ability to export the products of the cattle industry, mostly beef and hides, made possible by developments in preservation and shipping. As Buenos Aires grew it became one of the most important cultural centers in the New World and the most European of Latin American cities. A new generation of writers and intellectuals came to the fore in the 1830s, just as Rosas was assuming power. They rebelled by creating the Salón Literario in 1835 and, two years later, the "Association of May" (a reference to the May 1810 founding of the Republic), both institutions dedicated to overthrowing the dictator. European-educated and sophisticated to a fault, this group included Esteban Echeverría, a romantic poet and fiction writer, who wrote (but did not publish) in his short story "The Slaughterhouse" one of the most stinging indictments of Rosas's regime.[7] José Mármol, another prose writer and poet, published *Amalia* (1851), a widely read novel and a Latin American classic, which was also against Rosas. Other prominent members of the group were Bartolomé Mitre, a historian and a translator of Dante's *Divine Comedy*, who founded *La Nación*, one of the best newspapers in Latin America, which is still being published. Mitre eventually became president of the Republic. A political analyst and jurist, Juan Bautista Alberdi, wrote a pamphlet, *Bases para la organización política de la confederación argentina* (Bases for the political organization of the Argentine Federation), which influenced greatly the Constitution that was drafted in 1853 after the fall of Rosas. An admirer of the United States and England, Alberdi's social program was to foster European immigration to Argentina to people the vast expanses of rich, uninhabited lands. His motto was "gobernar es poblar," to govern is to populate.

Although a provincial from western San Juan province, hence not a

---

7. I included a translation of the story in my *Oxford Book of Latin American Short Stories* (New York: Oxford University Press, 1997), pp. 59–72.

member of this *porteño* elite, Sarmiento belongs to the group because of the affinity of his ideas with theirs as well as his untiring campaigns against Rosas. He too rose to the presidency, succeeding Mitre in 1868. Sarmiento was the best writer of them all and the one who left the most enduring literary works, particularly *Facundo*. Born on February 15, 1811, he was the fifth child and only son of a formerly comfortable family, now in economic decline, that encouraged him to read and educate himself.[8] This he did with unflinching devotion, first as an unruly but brilliant pupil in the Escuela de la Patria, in his native San Juan. This school, started by a Unitarist governor of Buenos Aires, was directed by two brothers, Ignacio Fermín and José Jenaro Rodríguez. Young Domingo Faustino was in the school from its inception in 1816 until its closing, because of political upheavals, in 1825. He was then tutored by his uncle, the priest José de Oro, with whom he learned Latin, Spanish grammar, and read the Bible. In his rich 1850 memoir, *Recuerdos de provincia* (Remembrances of provincial life), Sarmiento recalls fondly this teacher, to whom he owed many things, he said, most relevantly for his authorship of *Facundo* an enduring interest in the country's customs and traditions. Probably because of his haphazard instruction, the education of the young became Sarmiento's most abiding vocation, and for all his accomplishments in literature and politics, he is mostly revered today in Argentina as a model teacher.

His initiation into politics was early and painful. At sixteen, a member of the provincial militia by force, he was jailed for insubordination. He later joined the Unitarist bands fighting against regional boss Facundo Quiroga and was captured and sentenced to house arrest in San Juan. After four months he managed to escape to Chile, his first of several forced sojourns in that country, where even though he was a foreigner he was to have enormous influence. Sarmiento returned to San Juan after two months, when fighting against Facundo Quiroga resumed, but the caudillo again prevailed and Sarmiento returned to Chile with his father and a substantial group of Unitarists. For the next five years he taught reading at an elementary school, was a clerk at a store in Valparaíso, studied English so he could read Sir Walter Scott, was foreman at a mine, and fathered an illegitimate child, Emilia Faustina, in 1832. (His daughter, raised by Sarmiento's mother, provided much solace to him in his declining years.) Upon learning of Facundo Quiroga's

8. I follow, in the main, Allison Williams Bunkley's plodding but useful biography, *The Life of Sarmiento* (Princeton, N.J.: Princeton University Press, 1952).

murder in 1836, Sarmiento returned to his native San Juan, where he founded a school for young ladies, the Colegio de Santa Rosa de América. He also founded a newspaper, *El Zonda,* whose editorials reflected the democratic ideals of the Association of May. The new Federalist governor of the province, not taking kindly to these activities, closed the newspaper and imprisoned Sarmiento in 1840 under the charge of conspiracy. By November 18 of that year, barely surviving a Federalist lynch mob, Sarmiento crossed the Andes back to Chile.

Sarmiento's second exile in Chile was the most productive, and marks the period in which he came into his own as a writer, intellectual, and political figure. He was named editor of *El Mercurio,* in Valparaíso, and in Santiago founded *El Nacional*—both of which were important newspapers. Sarmiento continued his blistering and unrelenting attacks on Rosas, who tried unsuccessfully to get him extradited to Argentina, and wrote *Facundo,* first serialized in local newspapers and then published as a book in 1845. He also published *Travels through Europe, Africa, and America* and wrote *Remembrances of Provincial Life. Travels* was the result of his trips through Spain, France, England, Algiers, and the United States, a journey he undertook to study developments in education. It was also a pretext by his Chilean friends to get Sarmiento out of their hair for a while, since his presence attracted protests from the Argentine government for his persistent tirades against the regime. Full of himself, immoderate in his habits, exuding energy, Sarmiento had not endeared himself to many Chileans, who called him Don Yo ("Mr. Me," or "Mr. Ego"). Having a large head and the neck of a bull and being increasingly corpulent, Sarmiento was a presence to reckon with, so his hosts encouraged his going away. But the journey was indeed an education in itself, which had a lasting impact on Sarmiento. The United States fascinated him because he saw many parallels between it and Argentina (as is evident in *Facundo*)—vast territorial expanses to be populated and turned productive. Sarmiento found a model in Benjamin Franklin, whose autobiography he loved, and wrote incisively about Lincoln.[9] He admired the American school system, particularly as conceived by Horace Mann, the Massachusetts lawyer, poli-

9. In 1866 a *Vida de Abran Lincoln, décimo sesto presidente de los Estados Unidos* was published by Appleton in New York. It consisted of a series of journalistic pieces about Lincoln stitched together and translated into Spanish, with a long introduction by Sarmiento. I am using the second edition, published the same year. Sarmiento transposes the conflicts that brought about the Civil War in the United States to Argentina and its own, to him, similar circumstances and problems.

tician, and educator whom he befriended. Mrs. Mann (née Mary Pea-
body) was to publish in 1868 the first, and until the present one the only,
English translation of *Facundo*. Many of the ideas he learned in the
United States during this trip, and later during his three-year stint as Argentine minister plenipotentiary to Washington, he tried to adapt to his
native country.

In 1848, Sarmiento returned to Chile for his third exile there, which
was to last until 1851, when he heard of Justo José de Urquiza's rebellion against Rosas and hurried to Uruguay to join the insurgents. In the
three years of exile he continued his campaign against the tyrant and
wrote extensively about what he had seen in his travels and about European immigration to South America, which he saw as the solution to
the ills of the new countries. Following Alberdi, Sarmiento did not fail
to put this plan, which became his hobbyhorse, into practice during
his presidency. But that would have to wait, because once the dictator
was toppled and Urquiza assumed power, he slighted Sarmiento, who
returned to Chile to lick his wounds. But he came back in 1855 to edit a
newspaper, to serve as senator in the provincial legislature, and to run
the school system in the provinces with great success. Once Urquiza was
disposed of in 1862 and Mitre assumed the presidency, Sarmiento's star
rose again. He became governor of his native province of San Juan,
where he improved the schools and fought effective campaigns against
the new caudillo, Angel Vicente Peñaloza, "El Chacho." Wary of his rival's triumphs, Mitre sent Sarmiento to Washington in 1865 as minister
to the United States. When he returned to Buenos Aires in 1868, Sarmiento discovered that he had been elected president of Argentina.

Sarmiento's six-year term (1868–74) was marked by reform and progress, albeit some of it controversial. He completed Mitre's campaign to
eliminate the caudillos and won the Paraguayan war. In 1869 he organized and carried out the first census, which yielded the following results: the total population was 1,800,000, with 500,000 in the province
of Buenos Aires and 178,000 in the capital city. Of the total population,
212,000 were born abroad, mostly in Spain and Italy. Sarmiento accepted
the racialist "science" of his time, with its theories about Caucasian superiority and its corollary programs of social engineering. True to these
now discredited but long-held ideas, Sarmiento believed that European
immigration was the key to eradicate what he called barbarism; he was
impressed by the effect of such immigration on the United States and
therefore he systematically promoted it during his presidency. During
his term, 280,000 Europeans came to settle in Argentina.

Sarmiento's years in office coincided with developments in science and industry that he enthusiastically, undeniably successfully, imported to Argentina. He had a decisive impact on communications, increasing telegraph lines, linking Buenos Aires to Europe via a transatlantic cable, and extending railroad construction, thereby making uninhabited regions available for settlement. Agriculture was modernized, an academy of sciences was founded, exploration of the national territory was fostered to discover new resources, and a national observatory was established. Training schools were set up for the army and navy, and a national library commission made books available to public libraries, nearly one hundred of which were founded during Sarmiento's term. Because education continued to be Sarmiento's passion, school-building and teacher-training programs were high on his list of priorities. Educational facilities and school enrollment nearly doubled during his term, reaching figures far ahead of any Latin American country at the time. Sarmiento even brought sixty-three women teachers from the United States, chosen by Mrs. Horace Mann, to set up teachers schools in Argentina.

Nicolás Avellaneda, Sarmiento's youthful, frail, but effective minister of education, followed him in the presidency, having defeated Mitre in contested and divisive elections. Mitre revolted, and then was jailed and nearly executed. The transfer of power was a harbinger of evils that would beset Argentine politics in the future. Sarmiento served as senator during Avellaneda's presidency, was in charge of schools in the province of Buenos Aires, and became editor of *La Nación*. Under Julio Argentino Roca, the next president, he ran the country's schools and continued writing tirelessly. The state published his complete works, fifty-three volumes in all, during the last years of his life. Sarmiento died, at seventy-seven years of age, in 1888.

Few men have had a greater impact on their country's founding, both materially and intellectually. With *Facundo* in particular, Sarmiento had given Argentina a national discourse, a set of ideas and figures through which the country could think itself—a phenomenology of its spirit, as it were. The book is, among many other things, a modern national epic, cast in elevated romantic prose. Sarmiento's invocation of Facundo Quiroga's ghost, whom he asks to help him explain the internal convulsions and secret life of the motherland, is Homeric in its grandeur.

If *Facundo* began as a series of articles against Rosas published in a Chilean newspaper, hence as a political pamphlet, the book's intended form was probably that of a scientific treatise, or at least something like the report of a scientific traveler.[10] This is what determines its outer form: the beginning is a description of the land, which leads up to a description of the people within it, their customs and social organizations, and finally to the main specimen to be analyzed, Facundo Quiroga. From general to specific, from the broader determining factors to the particular result: the tyrant, the analysis of whose life will illuminate Rosas's life and will facilitate his elimination. Science is at the service of politics to change the course of history.

This scientific approach is not just the outer shell of *Facundo*: it is its very core. The scientific travelers to whom Sarmiento pays homage and whose works inform his were more literary in their approach than we are allowed to think from the perspective of contemporary science. Their quest for knowledge took the form of a journey, which in the best examples is reflected in their texts as the mind's movement from concrete observation of phenomena to the formulation of general principles and truth. Scientific method and literary form converge in this material and spiritual pilgrimage, a fusion often expressed in the rhetoric of the sublime. These travelers, Humboldt above all, were romantics, and shared with the poets of their age, especially with Goethe, a love of nature, because of its beauty and because it conceals the secrets of the universe. In *Facundo*—because Sarmiento is observing his native land, not a foreign country as in the case of the European travelers, and is attempting to discover its essence—the process is even more dramatic. Sarmiento is looking for and at himself as he gazes upon Argentina, Rosas, and ultimately upon Facundo Quiroga. As Enrique Anderson Imbert has written eloquently: "Sarmiento's originality lies in that the romantic philosophy of history came to be intimately fused with his feeling that his own life was an historical life. He felt that his self and the motherland were one and the same being, engaged in an historical mission within the unfolding of civilization."[11] This is the book's deep drama, the source of its somber beauty and shocking honesty—it is not a paean to the fatherland, but a probe of its innermost essence, including its most disturbing components.

10. I have expounded upon the relation of travel writing to *Facundo* in my *Myth and Archive: A Theory of Latin American Narrative* (Cambridge: Cambridge University Press, 1990), now available in paperback from Duke University Press (1998). The chapter on Sarmiento has also been reproduced in *Sarmiento: Author of a Nation*.

11. Enrique Anderson Imbert, *Historia de la literatura hispanoamericana* (Mexico: Fondo de Cultura Económica, 1954), vol. 1, p. 228; trans. mine.

Sarmiento's diagnosis is that Argentina is beset by the struggle between civilization and barbarism and that Rosas and his regime incarnate the latter. In other words, barbarism is prevailing. Hence the book's sense of urgency. Civilization for Sarmiento means modern European ideas and practices, and it is based in the cities, particularly Buenos Aires; barbarism, meanwhile, represents the backwardness of the countryside, especially the Pampas. This backwardness is the product of genetic, geographic, and historical factors, not the least of which is the Spanish legacy itself. *Facundo* both gains and loses by applying this dichotomy. Clarity is the first benefit, followed closely by the dramatic effect of the clash of opposing forces, which gives the whole struggle and its heroes an epic cast. It is like a biblical story about the fight between good and evil, with larger-than-life characters such as Facundo Quiroga and Rosas. The dichotomy's main drawback is oversimplification, a positive element as political propaganda but a weakness as intellectual construct. Rosas was not as primitive as Facundo Quiroga, and Facundo Quiroga himself was not an illiterate. In later years Sarmiento came to realize his error, and in *Facundo* there are contradictions that reveal his hesitations and inner doubts.

Fortunately for the book's energy but not for the logic of its principal argument, Sarmiento is more fascinated by barbarism than by civilization; he has a Miltonian passion for evil and its minions. The loving descriptions of the Pampas and its gauchos are among the most enduring pages in *Facundo*. It is a science of the concrete, of the minute, whose emblem perhaps could be two of its protagonists: the *rastreador* or "track finder," and the *baqueano* or "scout." The *rastreador* is capable of following a fugitive's trail no matter how faint and in spite of all the precautions the fugitive takes to erase it. The *baqueano* can tell where he is—even in the dark, when all else fails, by the flavor of the grass. This is savage knowledge at its highest, on a par with civilized man's most sophisticated capabilities. Sarmiento cannot hide his admiration for these rustic types, with their profound wisdom, self-assurance, and stoic curtness. Against the general laws that make up his science, these individuals are original and unique, as is their knowledge of that which is characteristic of their environment. In their description and analysis Sarmiento is displaying an analogous kind of learning, with its own intuitive method. This contradiction is at the heart of *Facundo*, energizing its most compelling literary qualities.

Sarmiento pursues what is original in the Pampas and in Facundo Quiroga, but slips over and over into comparisons with types and even archetypes drawn from the literary tradition, particularly the classics and the Bible. If the gauchos are an origin, mankind reduced to the beginning of time, they are so only because they repeat previous origins. The Pampas are like a blank page, an infinite, unfathomable void at the beginning of time and recorded history; but to be identified as such there has to be, as in a palimpsest, a series of previous beginnings that have been inscribed on it before: Thebes, Mesopotamia, Babylon, and biblical or Homeric stories. Sarmiento struggles with this contradiction in his quest to prove the originality of his subject, but the whole story is cast in an ancient genre, tragedy, where science and literature meet to shape the telling of Facundo's life.

"Life" is precisely the concept that informs Sarmiento's vision of Facundo Quiroga. It is a typically nineteenth-century scientific concept that subtends science and philosophy and is at the core of some of the century's most influential intellectual enterprises. Darwin's *Origin of Species* is based on the "struggle for life," as are, in different terms, philosophical systems like Schopenhauer's and Nietzsche's. Life is the instinct or volition to be, which often depends on the annihilation of others. Sarmiento studies Facundo Quiroga's life, he writes his biography, to search for his "life" in this sense—the spark of his will-to-be in his will-to-power. "Biography" here has the emphasis on *bio,* on the biological, material aspect. Hence the detailed description of Facundo Quiroga's facial and other physical features, which are expressions of his fierceness. What is unique about this life is its excess, which is Facundo Quiroga's tragic flaw. He is endowed with a surfeit of life that leads him inexorably to death—life leads to death, or death itself is lodged in the life instinct, as Freud was to theorize but a few decades later. This contrary force is stronger than Facundo Quiroga's conscious will; it drives him inexorably to meet his death at Barranca-Yaco in spite of the warnings and omens. Barbarism has the grandeur of tragedy, sharing its inevitability, which preempts Sarmiento's program to eradicate it with the aid of civilization. If, as he asserts, there is a gaucho hiding beneath the frock coat of every Argentine, where does that leave Sarmiento himself, if not on the side of the tragic? The life of Facundo Quiroga, both its unrestrained vital thrust and its originality, is also the life of Domingo Faustino Sarmiento. The book is both biography and autobiography, collective and individual analysis.

Life is also the deep design of history in *Facundo*. Like his European models, Sarmiento's conception of the unfolding of history follows a pattern of birth, infancy, maturity, decay, and death, with each period being characterized by the features of an individual's life at that stage. Hence nations have an "infancy." The pattern is repeated everywhere, as biological shapes are repeated from species to species, but at different moments in time: one region is in its infancy (Latin America) while another has reached maturity (Europe). While this analogy seems crude now, it was used and systematized by thinkers as diverse as Hegel, Spengler, and Toynbee, and has not been abandoned totally in political discourse—we still talk about "young" nations. In Latin America it was to have a long history, often with positive connotations, to propose optimistically that Europe was in decay while the New World, by virtue of its newness, was not and therefore could avoid the errors of the Old. This trend, called *mundonovismo,* flourished between the two world wars of the twentieth century. While Sarmiento did not view Argentina's "infancy" in such a hopeful way, it was he who most forcefully and lastingly articulated the metaphor of history as life. In *Facundo* life is tragic, like that of its protagonist, a pattern deeply embedded in the very biological makeup of the human race.

Facundo's literary character is what makes it such an enduring work and the beginning of a trend in Latin American social sciences, particularly in anthropology. Since then, influential figures have straddled literature and their disciplines and produced books that have found a place in the literary canon. In Brazil, for instance, Euclides da Cunha's *Rebellion in the Backlands* (1900), a book that owes much to *Facundo,* began as a sociological study of a religious rebellion in Canudos. The *sertões* in the Portuguese title *(Os Sertões)* is the Brazilian equivalent to the Argentine Pampa. Then there is the work of Gilberto Freyre about the slave-plantation world in the sugar-producing northeast of Brazil, *Casa grande e senzala* (1933), translated as *The Masters and the Slaves,* a literary masterpiece in its own right. In Cuba, Fernando Ortiz, a pioneer in the study of Afro-Cuban culture, essentially an anthropologist, wrote books like *Cuban Counterpoint: Tobacco and Sugar* that are a part of the Latin American literary tradition, as did his disciples Lydia Cabrera and Miguel Barnet. Historian and economist Manuel Moreno Fraginals's *The Sugarmill* is a classic of Cuban literature. In Peru, tragic José María Arguedas alternated between writing literature and writing anthropology. From the literature side, writers like Octavio Paz, in his *Labyrinth of Solitude* (1950), have practiced a kind of poetic anthropology that has its origin in *Facundo,* as did much of the work of Alfonso Reyes and other essayists interested in the topic of national and cultural identities in Mexico and the rest of Latin America.

Literature and the quest for self and collective knowledge have gone hand in hand in Latin America since Sarmiento: books like *Facundo* represent Latin America's form of thought, its poetic philosophy. In Latin America, truth—social, political, metaphysical—is sought through the aesthetic, in novels, essays, and poems—an approach that is evident in novels like Alejo Carpentier's *The Lost Steps* (1953) and in poems such as Pablo Neruda's *Canto general.* The enduring romantic legacy in Latin American culture fosters this approach, as does the relative weakness of academic disciplines as a result of economic underdevelopment. The best example of this blend of literature and social, political, and historical thought is Gabriel García Márquez's *One Hundred Years of Solitude.* All those Buendías founding Macondo in the midst of the jungle, becoming caudillos in interminable civil wars, receiving with astonishment the developments of modern science and attempting to apply them to their lives, are heirs to Sarmiento's formulations about civilization and barbarism.

The reading of such works alongside *Facundo* enhances and deepens the reader's comprehension of them. Sarmiento's classic is in all of them as in a filigree, with its cast of characters and figures and its defining landscape, the sublime and overwhelming beauty of the land that is both friend and foe, and with the tragic nature of life itself in all of its manifestations, from the most elementary to the cosmic. Sometimes authors pay direct homage to *Facundo.* For instance, in Carpentier's dictator novel, *El recurso del método* (1976), translated as *Reasons of State,* the counterpoint between the provincial city, called Nueva Córdoba, and the capital is a direct allusion to Sarmiento, as is the whole characterization of the tyrant—a barbarian who aspires pathetically to become civilized. And in Carlos Fuentes's novel *The Campaign,* Argentina's struggles for independence are portrayed in terms that could not be more indebted to *Facundo.* Carpentier was a Cuban and Fuentes is a Mexican. Sarmiento's legacy in Argentine literature is immense, both in the essay genre and in fiction. In trying to eradicate the gaucho, Sarmiento turned him into a national symbol. By the time José Hernández wrote his epic poem *Martín Fierro* (1872), the gaucho had become an object of nostalgia, a lost origin around which to build a national mythology. Facundo Quiroga endures, as all mythical figures do, because his contradictions represent our unresolved struggle between good and evil and our lives' inexorable drive toward death.

Translator's Introduction

A Foundational Text

Domingo Faustino Sarmiento was living in exile in Chile in 1845 when he wrote *Facundo: Civilization and Barbarism.* Today recognized as one of the foundational works of Spanish American literary history, *Facundo* marks a defining point in the evolution of a literature that was attempting to establish a cultural identity for the new, post-Independence Latin nations. A text controversial from its inception, this book remains required reading for any student of Latin American history and culture. Its liberal ideology and prescriptions for modernization, combined with a prose style of tremendous beauty and passion, make it reverberate powerfully even for the twenty-first century, as rapid change overtakes Argentina and the rest of the continent and region.

As a narrative, *Facundo* is hard to classify. Written in the expansive spirit of romantic, nineteenth-century historiography, it combines biography, sociology, geography, poetic description, and political propaganda in order to denounce the tyranny of the Argentine dictator Juan Manuel de Rosas, who held power from 1835 to 1852. Sarmiento's attack on Rosas in *Facundo* was carried out in several ways. The Argentine national character, the effects of land configuration on personality, the "barbaric" nature of the countryside versus the "civilizing" influence of the city, and the great future awaiting Argentina when it opened its doors wide to European immigration are all themes treated extensively in this text.

The political conflict between Buenos Aires and the provinces, which had been a cause of earlier civil wars, had reached a crucial point by 1845. The book's subtitle, *Civilization and Barbarism,* reflects both that split and the oppositional concept that guided Sarmiento's own thought. Juan Facundo Quiroga (1793–1835), a provincial caudillo loyal to Rosas, personifies the barbarism of the countryside; thus, his biography serves as the centerpiece of Sarmiento's argument, and a description of the land where he was born and reared introduces the life. Facundo, of course, also represents the violence and evil fostered by Rosas's tyranny, which favored the countryside at the expense of the supposedly superior values of the city.

The physical description of the countryside in chapter I is complemented by the character analyses of chapter II, probably the most famous and frequently anthologized section of *Facundo.* Here are introduced various types of gauchos in great detail, each accompanied by a portrait of his surrounding environment. Facundo's life, outlined in chapter V, is followed by several essays dealing with the political life of Argentina, leading up to Facundo's assassination in chapter XIII. The narrative ends with a vision of the country's possible future under a government by Sarmiento's party of opposition, the Unitarists.

The exiled Sarmiento was directing the Santiago newspaper *El Progreso* when he published *Facundo* in installments as part of that paper's literary supplement in 1845. The first and second editions were published in Chile in 1845 and 1851, respectively. In the second edition, the introduction and chapters XIV and XV were suppressed (see Sarmiento's letter to Valentín Alsina, included here following his introduction). These materials appear in English for the first time in the present volume.

Facundo in English Translation: 1868

Sarmiento in his time was a highly controversial figure, well remembered by his compatriots today as the man who founded the Argentine school system. Some remember him also for pushing back the Indian frontier, severely curtailing the culture of the gauchos, and opening the door to extensive European immigration. The key model for these reforms was the United States, a nation Sarmiento first visited during the late 1840s and to which he later returned as a diplomat posted to Washington during Lincoln's presidency. Thus, the publication of *Facundo* heralded a close association of Argentine ideas and policies with those of the United States. Sarmiento died in 1888, yet more than one hundred years later his influence is still being debated heatedly, as was made clear at various symposia that marked the centenary year, 1988, both in the United States and in Latin America.[1] It is fitting that this debate be extended to the English-reading U.S. audience, for by studying *Facundo* we may understand, through the words and vision of a Latin American writer and political figure, the history of both the Americas.

Facundo was first translated into English by Mary Mann, wife of the famous United States educator Horace Mann, in 1868. Sarmiento had traveled to Boston in 1847, two years after *Facundo*'s publication, and had observed Mann's school in that New England city. As has been shown by Diana Sorensen Goodrich in her study *Facundo and the Construction of Argentine Culture,* Mary Mann makes *Facundo* understandable to the North American and English reading public by framing it between two texts: a preface, devoted to Argentine history prior to 1845, and a lengthy follow-up biographical sketch of Sarmiento. Mann's efforts as the translator of *Facundo* into an Anglo-Saxon idiom, a translation she described to her friend Longfellow as "a work of love," had much to do with the fact that in 1868 Sarmiento was a candidate for the Argentine presidency.[2] Mary Mann wished to further her friend's cause abroad by presenting Sarmiento as an admirer and emulator of United States political and cultural institutions and an enlightened writer and statesman who would bring order to a chaotic South American country.

Reading this translation alongside the original Spanish, Mann's elimination of metaphor, the stylistic device perhaps most characteristic of Sarmiento's prose, is especially striking. Mann simply leaves out many instances of such embellishments to the narrative; in other cases, she interprets the sense but destroys the metaphor itself. Doris Sommer, in her *Foundational Fictions,* characterizes this absence as "dead metaphor" in Mann's work.[3] It seems clear that a double cause is operative here: both the translator's deficient command of Spanish and her politically motivated approach to *Facundo.* Mann's concern rested with

1. See, for example, Tulio Halperín Donghi, Gwen Kirkpatrick, and Francine Masiello, eds., *Sarmiento: Author of a Nation* (Berkeley: University of California Press, 1994).

2. Diana Sorensen Goodrich, *Facundo and the Construction of Argentine Culture* (Austin: University of Texas Press, 1996), p. 88.

3. Doris Sommer, *Foundational Fictions: The National Romances of Latin America* (Berkeley: University of California Press, 1991), p. 344n17.

Sarmiento's ambitions as a politician, not as a writer. Moreover, the hegemony of North over South America informed that concern.

Mann's biography of Sarmiento alludes in this way to his as yet un-realized presidential candidacy, as she declares: "it is evident that there are everywhere some who appreciate the true value of his labors, and there is a party there that understands how much it might be benefited by putting the reins of government into such able and experienced hands."[4] However, the biographical sketch ends on a somber note: "In countries so little experienced in republican practices as South America must be, the material facts of an election are not always the expression of the most dominant opinion of the best minds, but rather of the acci-dental influences of the moment" (280). But her preface can be more optimistic, and more openly partisan: "Colonel Sarmiento . . . has by an almost unanimous movement been made the candidate *par excellence* for the Presidency of the Argentine Republic, and the returns are al-ready known from the province of Buenos Ayres, which contains one third of the population of the whole Republic. . . . Doubtless before these pages see the light, the favorable result will be confirmed" (7).

Reviewers in the United States responded to *Facundo* from the con-text of their own post–Civil War concerns. According to Sorensen Goodrich, "the overall effect of reading it was to bolster America's sense of nationhood by setting it off against the upheaval which still held many of the South American republics in its grip. The spectacle of barbar-ism reinforced the experience of civilization which the mid-nineteenth-century American public was seeking to solidify."[5] *Facundo,* then, made the U.S. audience feel confident in its superior institutions and its se-cure, bright future, so recently threatened with extinction by its own devastating Civil War.

Sarmiento's book was retitled for the English-language readership from *Facundo; o, Civilización y barbarie* to *Life in the Argentine Repub-lic in the Days of the Tyrants; or, Civilization and Barbarism.* Sorensen Goodrich refers to this as the "repackaging" of *Facundo* from biograph-ical essay into something resembling a travel book, a nineteenth-century genre familiar to the metropolitan reader. The violence and tyranny of South America thus are filtered through this grid for the consumption of the North American reader. Moreover, Sarmiento's language itself

---

4. In Domingo Faustino Sarmiento, *Life in the Argentine Republic in the Days of the Tyrants; or, Civilization and Barbarism,* trans., with a biographical sketch of the author, by Mrs. Horace Mann (New York, 1868; reprint, New York: Gordon Press, 1976), p. 280.

5. Sorensen Goodrich, *Facundo and the Construction of Argentine Culture,* p. 95.

aids in this transformation, given his reliance in *Facundo* on the dominant discourse of European travel literature and its Orientalist images, employed by Sarmiento to explain Argentine "barbarism" to an ideal "civilized" reader.

Metaphor in *Facundo*

In light of these twin impulses behind Mann's translation—one being the presentation of Sarmiento as a presidential candidate the reader can identify (and identify with) as enlightened and "civilized," the other the presentation of the essay itself as a travel book with the dangerous South neatly confined—let us consider metaphor in *Facundo*. Perhaps it would be more precise to speak of metaphor as the key ingredient of something more generalized in the text, what the Argentine critic Noé Jitrik, in the prologue to the 1977 edition of the book, calls "drive" *(empuje)*. This is a rhythm in the text that Sarmiento himself compared to the production of thread by a silkworm, with long-incubated ideas spilling effortlessly over the paper into an entire book.[6] To quote Jitrik: "To unfold, to produce a thread, this is the secret of its rhythm, which in its drive we feel to be very breathlike, pulmonary, threatening to go on while life, or writing, continue; never as in this text has rhythm become so material for us: rhythm appears as if in its pure state" (xvi; trans. mine).

Carlos Alonso, another reader of Sarmiento, has also explored this aspect of the Argentine's writing, which he identifies as its "passion": "in it, discourse is depicted as being ultimately ruled by the relentless, contradictory drives of a desiring subject."[7] By this formulation Sarmiento's discourse is a performance, "an *activity* in which intentionality and language intersect in the uninterrupted flow of writing" (40; Alonso's emphasis). Thus Alonso argues for a critical reading that will be "attentive" to the passion of the text, rather than "circumventing, taming or overlooking it" (48).

It is this drive, poetry, and passion that Mary Mann often destroys or omits in her translation and that I have attempted to recoup in this new translation. Mann intended for her U.S. readers to get a geography and

6. In Domingo Faustino Sarmiento, *Facundo,* prologue by Noé Jitrik, notes and chronology by Nora Dottori and Silvia Zanetti (Caracas: Biblioteca Ayacucho, 1977), p. xvi.

7. Carlos J. Alonso, "Reading Sarmiento: Once More, with Passion," *Hispanic Review* 62 (1994): 46.

history lesson and to acquire an elevated idea of Sarmiento, the future president. To those ends, she sacrificed much of what makes the text compelling and unique to the Spanish-language reader. By restoring metaphoric, rhythmic language to the English translation of *Facundo,* my intention is to translate the interior meaning of Sarmiento's prose, or at least to present a range of metaphorical possibilities so that the reader may grasp the richness of this language.

Doris Sommer's *Foundational Fictions* gives us a powerful reading of Sarmiento's use of this kind of language as part of the conflicted response to a wild land in need of taming in the name of progress: "Demanding to be admired wild and shapeless as she is, the land lies ready for the man who dares to make her productive. . . . Sarmiento is saying that Argentina needs the manageable, recognizably demarcated body that a modern subject could love, because his real passion was for progress."[8] As she explicates this, Sommer castigates the "chaste" translation of Mary Mann, and provides her own revision of the English, marking the land as feminine, as *she* "flaunts her smooth, infinite, downy brow without frontiers" (Sommer's translation of Sarmiento, 61; my emphasis).

In translating the land in *Facundo* as "she," Sommer wishes to highlight the erotic charge of a nineteenth-century literary discourse that defined the nation through romantic novels. The result is a translation that takes the necessarily gendered Spanish of *la pampa* and *la tierra* from a subconscious to a conscious level of decision. I have had to think through these metaphors of romance, possession, and eroticism constantly in my translation. What I have done is, again, to follow Sarmiento's passionate language as literally as possible but not to produce gendered English where that would mean an imposition of one reading. Thus I did not feminize the land or the Pampas, leaving them neutral as would be normal in English, and the Pampas to "display their smooth, downy brow." The reader, I believe, will discover the erotic tendencies of Sarmiento's prose through his or her own effort. And that, indeed, was my experience more often than not with *Facundo:* letting the text go, literally, where Sarmiento's discourse sends it was usually enough. For this reason, while in places I modernize punctuation and divide some long sentences, I do so only when necessary for effective comprehension and when the integrity of the original is not compromised.

8. Sommer, *Foundational Fictions,* p. 61.

Facundo in English Translation: 2003

The question of a current political context for a new translation of *Facundo* should be addressed. In today's Argentina, of course, *Facundo* still inspires controversy and debate regarding its contribution to national myths of modernization, its antipopulism, and its racist ideology; in Diana Sorensen Goodrich's words, "No one treats *Facundo* as a neutral text."[9] Only Sarmiento's full, metaphorical text will enable the English-language reader to understand this lack of neutrality and to comprehend the debate. As Doris Sommer's examination of Sarmiento as a reader of Fenimore Cooper shows, however, the North American reader might also consider the connection of *Facundo* to racist ideology in the United States, to a nineteenth-century discourse of expansion and progress that engendered the nation of the North through war, slavery, and genocide. I hope the reader of this new translation will engage in a process that simultaneously recognizes difference and sameness, and will imagine nineteenth-century Latin America from a position other than that of the smug northern superiority rampant in 1868.

Translations, as Lawrence Venuti tells us in his book *The Scandals of Translation,* "inevitably perform a work of domestication. Those that work best, the most powerful in recreating cultural values and the most responsible in accounting for that power, usually engage readers in domestic terms that have been defamiliarized to some extent, made fascinating by a revisionary encounter with a foreign text."[10] What has been so challenging in the case of *Facundo* is that, despite the necessary inequality of a South-to-North domestication, this is a master narrative and not a minority discourse. Thus, while trying to re-create the cultural values it represents, I have also wished to break down the unity of the master's voice, to make many readings possible by letting the words signify in multiple ways. In this way I hope the defamiliarization of the text will make the North American reader stop and consider the implications, across the Americas, of what he or she is reading.

Methodology and Acknowledgments

For this translation, several modern editions were used. They are: (1) the critical and annotated edition of Alberto Palcos, published in

---

9. Sorensen Goodrich, *Facundo and the Construction of Argentine Culture,* p. 1.

10. Lawrence Venuti, *The Scandals of Translation: Towards an Ethics of Difference* (London: Routledge, 1998), p. 5.

1938 at the University of La Plata (Argentina) on the occasion of the fiftieth anniversary of Sarmiento's death; (2) the edition of Roberto Yahni, published in Madrid in 1997, also annotated for the general reader; (3) the edition of Noé Jitrik, published in 1977 in Caracas with a strong locating introduction, chronology, and notes (see the bibliography below for complete information). The translation has notes at the end of the book as needed to explain specific vocabulary choices and cultural or historical references. Additionally, a glossary of historical names explains references made in *Facundo* to specific key figures.

I would like to acknowledge the help of two research assistants in the preparation of this volume. Ariadna García aided in researching the sources of Sarmiento's epigraphs. Matthew W. Stevens compiled information for the glossary. I thank them both for their work.

My colleague and friend Sylvia Molloy has been generous with her time and expertise as a reader of this work. Carol Maier gave suggestions and a ready ear.

To Roberto González Echevarría, academic editor of this series for the University of California Press, I owe a great debt for his proposal of this translation and his constancy during its preparation.

Finally, I wish to thank Daniel, Demian, and Ana Szyld, Argentines all, for their support and encouragement as this translation slowly emerged.

Bibliography

PRIMARY SOURCES

Sarmiento, Domingo Faustino. *Facundo*. Prologue by Noé Jitrik. Notes and chronology by Nora Dottori and Silvia Zanetti. Caracas: Biblioteca Ayacucho, 1977.

———. *Facundo*. Ed. Alberto Palcos. La Plata, Argentina: Universidad Nacional de La Plata, 1938.

———. *Facundo: Or, Civilization and Barbarism*. Trans. Mary Mann. Introduction by Ilan Stavans. New York: Penguin Books, 1998.

———. *Facundo: Civilización y barbarie*. 3rd ed. Ed. Roberto Yahni. Madrid: Cátedra, 1997.

———. *Life in the Argentine Republic in the Days of the Tyrants; or, Civilization and Barbarism*. Trans., with a biographical sketch of the author, by Mrs. Horace Mann. New York: Hurd and Houghton, 1868. Reprint, New York: Gordon Press, 1976.

SECONDARY SOURCES

The bibliography on Sarmiento is vast. This is a highly selective list of criticism, primarily in English, meant to direct the reader to sources for further reading on *Facundo*, Argentina, and Sarmiento.

Alonso, Carlos J. *The Latin American Regional Novel: Modernity and Autochthony.* Cambridge: Cambridge University Press, 1989.
―――. "Reading Sarmiento: Once More, with Passion." *Hispanic Review* 62 (1994): 35–52.
Altamirano, Carlos, and Beatriz Sarlo. *Ensayos argentinos de Sarmiento a la vanguardia.* Buenos Aires: Centro Editor de América Latina, 1983.
Bethell, Leslie, ed. *Argentina since Independence.* New York: Cambridge University Press, 1993.
Botana, Natalio R. *Domingo Faustino Sarmiento.* Buenos Aires: Fondo de Cultura Económica, 1996.
Bunkley, Allison Williams. *The Life of Sarmiento.* Princeton, N.J.: Princeton University Press, 1952.
Carilla, Emilio. "Los epígrafes y la elaboración del *Facundo.*" *Academia Argentina de Letras* 54 (1989): 131–69.
Foster, David William. *The Argentine Generation of 1880: Ideology and Cultural Texts.* Columbia: University of Missouri Press, 1990.
González Echevarría, Roberto. *Myth and Archive: A Theory of Latin American Narrative.* Cambridge: Cambridge University Press, 1990.
―――. *The Voice of the Masters: Writing and Authority in Modern Latin American Literature.* Austin: University of Texas Press, 1985.
―――, ed. *Oxford Book of Latin American Short Stories.* New York: Oxford University Press, 1997.
González Echevarría, Roberto, and Enrique Pupo-Walker, eds. *The Cambridge History of Latin American Literature.* Cambridge: Cambridge University Press, 1996.
Halperín Donghi, Tulio, Gwen Kirkpatrick, and Francine Masiello, eds. *Sarmiento: Author of a Nation.* Berkeley: University of California Press, 1994.
Jitrik, Noé. *Muerte y resurrección de "Facundo."* Buenos Aires: Centro Editor de América Latina, 1968.
Ludmer, Josefina. *The Gaucho Genre: A Treatise on the Motherland.* Trans. Molly Weigel. Durham, N.C.: Duke University Press, 2002.
Molloy, Sylvia. *At Face Value: Autobiographical Writing in Spanish America.* Cambridge: Cambridge University Press, 1991.
Ramos, Julio. *Divergent Modernities: Culture and Politics in Nineteenth-Century Latin America.* Trans. John D. Blanco. Foreword by José David Saldívar. Durham, N.C.: Duke University Press, 2001.

Rock, David. *Argentina, 1516–1982: From Spanish Colonization to the Falklands War*. London: I. B. Tauris, 1986.

Shumway, Nicolas. *The Invention of Argentina*. Berkeley: University of California Press, 1991.

Sommer, Doris. *Foundational Fictions: The National Romances of Latin America*. Berkeley: University of California Press, 1991.

Sorensen Goodrich, Diana. *Facundo and the Construction of Argentine Culture*. Austin: University of Texas Press, 1996.

Facundo

CIVILIZATION AND BARBARISM

Domingo Faustino Sarmiento

Author's Note

Since this work was published, I have received from several friends corrections of several facts it relates. Some inaccuracies will have necessarily slipped through in a work done quickly, far from the scene of events, and on a topic about which nothing had been written until now. Bringing together incidents that took place in different and distant provinces and at diverse times, consulting an eyewitness on some point, searching through rapidly written manuscripts, or invoking personal recollections, it is not unusual if here and there the Argentine reader may feel that something he himself knows about is missing, or may disagree about some proper name, some date, changed or out of place.

But I do state that in the notable events to which I refer, and which serve as the basis for the explanations I give, there is irreproachable accuracy, to which the existing public documents about those events will attest.

Perhaps there will be a moment when, unburdened by the worries that have precipitated the writing of this little work, I may remold it according to a new plan, stripping it of all accidental digression and supporting it with the numerous official documents to which I now make only passing reference.

1845

. . .

On ne tue point les idées.
Fortoul[1]

A los hombres se degüella: a las ideas no.

Toward the end of 1840 I was leaving my homeland, pitifully exiled, broken, covered with bruises, kicks, and blows received the day before in one of those bloody bacchanals of unruly soldiers and *mazorqueros*.[2] Passing the Baths of Zonda, beneath a national coat of arms that in happier days I had painted in a room, I wrote these words with charcoal:

On ne tue point les idées.

The government, informed of this deed, sent a commission in charge of deciphering the hieroglyph, which was said to contain base venting, insults, and threats. Upon hearing the translation, "So!" they said, "what does this mean?"

It simply meant that I was coming to Chile, where freedom was still shining, and that I intended to make the rays of light of its press project over to the other side of the Andes. Those familiar with my conduct in Chile know if I have kept that promise.

Introduction

Je demande à l'historien l'amour de l'humanité ou de la liberté;
sa justice impartiale ne doit être impassible. Il faut, au contraire,
qu'il souhaite, qu'il espère, qu'il souffre, ou soit heureux de ce
qu'il rencontre.

Villemain, Cours de littérature[1]

Terrible specter of Facundo, I will evoke you, so that you may rise, shaking off the bloody dust covering your ashes, and explain the hidden life and the inner convulsions that tear at the bowels of a noble people! You possess the secret: reveal it to us! Even ten years after your tragic death, the men of the cities and the gauchos of the Argentine plains, following different paths in the desert, were saying: "No! he has not died! He still lives! He will return!" True! Facundo has not died. He lives on in popular traditions, in Argentine politics and revolutions, in Rosas, his heir, his complement; his soul has moved into that new mold, one more perfect and finished, and what in him was only instinct, impulse, and a tendency, in Rosas became a system, means, and end. Rural nature, colonial and barbarous, was changed through this metamorphosis into art, into a system, and into regular policy, able to present itself to the world as the way of being of a people, incarnated in one man who has aspired to take on the airs of a genius, dominating events, men, and things. Facundo—provincial, barbarous, brave, bold—was replaced by Rosas, son of cultured Buenos Aires without being so himself; by Rosas, traitorous, cold-hearted, calculating soul, who does evil without passion, and slowly

organizes despotism with all the intelligence of a Machiavelli. Tyrant
without rival today on earth, why should his enemies dispute the title
of "Great One" proclaimed by his courtiers? Yes, great and very great
he is, to the glory and the shame of his homeland; for, though he has
found thousands of degraded beings willing to yoke themselves to his
cart and drag it over dead bodies, there are also generous souls by the
thousand who, in fifteen years of bloody battle, have not despaired of
vanquishing the monster that the enigma of the political organization
of the Republic presents to us. The day will finally come when they will
solve that riddle, and the Argentine Sphinx, half cowardly woman, half
bloodthirsty tiger, will die at their feet, giving the Thebes of the Plata
the high rank it deserves among the nations of the New World.

However, to untie this knot that no sword has been able to cut, it is
necessary to study extensively the twists and turns of the threads that
form it, and to look to national precedent, to the physiognomy of the
land, to popular traditions and customs, for the points where they are
bound together.

Today the Argentine Republic is the area of Spanish America whose
outward manifestations have most come to the attention of the European nations, which often find themselves embroiled in its disorder, or
else pulled, as to a vortex, toward its center where opposing elements
swirl. France was on the brink of yielding to that attraction, and not
without great effort of sail and oar, not without losing the rudder, did
it succeed in removing itself and keeping its distance. Its most skilled
politicians have not been able to understand anything of what they saw
with their own eyes when they took a quick glimpse at the American
power challenging their great nation. Seeing the waves of burning lava
roaring in this great focus of intestine struggle, rolling, shaking, and
crashing into each other, even those who think themselves most informed have said: "It is just a nameless, subaltern volcano, one of many
that appear in America; soon it will be extinguished"; and then they
have looked elsewhere, satisfied to have given a solution so easy and precise for social phenomena they have seen only superficially and grouped
together. South America in general, and the Argentine Republic above
all, has lacked a Tocqueville who, previously equipped with a knowledge of social theory just as a scientist travels with barometer, compass,
and octant, would have penetrated the interior of our political life as a
vast field still unexplored and undescribed by science, and revealed to
Europe and France, so eager for knowledge of new phases in the lives of
different segments of humanity, this new way of being that has no well-

marked or known precedent. Then the mystery of the obstinate struggle tearing that Republic to pieces would have been explained; the opposing, invincible elements crashing into one another would have been
distinctly classified; the configuration of the land and the customs it engenders would have been assigned their proper part; the Spanish traditions and the iniquitous, plebeian national consciousness that the Inquisition and Hispanic absolutism have left, their part; the influence of
the opposite ideas that have disturbed the political world, its part; indigenous barbarism, its part; European civilization, its part; and finally,
the democracy consecrated by the 1810 revolution, and equality, whose
dogma has penetrated down to the lowest levels of society, their part.
Done by competent observers, this study, which we ourselves cannot
yet do because of our lack of philosophical and historical instruction,
would have revealed to the stunned eyes of Europe a new world of politics, an ingenuous, open, and primitive struggle between the latest
progress of the human spirit and the rudiments of savagery, between the
populous cities and the gloomy forests. Then the problem of Spain
could have been clarified a bit, that straggler behind Europe, which lying between the Mediterranean and the ocean, between the Middle
Ages and the nineteenth century, united to cultured Europe by a broad
isthmus and separated from barbarous Africa by a narrow strait, sways
in the balance between two opposing forces, now rising on the side of
free peoples, now falling with peoples ruled by despotism; now impious,
now fanatical; now declaredly constitutionalist, now impudently despotic; sometimes cursing its broken chains, then standing still and crying out for the yoke which seems to be its condition and way of being.
So! Could not the problem of European Spain be resolved by closely examining American Spain, just as through the upbringing and habits of
their children the ideas and morals of parents may be traced? So! Does
not this eternal struggle of the peoples of Spanish America signify something for history and philosophy, this supine lack of political and industrial ability which afflicts them and has them spinning with no fixed
pole, no precise objective, without knowing why they cannot get a day
of rest, or which enemy's hand pushes and tosses them into the fatal
whirlwind dragging them against their will, with no chance to resist its
evil influence? Would it not be worthwhile to know why in Paraguay, a
land taken apart by the *wise* hand of the Jesuits, a *wise* man,[2] educated
in the classrooms of the old University of Córdoba, opens a new page
in the history of aberrations of the human spirit, closes up a people
inside its primitive forest, and, erasing the paths leading to this recon-

dite China, hides and conceals his prisoner for thirty years in the depths of the American continent, not allowing it to cry out even once, until, dead himself from old age and from the quiet fatigue of standing immobile with his foot on a submissive people, it can finally say to those wandering nearby, in an exhausted and barely intelligible voice: I am still alive! But how I have suffered, *quantum mutatus ab illo!* What a transformation Paraguay has suffered; what bruises and lesions the yoke has left on its neck, which offered no resistance! Does not the spectacle of the Argentine Republic merit study, when after twenty years of internal convulsion, of attempts at organization of every sort, from the depths of its bowels, from its innermost heart, it produces that same Dr. Francia in the person of Rosas, but greater, more confident, and more hostile, if that is possible, to the ideas, customs, and civilization of European peoples? Does not one discover in him the same rancor toward foreign elements, the same idea of government authority, the same insolence that defies the world's disapproval, with the addition of his own savage originality, his coldly ferocious character, and his will, implacable to the point of sacrificing his homeland as did Sagunto and Numancia, to the point of abjuring the future and the rank of a cultured nation as did the Spain of Philip II and Torquemada?[3] Is this an accidental quirk, a mechanical deviation caused by the appearance on the scene of a powerful genius, like when the planets leave their regular orbit, attracted by the approach of another planet, but not totally resisting the force of their center of attraction, which then assumes its preponderance and causes them to reenter the ordinary route? M. Guizot has said from the French tribunal: "In America there are two parties, the European party and the American party: the latter is stronger"; and when he is advised that the French have taken up arms in Montevideo, and that they have joined their future, their lives, and their well-being to the triumph of the civilized European party, he contents himself by adding: "The French are very meddlesome, and put their nation in jeopardy with other governments." Good Lord! M. Guizot, the historian of European *civilization,* the one who has outlined the new elements that modified Roman civilization, and who has penetrated the tangled labyrinth of the Middle Ages to show how the French nation has been the crucible in which the modern spirit has been developed, blended, and recast; M. Guizot, minister of the king of France, gives as his only explanation for this demonstration of profound sympathy between the French and the enemies of Rosas: "The French are very meddlesome"! The other American peoples in their turn exclaim, full of indignation: "Those Argentines are very friendly with the Europeans!" as they watch, indifferently and impassively, the struggle of an Argentine party and its alliance with any European element that offers assistance. And the tyrant of the Argentine Republic officiously takes it upon himself to complete their sentence, adding: "Traitors to the American cause!" True! they all say; traitors! that is the word! True! we say; traitors to the American, Spanish, absolutist, barbarous cause! Have you not heard the word *savage*, which flutters about over our heads?

That is the point: to be or not to be *savages*. According to this, is not Rosas an isolated case, an aberration, a monstrosity? Or, on the contrary, is he a social manifestation, a formula for the way of being of a people? Why should you fight him so obstinately, then, if he is logical, natural, fatal, inevitable? My God! why do you fight him! . . . Just because the undertaking is arduous, does that make it absurd? Just because the evil principle triumphs, is the field to be abandoned to it in resignation? Just because Italy moans under the weight of all its despotisms, and Poland goes wandering over the earth begging for a bit of bread and a bit of freedom, are civilization and liberty weak in the world today? Why do you fight him! . . . Aren't those of us who still survive after so many disasters still living, or have we lost our sense of justice and of the future of our native land, just because we have lost some battles? So! Are ideas too part of the spoils of combat? Is it within our power to do anything other than what we are doing, no more nor less than Rosas cannot stop being what he is? Is there nothing providential in these struggles among peoples? Was triumph ever granted to the one who could not persevere? Moreover, are we to abandon one of the most privileged soils in America to the devastations of barbarism, to leave one hundred navigable rivers abandoned to the aquatic birds that calmly possess and furrow them all alone *ab initio*?

Are we to close our doors voluntarily to the European immigrants who knock repeatedly, wanting to populate our deserts and to make us, in the shadow of our own flag, a people as innumerable as the ocean sands? Are we to give up as illusory and vain the dreams of power, glory, and development with which we have been rocked to sleep since childhood, the predictions enviously made for us by those in Europe who study the needs of humanity? After Europe, is there any other uninhabited and civilizable Christian world besides America? Are there any other peoples in America who, like the Argentines, are now being called upon to receive a European population that overflows like liquid from a glass? And finally, do you not want us to invoke the names of science and industry to come to our aid, to call on them with all our might so that they may take their place among us, the one freed of all fetters placed on thought, the other safe from all violence and coercion? Oh! This future will not be surrendered so easily! It will not be surrendered because an army of twenty thousand men may guard our homeland's borders; soldiers die in combat, they desert or change allegiances. It will not be surrendered because fortune may have favored a tyrant through long and hard years; fortune is blind, and one day when it cannot find its favorite amid the dense smoke and the suffocating dust clouds of combat, farewell tyrant! farewell tyranny! It will not be surrendered because all those brutal, ignorant colonial traditions may have overtaken, in a misguided moment, the minds of the inexperienced masses; political convulsions also bring experience and knowledge, and it is a law of humanity that new interests, fecund ideas, and progress will triumph in the end over aging traditions, ignorant habits, and fixed prejudices. It will not be surrendered because there may be thousands of ingenuous men among a people who see good where there is evil, egotists who take advantage of that evil for themselves, indifferent men who see it but take no personal interest, timid men who dare not fight it, and finally, corrupt men who unknowingly give themselves over to it because they are inclined to evil through their depravity; all of this has always existed among peoples, and evil has never definitively triumphed. It will not be surrendered because other peoples of America cannot help us; because governments can only see from afar the glitter of organized power, and cannot distinguish, in the humble, unprotected darkness of revolutions, the great elements that are striving to unfold; because the supposedly liberal opposition may abjure its principles, silence its conscience, and, in order to smash underfoot an insect that vexes it, bring down the noble sole on which that insect had attached itself. It will not be surrendered because other peoples en masse may turn their backs on us, since our miseries and our greatness are too far out of their sight to reach and move them. No! a future so unlimited, a mission so exalted, will not be surrendered because of this accumulation of contradictions and difficulties. Difficulties can be vanquished, and contradictions are ended by contradicting them!

From Chile, there is nothing we can give *to those who persevere* in the struggle with all the rigors of privation, and with the exterminating blade constantly hanging over their heads like the sword of Damocles. Nothing! except for ideas, except for consolation, except for encouragement; no weapon is ours to bring to those combatants beyond the one that the *free press* of Chile provides to all free men. The press! The press! Behold, tyrant, the enemy you suffocated among us. Behold the golden fleece we try to win. Behold how the presses of France, England, Brazil, Montevideo, Chile, and Corrientes will disturb your slumber, amid your victims' sepulchral silence; behold how you have been compelled to steal the gift of language in order to excuse your evil, a gift given only to promote good. Behold how you stoop to justify yourself, and how you go among all the peoples of Europe and America begging for a venal, fratricidal pen to defend, through the press, the one who put it in chains! Why don't you permit in your homeland the discussion you maintain with all other peoples? For what were so many thousands of victims sacrificed by the dagger? What were so many battles for if, in the end, you had to decide on a peaceful discussion in the press?

The reader of the preceding pages will think that my intention is to draw an impassioned picture of the acts of barbarism that have dishonored the name of Don Juan Manuel Rosas. Those who harbor such fears should not worry. The last page of that immoral biography is not yet shaped; the cup is not yet filled; not yet numbered are the days of its hero. Moreover, the passions he arouses in his enemies are still too rancorous for them to trust in their own impartiality or fairness. I must concern myself with another character: Facundo Quiroga is the caudillo whose deeds I want to consign to paper.

Ten years has the earth weighed upon his ashes, and cruel and poisoned would prove the calumny that would dig up graves in search of victims. Who fired the *official* bullet that ended his career? Did it come from Buenos Aires, or from Córdoba? History will explain this arcanum. Facundo Quiroga, however, is the simplest example of the character of civil war in the Argentine Republic; he is the most American figure the revolution offers. Facundo Quiroga links and ties together all the elements of disorder that were stirring up separately in every province, even before his appearance; he makes a national, Argentine war out of a local war, and at the end of ten years of toil, devastation, and combat, triumphantly presents the result, which only the one who murdered him knew how to put to use.

It has occurred to me to explain the Argentine Revolution with the biography of Juan Facundo Quiroga because I believe he sufficiently explains one of the tendencies, one of the two different aspects that struggle in the bosom of that singular society.

I have evoked, then, my memories, and to complement them, have searched out the details that could be furnished me by men who knew him as a child, who were his partisans or his enemies, who have seen some deeds with their own eyes, have heard of others, and have had precise knowledge of a particular time or situation. I await yet more facts than those I now possess, which already are numerous. If some inaccuracies escape through, I beg those who take note of them to inform me, because in Facundo Quiroga I do not see simply a caudillo, but rather a manifestation of Argentine life as it has been made by colonization and the peculiarities of the land, to which I believe serious attention must be devoted, because without it the life and deeds of Facundo Quiroga are vulgarities that would merit but episodic entry into the domain of history. But Facundo, in relation to the physiognomy of the magnificently wild nature that prevails in the immense expanse of the Argentine Republic; Facundo, true expression of the way of being of a people, of its prejudices and instincts; Facundo, finally, being what he was not through an accident of character, but rather through inevitable causes apart from his own will, is the most singular, most notable historical character that can be offered for contemplation by men who understand that a caudillo who leads a great social movement is nothing more than a mirror in which the beliefs, the needs, the prejudices, and customs of a nation in a given era of its history are reflected in colossal dimensions. Alexander is the picture, the reflection, of a warlike, literary, political, and artistic Greece, of a skeptical, philosophical, and enterprising Greece that spills over Asia in order to extend the sphere of its civilizing actions.

This is why it is necessary for us to stop and consider the details of the interior life of the Argentine people, in order to understand its ideal, its personification.

Without these causes, no one will understand Facundo Quiroga, just as no one, in my judgment, has yet understood the immortal Bolívar, owing to the incompetence of the biographers who have drawn the picture of his life. I have read a brilliant work about General Bolívar in the *Enciclopedia nueva,* in which all the justice he deserves is done to that American caudillo for his talent and for his genius; but in this biography, as in all others written about him, I have seen the European general, the marshals of the empire, a less colossal Napoleon, but I have not seen the American caudillo, the leader of a mass uprising; I see the imitation of Europe, and nothing that reveals America to me.

Colombia has plains, pastoral life, barbarous, purely American life, and from there came the great Bolívar; from that mud he made his glorious edifice. How can it be, then, that his biography makes him seem like any European general of illustrious gifts? Because the writer's classical, European prejudices distort the hero, from whom they remove the poncho to present him from the first wearing a tailcoat, just as the lithographers of Buenos Aires have painted Facundo wearing a coat, believing inappropriate the jacket that he never stopped wearing. Very well: they have made a general, but Facundo disappears. Bolívar's war may be studied in France, in that of the *chouans:* Bolívar is a Charette of broader dimensions.[4] If the Spanish had penetrated the Argentine Republic in 1811, perhaps Artigas would have been our Bolívar, if that caudillo had been as prodigiously gifted by nature and education.

The way in which the history of Bolívar is treated by European and American writers suits San Martín and others of his class. San Martín was not a popular caudillo; he really was a general. He was educated in Europe and then arrived in America, where there was a revolutionary government, and he was able to form at his leisure a European army, to drill it and to wage regular battle, according to scientific rules. His expedition into Chile is a conquest done by the rules, like that of Italy by Napoleon. But if San Martín had had to lead *montoneras,* getting beaten in one place then having to pull together a group of plainsmen in another, they would have hanged him on his second try.[5]

Bolívar's drama, then, is made up of elements other than the ones we know today: the American scenery and costumes must be in place first, for the character then to be shown. Bolívar is still a tale, forged out of some real facts: Bolívar, the true Bolívar, is still unknown to the world, and it is very likely that, when he is translated into his native language, he will appear even greater and more surprising.

Reasons of this kind have moved me to divide this hasty work into two parts: one in which I draw the terrain, the landscape, the theater where the action will be performed; the other where the character appears, with his costume, his ideas, his method of operating. In this manner, the first will already be revealing the second, without need of commentary or explanation.

· · ·

LETTER TO SR. VALENTÍN ALSINA (2ND EDITION, 1851)

I dedicate to you, my dear friend, these pages that once again see public light, not so much for their own worth, as for your efforts to reduce, with your notations, the many blemishes that marred the first edition. An essay and a revelation, even for me, of my own ideas, Facundo *suffered from the defects of all fruits of spontaneous inspiration, with no aid from documents at hand, carried out scarcely was it conceived, far from the theater of events, and with the purpose of immediate, militant action. Even as it was, my poor little book has had the good fortune to find passionate readers in that land closed off to discussion and the truth, slipping furtively from hand to hand, kept in some secret hiding place to halt in its wanderings, setting out on long journeys, and copies by the hundreds arrive, faded and crushed from being read so much, all the way to Buenos Aires, to the office of the poor tyrant, to the soldiers' camps, and to the gauchos' huts, until it has itself become, in popular lore, a myth like its hero.*

I have used your precious notes sparingly, saving the most substantial ones for better times and more careful works, fearful that by retouching such a formless work, its primitive physiognomy might disappear and with it the fresh, willful audacity of its undisciplined conception.

This book, like so many others born in the struggle for liberty, soon will become confused with an immense farrago of material, out of whose discordant chaos one day will emerge the history of our homeland, cleansed of all its unpleasantness, the liveliest drama, most fecund in lessons, richest in peripeteia, that the hard, painful American transformation has offered. How happy I would be if, as I wish, one day I might devote myself successfully to such a great task! Then I would gladly throw into the fire all the hasty pages I have let slip through in the battle in which you and so many other brave writers have won the freshest laurels, wounding our homeland's powerful tyrant from closer range and with better-tempered weapons.

I have omitted the introduction as useless, and the last two chapters as superfluous today, recalling something you indicated in Montevideo in 1846, when you insinuated to me that the book was finished with the death of Quiroga.

I have literary ambitions, my dear friend, and dedicate many long nights, extensive research, and careful study toward satisfying them. Facundo died in body at Barranca-Yaco, but his name in History was able to escape and survive for some years, without the exemplary punishment it deserved. The judgment of History has now fallen on him, and the repose of his grave is maintained through the suppression of his name and the scorn of the people. Writing the life of Rosas would be an affront to History, and to remind our homeland, after its rehabilitation, of the degradation it has gone through would be humiliating. But there are other peoples and other men who should not remain without humiliation or without learning a lesson. Oh! France, so justly proud of its competence in the social, political, and historical sciences; England, so attentive to its commercial interests; those politicians of all countries, those writers who consider themselves so informed, if a poor American narrator presented himself to them with a book, to show them, as God shows the things we call evident, that they have prostrated themselves before a phantom, that they have been accommodating an impotent specter, that they have venerated a pile of garbage, calling stupidity, energy; blindness, talent; crapulence and intrigue, virtue; and the grossest cunning, diplomacy; if this could be done, as it is possible to do, with earnest words, with irreproachable impartiality in the appraisal of events, with a lucid, animated exposition, lofty sentiments, and a profound knowledge of the interests of the people, and an intuition, founded on deductive logic, of the good that they suffocated with their mistakes and the bad that they propagated in our country and made overflow into others . . . do you not feel that the one who did so could present himself in Europe with his book in hand, and say to France and England, to the Monarchy and the Republic, to Palmerston and Guizot, to Louis Philippe and Louis Napoleon, to the Times *and the* Presse: *"Read it, wretches, and be humiliated! There is your man!" and make real that ecce homo, so wrongly celebrated by the powerful, to the scorn and disgust of the people!*

The history of Rosas's tyranny is the most solemn, the most noble, and the saddest page of the human species, as much for the peoples who have been its victims as for the European and American nations, governments, and politicians who have been actors in the drama or interested witnesses.

There, the events are consigned, classified, proven, documented; they need, however, the thread that will tie them together as one sole event, the breath of life that will make them all stand up at once for the onlooker to see, and change them into a living portrait, with perceptible primary planes and the necessary background. They need the color given by the landscape and sunbeams of our homeland; they need the evidence given by statistics that count up the numbers, that silence the presumptuous phrasemakers and make impudent, powerful men go mute. To attempt this, I need to examine the ground and visit the scenes of action, hear the accomplices' revelations, the victims' depositions, the old people's recollections, the painful stories of mothers who speak from the heart; I need to hear the confused echo of the common people, who have seen but have not understood, who have been victim and executioner, actor and witness. The maturity of a finished event and the passing of one era to another, a change in the fortune of the nation, are needed in order to look backward fruitfully, making of history an example rather than a revenge.

If this is the treasure I covet for myself, you may imagine, my dear friend, the great attention I must pay to the faults and inaccuracies in the life of Juan Facundo Quiroga, or in anything I have released to the public. There is exemplary justice to be done, and glory to be attained, as an Argentine writer: to whip the world and humiliate the arrogance of the great of the earth, whether they call themselves governments or sages. If I were wealthy, I would fund a Montyon Prize for the one who could achieve that.⁶

I send you Facundo, *then, without further delay, and may it continue the work of rehabilitating what is just and worthy, which was its aim from the start. We have what God grants to those who suffer: hopes and years ahead of us. I myself have but an atom of that which to you and to Rosas, to virtue and to crime, He grants at times: perseverance. Let us persevere, my friend; we may die, you there and I here; but let no act, no word of ours reveal that we are aware of our weakness, and that tribulations and dangers threaten us now and tomorrow. I remain,*

Your devoted friend,
Domingo F. Sarmiento
Yungay, 7 April 185

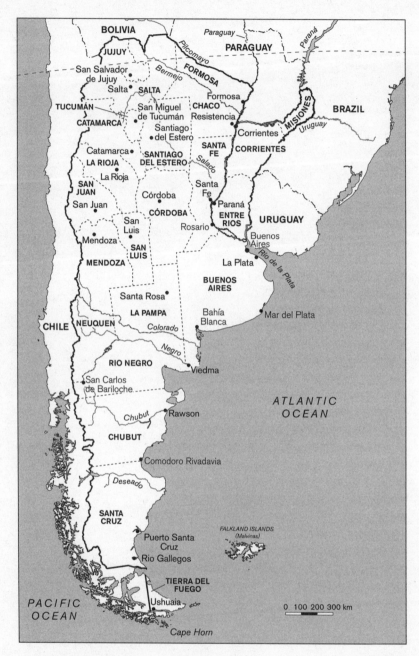

Argentina and neighboring countries

CHAPTER I

Physical Aspect of the Argentine Republic, and the Ideas, Customs, and Characters It Engenders

---

L'étendue des Pampas est si prodigieuse qu'au nord elles son bornées par des bosquets de palmiers, et au midi par des neiges éternelles.

Head[1]

The American continent ends to the south in a point, at whose extreme end the Strait of Magellan is formed. To the west, and at a short distance from the Pacific, the Chilean Andes run parallel to the coast. The land that lies to the east of that chain of mountains and to the west of the Atlantic, following the Río de la Plata toward the interior upstream along the Uruguay, is the territory formerly called the United Provinces of the Río de la Plata, and there, blood is still being shed in order to name it either the Argentine Republic or the Argentine Confederation. To the north are Paraguay, the Gran Chaco, and Bolivia, its alleged borders.

The immense expanse of land is entirely unpopulated at its extreme limits, and it possesses navigable rivers that no fragile little boat has yet plowed. The disease from which the Argentine Republic suffers is its own expanse: the desert wilderness surrounds it on all sides and insinuates into its bowels; solitude, a barren land with no human habitation, in general are the unquestionable borders between one province and another. There, immensity is everywhere: immense plains, immense forests, immense rivers, the horizon always unclear, always confused with the earth amid swift-moving clouds and tenuous mists, which do not allow the point where the world ends and the sky begins to be marked in a far-off perspective. To the south and the north, savages lurk, waiting for moonlit nights to descend, like a pack of hyenas, on the herds that graze the countryside, and on defenseless settlements. In the solitary caravan of wagons slowly traversing the Pampas that stops to rest for a few moments, the crew, gathered around a poor fire, mechanically turn their eyes toward the south at the least murmur of wind blowing the dry grass, to bore their gaze into the profound darkness of the night, searching out the sinister bulks of savage hordes that from one moment to the next can surprise them unprepared. If their ears hear no sound, if their eyes cannot pierce the dark veil that covers this quiet solitude, to be absolutely sure they turn their gaze to the ears of some horse next to the fire, observing if these are at rest and easily folded back. Then their interrupted conversation continues, or they put the half-singed strips of dried beef that are their food into their mouths. If it is not the proximity of savages that worries the man of the countryside, it is the fear of a tiger stalking him, of a viper he might step on.[2] This insecurity in life, which is customary and permanent in the countryside, imprints upon the Argentine character, to my mind, a certain stoic resignation to violent death, making it one of the misfortunes that are inseparable from life, a manner of dying just like any other, and perhaps this may explain, in part, the indifference with which death is given and received, without leaving any deep or lasting impression on those who survive.

The inhabited part of this country, so privileged in riches and containing all manner of climates, may be divided into three distinct physiognomies that imprint different qualities on the populace, according to the way in which it must come to terms with the nature that surrounds it. In the north, melding into the Chaco, a dense forest with impenetrable branches covers expanses we would call unheard of, were there anything unheard of about colossal forms anywhere in the entire expanse of America. In the center, parallel zone, the Pampas and the jungle dispute the land for a long while; the forest dominates in places, then breaks down into sickly, spiny bushes; the jungle appears again thanks to some river that favors it, until in the south the Pampas finally triumph and display their smooth, downy brow, infinite, with no known limit, no noteworthy break. It is an image of the sea on land, the land as it looks on the map, the land still waiting for a command to produce plants and all kinds of seed.

As a notable feature of the physiognomy of this country, one could indicate the agglomeration of navigable rivers that meet in the east, from all points on the horizon, to unite in the Plata and gravely present their stupendous tribute to the ocean, which takes it on the flank, not without visible signs of turbulence and respect. But these immense canals, excavated by the solicitous hand of nature, do not bring about any changes at all in national customs. The son of the Spanish adventurers that colonized the country detests navigation, and feels himself imprisoned within the narrow confines of a boat or launch. When a large river cuts off his path, he calmly undresses, prepares his horse, and directs it to swim toward some barren island out in the distance; arriving there, horse and horseman rest, and from island to island, the crossing is finally completed.

In this manner, the greatest favor that divine providence grants to a people is disdained by the Argentine gaucho, who sees it as an obstacle opposing his movement, rather than the most powerful medium for facilitating it. In this manner, the source of the greatness of nations which brought celebrity to remote Egypt, which made Holland great and is the cause of the rapid development of North America—navigation through rivers or canals—is a dead resource, unexploited by the inhabitant of the margins of the Bermejo, Pilcomayo, Paraná, Paraguay, and Uruguay Rivers. From the Plata, a few little ships with Italian and Genoese crews sail upstream; but this movement goes only a few leagues, and then ceases almost entirely. The instinct for navigation, possessed to such a high degree by the Saxons of the north, was not given to the Spanish. A different spirit is needed to stir up those arteries, in which the vivifying fluids of a nation today lie stagnant. Of all these rivers that should be bringing civilization, power, and wealth to even the most hidden depths of the continent, making Santa Fe, Entre Ríos, Corrientes, Córdoba, Salta, Tucumán, and Jujuy peoples swimming in riches and overflowing with population and culture, there is only one that is fecund in its benefits for those who live on its banks: the Plata, which sums up all of them.

At its mouth are situated two cities: Montevideo and Buenos Aires, today alternately reaping the advantages of their enviable position. Buenos Aires is destined one day to be the most gigantic city of both Americas. With a benign climate, mistress of the navigation of the hundred rivers that flow at its feet, leisurely reclining over an immense territory, and with thirteen interior provinces knowing no other outlet for their products, it already would be the American Babylon, had not the spirit of the Pampas blown over it and the riches that the rivers and provinces must always bring to it in tribute been strangled at their source. It alone, in the vast expanse of Argentina, is in contact with European nations; it alone exploits the advantages of foreign commerce; it alone has power and income. In vain, the provinces have asked it to allow a little bit of European civilization, industry, and immigration to reach them; stupid, colonial policies have turned a deaf ear to this clamor. But the provinces avenged themselves by sending Buenos Aires, in Rosas, much and too much of the barbarism they have to spare.

Very dearly have those who used to say, "The Argentine Republic ends at Arroyo del Medio," paid the price.[3] Now it goes from the Andes to the sea: barbarism and violence have brought Buenos Aires down to a level even lower than that of the provinces. We should not complain about Buenos Aires, which is great and will become more so, because this is its fate. First we would have to complain about divine providence, and ask that it rectify the configuration of the earth. As this is not possible, let us accept as made well that which the Master's hand has made. Let us complain about the ignorance of this brutal power that makes sterile, for himself and for the provinces, the gifts that nature wasted on a people who have strayed. Buenos Aires, instead of sending prosperity, riches, and knowledge to the interior, now sends only chains, exterminating hordes, and little subordinate tyrants. It too avenges the evil the provinces did to it when they trained Rosas![4]

I have indicated this circumstance of the monopolizing position of Buenos Aires to show how in that country[5] there is an organization of the land so central and so unitary, that although Rosas might have cried in good faith: "Confederation or death!" he would have ended up with the Unitarist system that he has established today. We, however, wanted unity in civilization and liberty and have been given unity in barbarism and slavery. But another time will come in which things will return to their normal course. For now, what concerns us is to know that the progress of civilization accrues only in Buenos Aires: the Pampas are a very bad means of bringing and distributing it to the provinces, and later we shall see what results from this. But, beyond all these features peculiar to certain parts of that territory, one general, uniform, and constant trait predominates: whether the land is covered with the lush, colossal vegetation of the tropics, or sickly, spiny, rough bushes reveal the scarce moisture that gives them life, or, finally, whether the Pampas display their clear, monotonous face, the surface of the land is generally flat and unified, without even the sierras of San Luis and Córdoba in the center, and some outlying branches of the Andes in the north, being enough to interrupt this limitless continuity. A new unifying element for the nation that one day will populate those vast solitudes, since it is well known that mountains interposed between countries, and other natural obstacles, maintain the isolation of peoples and preserve their primitive peculiarities. North America is destined to be a federation, less because of the initial independence of its settlements, than because of her broad exposure to the Atlantic and the many routes that lead from it to the interior: the St. Lawrence in the north, the Mississippi in the south, and the immense system of canals in the center. The Argentine Republic is "one and indivisible."

Many philosophers, too, have thought that the plains prepare the way for despotism, in the same way that the mountains have lent support to the forces of liberty. This limitless plain, which from Salta to Buenos Aires and from there to Mendoza, for a distance of more than seven hundred leagues, allows enormous, heavy wagons to roll without meeting a single obstacle on roads where human hands have scarcely needed to cut down more than a few trees and shrubs, this plain constitutes one of the most notable features of the Republic's interior physiognomy. To prepare routes of communication, all that is needed are individual effort and the results of raw nature; even if skill were to lend nature its assistance, even if the forces of society tried to supplant the weakness of the individual, the colossal dimensions of the task would terrify the most enterprising, and the inadequacy of the effort would make it inopportune. So, in the matter of roads, wild nature will make the laws for a long time to come, and the actions of civilization will remain weak and ineffective.

This expanse of the plains, moreover, imprints a certain Asiatic tinge on life in the interior that is not at all unpronounced. Many times, when a tranquil, resplendent moon appears from amid the grassland, I have saluted it mechanically with these words of Volney, describing the Ruins: "La pleine lune à l'Orient s'élevait sur un fond bleuâtre aux plaines rives de l'Euphrate."[6] And, in effect, there is something in the Argentine solitudes that brings to mind the Asian solitudes; there is some analogy to be found between the spirit of the Pampas and the plains that lie between the Tigris and the Euphrates; some relation between the troop of solitary wagons crossing our solitudes to arrive, after a march of months, in Buenos Aires, and the caravan of camels heading for Baghdad or Smyrna. Our traveling wagons are a kind of squadron of small vessels, whose people have their own customs, languages, and dress that distinguish them from other inhabitants, as the sailor may be distinguished from men of the land.

The foreman is a caudillo, as is the caravan chief in Asia. To reach this position, he needs a will of iron and a character so bold as to be rash, in

order to control the audacity and turbulent nature of the land bucca-
neers that he alone will govern and dominate, in the abandoned wilds
of the desert. At the least sign of insubordination, the foreman raises his
iron *chicote* and lets loose blows causing contusions and wounds on
the insolent one; if the resistance continues, before resorting to pistols,
whose aid he generally disdains, he jumps from his horse with his formidable knife in hand, and very quickly reclaims his authority by the
superior dexterity with which he handles it.[7] He who dies in these executions by the foreman leaves behind no rights to any kind of complaint, since the authority that has murdered him is considered to be
legitimate.

This, then, is how, in Argentine life, the predominance of brute force,
the preponderance of the strongest, authority with no limits and no
accountability for those in command, justice administered without
formality and without debate, begin to be established because of these
peculiar characteristics. In addition, the wagon troop carries firearms: a
rifle or two in each wagon and sometimes a small, swiveling cannon in
the lead one. If barbarians attack the troop, it forms a circle by tying one
wagon to the next, and almost always victoriously resists the greed of
the savages, avid for blood and plunder.

Mule trains frequently fall, defenseless, into the hands of these American Bedouins, and it is a rare instance when the muleteers escape having their throats cut. On these long trips, the Argentine proletarian
acquires the habit of living far from society and of struggling alone with
nature, hardened by privation, with no resources but his own personal
cleverness and ability to guard against all the risks that continually surround him.

The people who inhabit these extensive territories are made up of
two distinct races, Spanish and indigenous, which, by mixing, form imperceptible halfway points. In the rural areas of Córdoba and San Luis
the pure Spanish race predominates, and it is common to find in the
countryside, tending sheep, girls as white, as rosy and beautiful as the
elegant women of a capital city might wish to be. In Santiago del Estero, the majority of the peasant population still speaks Quechua, revealing its Indian origins. In Corrientes, the peasants use a very amus-
ing Spanish dialect: "General, give me a *chiripá*," Lavalle's soldiers used
to say to him.[8]

In the rural areas of Buenos Aires the Andalusian soldier still can be
recognized, and in the city foreign surnames predominate. The black
race, now almost extinct except in Buenos Aires, has left its *zambos* and

mulattoes, inhabitants of the cities, as a link connecting civilized with rustic man; a race inclined to civilization, gifted with talent and with the finest instincts for progress.[9]

Apart from this, the fusion of these three families has resulted in a homogenous whole, distinguished by its love for idleness and incapacity for industry, except when education and the exigencies of social position put the spurs to it and pull it out of its customary pace. The incorporation of indigenous races caused by colonization has contributed much to produce this unfortunate result. The American races live in idleness, and demonstrate an incapacity, even when forced, to apply themselves to hard, uninterrupted work. This prompted the idea of bringing blacks to America, which has produced such fatal results. But the Spanish race has not shown itself to be any more given to action when, in the American deserts, it has been left to its own instincts.

In the Argentine Republic, it makes one feel pity and shame to compare the German or Scottish colonies to the south of Buenos Aires with the towns existing in the interior. In the first, the little houses are painted, always clean in front, adorned with flowers and nice little shrubs; the furnishings, simple but complete; the dishes made of copper or tin, always shining; the bed with nice curtains; and the inhabitants in constant motion and action. Milking cows, making butter and cheese, some families have been able to amass colossal fortunes, retiring to the city to enjoy its conveniences.

The native town is the disgraceful reverse side of this coin: dirty children covered in rags, living amid packs of dogs; men stretched out on the ground, in utter inactivity; filth and poverty everywhere; a little table and leather chests, the only furnishings; miserable huts for habitation, notable for their generally barbaric and neglected appearance.

This misery, which is now disappearing as a feature of the rural, pastoral areas, doubtless motivated the words wrested out of Sir Walter Scott by spite and the humiliation of the English forces: "The vast plains of Buenos Aires," says he, "are populated solely by Christian savages, known by the name of guachos"—that is, gauchos—"whose principal furnishings are horses' skulls, whose food is raw meat and water, and whose favorite pastime is racing horses until they burst. Unfortunately," adds the good gringo, "they preferred national independence over our cottons and muslins." * It would be good to make a proposal to

---

*Life of Napoleon Buonaparte, vol. II, chap. I. (Author's note to the first edition.)

England, just to see how many yards of linen and how many pieces of muslin it would give to own the plains of Buenos Aires!

Throughout that limitless expanse, as we have described it, are scattered here and there fourteen provincial capitals, which, were we to follow their obvious order, we could classify by geographical location: Buenos Aires, Santa Fe, Entre Ríos, and Corrientes, along the banks of the Paraná River; Mendoza, San Juan, Rioja, Catamarca, Tucumán, Salta, and Jujuy, in a line almost parallel to the Chilean Andes; Santiago, San Luis, and Córdoba, in the center. But this way of enumerating Argentine towns doesn't lead to any of the social outcomes I am looking for. The classification that suits my objective emerges from the way of life of country people, which is what influences their character and spirit. I have already said that proximity to rivers imprints no modification at all, since they are unnavigated, except to an insignificant degree of no influence. However, all the Argentine towns, except for San Juan and Mendoza, live off the products of pasturage; Tucumán exploits, as well, its agriculture; and Buenos Aires, besides grazing millions of head of cattle and sheep, dedicates itself to the multiple and varied occupations of civilized life.

Argentine cities have the regular physiognomy of almost all American cities: their streets are cut at right angles and their population disseminated across a broad area, with the exception of Córdoba, which, built within a limited, narrow district, has all the appearances of a European city, made even more striking by the multitude of spires and cupolas of its numerous, magnificent churches. The city is the center of Argentine, Spanish, European civilization; the artisans' workshops are there, the commercial stores, the schools and academies, the courthouses: in short, everything that characterizes cultured peoples.

There, elegant manners, the conveniences of luxury, European clothing, the tailcoat, and the frock coat have their theater and their appropriate place. Not without purpose do I make this trivial enumeration. The capital city of the pastoral provinces sometimes exists by itself, without any smaller cities, and in more than one of them the uncivilized region reaches right up to its streets. The desert surrounds the cities at a greater or lesser distance, hems them in, oppresses them; savage nature reduces them to limited oases of civilization, buried deep into an uncivilized plain of hundreds of square miles, scarcely interrupted by some little town or other of any consequence. Buenos Aires and Córdoba are the cities that have been able to sprout the greatest number of small towns in the countryside, to be additional focuses of civilization and municipal interests; this in itself is noteworthy.

The man of the city wears European dress, lives a civilized life as we know it everywhere: in the city, there are laws, ideas of progress, means of instruction, some municipal organization, a regular government, etc. Leaving the city district, everything changes in aspect. The man of the country wears other dress, which I will call American, since it is common to all peoples; his way of life is different, his needs, specific and limited. They are like two distinct societies, two peoples strange to one another. And more still: the man of the country, far from aspiring to resemble the man of the city, rejects with scorn his luxuries and his polite manners; and the clothing of the city dweller, his tailcoat, his cape, his saddle—no such sign of Europe can appear in the countryside with impunity. All that is civilized in the city is blockaded, banished outside of it, and anyone who would dare show up in a frock coat, for example, and mounted on an English saddle, would draw upon himself the peasants' jeers and their brutal aggression.

Now let us study the external physiognomy of the extensive countryside surrounding the cities, and let us penetrate the internal life of its inhabitants. I have already said that, in many provinces, the compulsory border is an interposed, waterless desert. In general, this is not the case for the countryside of a province when the greatest part of its population resides there. In Córdoba, for example, where 160,000 souls live, scarcely 20,000 of them are within the isolated city district; all the rest of the population is in the country, which, since it is commonly a flat plain, is grassy in almost all areas, whether covered with forests or denuded of significant vegetation, and in some areas with such abundance and such exquisite quality that an artificial meadow would not surpass it. Mendoza and San Juan above all are exceptions to this peculiar characteristic of uncultivated areas, since their inhabitants principally live off the products of agriculture. Everywhere else, with grass in abundance, the raising of livestock is not the occupation of the inhabitants, but rather their means of subsistence. Once again, pastoral life unexpectedly brings to mind the recollection of Asia, whose plains we always imagine to be covered, here and there, with the tents of Kalmyks, Cossacks, and Arabs. The primitive life of the settlers, the eminently barbaric and unchanging life, the life of Abraham which is that of today's Bedouin, looms in the Argentine countryside, although modified by civilization in an odd way.

The Arab tribe, roaming through Asian solitudes, lives united under the command of an elder of the tribe or a warrior chief. A society exists, although it may not be permanently set in a certain place on earth; religious beliefs, traditions immemorial, the invariability of customs, respect for elders, together form a code of law, of customary ways and practices of government, that maintains order, morality as they understand it, and association within the tribe. But progress is suffocated, because there can be no progress without permanent ownership of land, without the city, which develops the capacity of man for industry and permits him to extend his acquisitions.

On the Argentine plains, the nomad tribe does not exist. The herdsman owns the land as a proprietor, he stays in one place which belongs to him; but it has been necessary to dissolve association within the group, and to spread families out over an immense surface, in order for him to occupy it. Imagine an expanse of two thousand square leagues, totally populated but with homesteads set apart from each another by four leagues, sometimes eight, two at the closest. The development of property and furnishings is not impossible; articles of luxury are not totally incompatible with this isolation, and riches could construct a fine edifice in the desert. But the stimulus is lacking, the example has disappeared, the need to maintain a dignified appearance, which is felt in the cities, is not felt there, amid isolation and solitude. Unavoidable privations justify natural laziness, and a frugality of pleasures quickly brings with it all the exterior aspects of barbarity. Society has completely disappeared; all that is left is the feudal family, isolated, enclosed within itself, and with no collective society; all forms of government are made impossible, the municipality does not exist, the police cannot do their work, and civil justice has no means of catching delinquents.

I am not aware of the modern world offering a type of association as monstrous as this one. It is the exact opposite of the Roman municipality, which concentrated within one district the whole population, which from there went out to work the surrounding fields. So a strong social organization did exist, and its beneficial effects are felt even today, having prepared the way for modern civilization. The Argentine type is similar to the old Slavonic *sloboda,* the difference being that the latter was agricultural and therefore more easily governed; the spreading out of the population was not as extensive as it is in the former. It is different from the nomad tribe, in that the latter hardly even passes as a society since it does not own land. And finally, it is somewhat similar to the feudal system of the Middle Ages, where barons resided in the country and from there made war on the cities and devastated the countryside; but here, the baron and his feudal castle are missing. If some power rises up in the country, it is momentary, it is democratic; it cannot be inherited or preserved, owing to a lack of mountains and natural strongholds.

That is why even the savage tribes of the Pampas are better organized for moral development than is our countryside.

But what is noteworthy in this society, in terms of its social aspects, is its affinity with ancient life, with Spartan or Roman life, were it not for a radical difference. The free citizen of Sparta or Rome lay the burden of material life, the worry of providing for subsistence, upon his slaves, while he himself lived free of worry in the forum and in the public square, occupying himself only with interests of the state, of peace, war, and partisan struggles. Pasturage provides the same advantages, with the inhuman function of the ancient Helot assumed by livestock. Spontaneous procreation makes a fortune accumulate indefinitely; the hand of man is unnecessary, his work, his intelligence, his time are not needed for the preservation and growth of his means of living. But although he needs none of this for the material side of life, he cannot put to use the effort he saves as the Romans did: he lacks a city, a municipality, intimate association, and therefore lacks the basis for all social development; since the ranchers do not meet together, they have no public needs to satisfy; in a word, there is no *res publica*.

Moral progress, the culture of intelligence neglected in the Arab or Tartar tribe, is thus here not only neglected, but impossible. Where could a school be placed so that children disseminated over ten leagues in every direction could attend classes? Civilization, then, can never be attained, barbarism is the norm, and we can be thankful if domestic customs preserve a small measure of morality.* Religion suffers the consequences of society's dissolution; there is only a nominal parish, the pulpit has no audience, the priest flees from his isolated chapel or becomes demoralized by inactivity and solitude; vices, simony, and accepted barbarism penetrate his cell and turn his moral superiority into a source of fortune and ambition, for, in the end, he winds up becoming a partisan caudillo.

I have witnessed a rural scene worthy of primitive times in the world, before the establishment of the priesthood. In 1838, I was in the sierra of San Luis, in the home of a rancher whose two favorite occupations were praying and gambling. He had built a chapel in which, on Sunday afternoons, he himself recited the rosary, to substitute for the priest and the holy service that had been lacking for years. That was a Homeric

---

*In 1826, during a yearlong stay in the sierra of San Luis, I taught six young men from prominent families to read, the youngest of whom was twenty-two years old. (Author's note to the first edition.)

picture: the sun setting in the west; the sheep returning to the fold, splitting the air with their bleats; the master of the house—a man of sixty with a noble appearance, in which his pure European race was displayed by the whiteness of his skin, his blue eyes, his wide, smooth brow—reciting the service, to which responded a dozen women and a few young boys whose horses, still not entirely broken, were tied up near the chapel door. The rosary concluded, he made a fervent offering. I have never heard a voice more full of devotion, a fervor more pure, a faith more firm, or a prayer more beautiful, more appropriate to the circumstances, than the one he recited. In it, he asked God for rain for the fields, fertility for the livestock, peace for the Republic, safety for travelers. . . . I am very prone to weeping, and that day I wept until I sobbed, because religious sentiment had awakened in my soul with exaltation and like an unknown sensation, for I have never observed a more religious scene. I thought I was back in the times of Abraham, in his presence, in that of God and of the nature which reveals Him. The voice of that honest and innocent man made every fiber in me shake, and penetrated into my very bone.

This, then, is what religion is reduced to in the pastoral countryside: to natural religion. Christianity exists, like the Spanish language, as a sort of tradition that is carried on, but corrupted, embodied in coarse superstitions, with no instruction, rites, or conviction. Almost everywhere in the countryside far from the cities, it happens that, when merchants from San Juan or Mendoza arrive, they are presented with three or four babies a few months or a year old to baptize, people being convinced that because of their education, they can do this validly; and it is not unusual that when a priest arrives, they bring him young boys already breaking colts, so that he may anoint them and administer baptism *sub conditione.*

Lacking all means of progress and civilization, which cannot develop unless men are grouped together in populous societies, consider the education of men in the country. The women keep the home, prepare the meals, shear the sheep, milk the cows, make cheese, and weave the coarse material from which they make clothing. All the domestic chores, all the production of the home is the woman's job; almost all the burden of work is on her, and she can be thankful if some of the men decide to grow a little corn to feed the family, since bread is unusual as an ordinary staple. The boys exercise their physical strength, and for pleasure become skilled in the handling of the lasso and the bolas, with which they endlessly harass and chase the calves and goats. When they become riders—and this happens almost as soon as they learn to walk—they do a few tasks on horseback; later on, when they have grown in strength, they race through the fields, falling off horses and getting up again, tumbling on purpose over viscacha holes, jumping off cliffs, and becoming skilled horsemen. When puberty arrives, they devote themselves to breaking wild colts, and death is only the least of the punishments that await them, if at any moment they lack in strength or courage. With young manhood comes complete independence—and idleness.

Here is where what I will call the public life of the gaucho begins, for his education is now finished. We must see these men as Spanish only in language, and in the confused religious notions they maintain, to be able to appreciate their indomitable, haughty character, born of the struggle of isolated man with savage nature, of rational man with the brute. We must see these heavily bearded faces, these grave, serious countenances like those of Asian Arabs, to judge the pitying disdain inspired in them by the sight of a sedentary city dweller, who may have read many books but does not know how to pull down a fierce bull and kill it; who would not know how to provide himself with a horse in the open country, on foot and without help from anyone; who has never stopped a tiger, facing it with a dagger in one hand and a poncho wrapped around the other to stick in its mouth, while he runs it through the heart and leaves it lying at his feet. This habit of triumphing over all resistance, of always proving himself superior to nature, challenging and conquering it, develops a prodigious feeling of individual importance and superiority. The Argentines, civilized or ignorant, of whatever class they may be, have a high awareness of their worth as a nation; all the other peoples of America accuse them of this vanity and are offended by their presumption and arrogance. I think the charge is not totally unfounded, and it causes me no regret. Woe to the nation without faith in itself! It was not meant for great things! How much did the arrogance of these Argentine gauchos, who have never seen anything under the sun better than themselves, not even learned or powerful men, surely contribute to the independence of a whole region of America? The European, for them, is the least of all, for he cannot even stand a couple of plunges on a horse.* If the origin of this national vanity in the lower classes is a mean one, its results are no less noble for that reason, just as the water of a river is no less pure because it may be born at a marshy,

---

*General Mansilla said in the House, during the French blockade: "And why should we fear these Europeans who can't even ride all night?"; and the immense, plebeian crowd of supporters drowned out the orator's voice with a clamor of applause. (Author's note to the first edition.)

infected source. The hatred that cultured men inspire in them is implacable, and their repugnance for the dress, ways, and manners of those men unyielding. From this clay are molded Argentine soldiers, and it is easy to imagine what these sorts of customs can produce in valor and tolerance for war. Add to this that from earliest childhood they are accustomed to slaughtering cattle, and that this act of necessary cruelty familiarizes them with the spilling of blood and hardens their hearts against the victims' moans.

Country life, then, has developed the gaucho's physical faculties, but none of his intelligence. His moral character is affected by his custom of triumphing over obstacles and the power of nature: he is strong, haughty, vigorous. Without instruction, without need of it either, without a means of subsistence and without needs, he is happy in the midst of his poverty and privations, which are not many for one who has never known greater pleasures or set his desires any higher. So, although this dissolution of society deeply implants barbarism because of the impossibility and uselessness of moral and intellectual education, in another way it is not without its attractions. The gaucho does not work; he finds food and clothing at hand in his home. Both of these are provided by his livestock, if he is a proprietor, or the house of his employer or relatives, if he owns nothing. The attention the livestock require boils down to excursions and pleasurable games. The branding, which is like the grape harvest for farmers, is a celebration whose arrival is greeted with transports of joy: this is the place where all the men within a twenty-league radius meet, where they show off incredible skill with the lasso. The gaucho arrives at the branding on his best racing horse with a slow, measured step, halting some distance away, and to better enjoy the spectacle, crosses his leg over the horse's neck. If enthusiasm so moves him, he descends slowly from his horse, unrolls his lasso, and throws it over a bull going by at the speed of lightning, forty paces away: he catches it by a hoof, as he intended, and calmly rolls his rope up again.

CHAPTER II

Argentine Originality and Characters

Ainsi que l'océan, les steppes remplissent l'esprit du sentiment de l'infini.

Humboldt[1]

Although the conditions of pastoral life, as constituted by colonization and negligence, give rise to grave difficulties for any sort of political organization and many more for the triumph of European civilization, its institutions, and the wealth and liberty that come from it, it cannot be denied that this situation also has a poetic side, and aspects worthy of the novelist's pen. If the glimmer of a national literature momentarily shines in new American societies, it will come from descriptions of grand scenes of nature, and above all, from the struggle between European civilization and indigenous barbarism, between intelligence and matter. This is an awesome struggle in America, which gives rise to scenes that are very peculiar, very characteristic, and very alien to the sphere of ideas within which the European spirit is educated, since dramatic forces become unfamiliar, customs surprising, and characters original outside the region where they occur.

The only North American novelist who has succeeded in making a name for himself in Europe is Fenimore Cooper, and this is because he transported the scene of his descriptions outside the sphere occupied by the settlers, to the borderland between barbarous and civilized life, to the theater of war where the indigenous races and the Saxon race are fighting for possession of the territory.

In a similar way, our young poet Echeverría has successfully gained the attention of the Spanish literary world with his poem *La cautiva*. This Argentine bard set aside Dido and Argos—which his predecessors the Varela brothers had treated with classic mastery and poetic ardor, but without success or consequence, since they added nothing to the stock of European ideas—and turned his gaze to the desert. There in the immensity without limit, in the solitudes where the savage roams, in the far-off zone of fire that the traveler sees coming toward him when the fields burn, he found the inspiration that the spectacle of a solemn, grand, incommensurate, silent nature provides to the imagination; and then the echo of his verse could make itself heard, applauded even in the Spanish peninsula.

In passing, a fact must be noted that explains many of the social phenomena of nations. The features of nature produce customs and ways peculiar to those features, so that where those features reappear, the same means of controlling them are found again, invented by different peoples. This explains for me why the bow and arrow are found among all savage peoples, whatever their race, their origin, or their geographic location. When I read in Cooper's *The Last of the Mohicans* how Hawkeye and Uncas had lost the trail of the Mingos in a stream, I said to myself: "They're going to dam up the stream." When, in *The Prairie*, the Trapper waits in uncertainty and agony while the fire threatens, an Argentine would have counseled the same thing that the Trapper finally suggests, which is to clear a space and then burn it, so as to be able to retreat from the invading fire onto the ashes of the burned-out area. The practice for escaping grass fires of people crossing the Pampas is the same. When the fugitives in *The Prairie* arrive at a river, and Cooper describes the mysterious operation of the Pawnee with the buffalo hide he gathers up, "He's going to make a *pelota*," I said to myself; it was a shame there was no woman to pull it, for among us the women are the ones who cross rivers with the *pelota* held in their teeth by a lasso. The procedure for roasting a buffalo's head in the desert is the same one we use to *batear* a cow's head or a loin of veal.[2] In short, a thousand other features that I omit prove the truth that analogies in the land bring analogous customs, resources, and expediencies. There is no other reason for finding, in Fenimore Cooper, descriptions of customs and ways that seem to be plagiarized from the Pampas; just as we find reproduced in the pastoral habits of America the same grave countenances, hospitality, and dress of the Arabs.

There exists, then, an underlying poetry, born of the natural features of the country and the unique customs it engenders. Poetry, in order to awaken (for poetry is like religious feeling, a faculty of the human spirit), needs the spectacle of beauty, of terrible power, of immensity, of expanse, of vagueness, of incomprehensibility, because only where the palpable and vulgar ends, can the lies of the imagination, the ideal world, begin. Now I ask: what impression must be left on the inhabitant of the Argentine Republic by the simple act of fixing his eyes on the horizon and seeing . . . seeing nothing, because the more he sinks his eyes into that uncertain, vaporous, indefinite horizon, the farther away it gets from him, the more it fascinates him, confuses him, and plunges him into contemplation and doubt? Where does the world end that, in vain, he wishes to penetrate? He does not know! What is out there beyond what he can see? Solitude, danger, savages, death! This then is poetry: the man who moves among these scenes feels assaulted by fears and fantastic uncertainties, by dreams that disturb him while he is awake.

The result is that the Argentine people are poets by character, by nature. How could they not be, when, in the middle of a serene, pleasant afternoon, a grim, black cloud appears from who knows where, stretches itself across the sky before two words can be said, and suddenly a stampede of thunder announces a storm that leaves the traveler cold and holding his breath, for fear of attracting one of the thousands of lightning bolts coming down around him? Darkness is followed by light; death is everywhere; a terrible, incomparable power in one moment has made him go inside himself and feel his nothingness in the midst of that disturbed nature, to feel God, to put it plainly, in the terrifying magnificence of His works. Is this color enough for the palette of fantasy? Masses of darkness that cloud the day, masses of trembling, livid light that illuminate the darkness for an instant and show the infinite distance of the Pampas, lightning flashing across them, the final symbol of power. These images are meant to stay deeply engraved. Thus, when the storm passes, the gaucho is left sad, pensive, serious, and the succession of light and darkness continues in his imagination, in the same way that the disk of the sun stays on the retina for a long time when we stare at it.

Ask the gaucho whom the lightning bolts prefer to kill, and he will introduce you to a world of moral and religious idealization, mixed with badly understood facts of nature and superstitious, crude traditions. Add to this, if it is true that electric fluid is part of the economy of human life and is the same as what they call nervous fluid, which when excited, arouses passions and sparks enthusiasm, that a people inhabiting an atmosphere charged with electricity to the point where clothing, if rubbed, gives off sparks like a cat's fur stroked the wrong way, must be quite disposed to the workings of the imagination.

How could he who witnesses these impressive scenes not be a poet?

> The eye turns in vain, focuses
> on its immensity, and
> like a bird over the sea
> cannot find in its intense desire
> a place to fix its brief flight.
> Everywhere, fields and countryside
> havens of bird and beast;
> everywhere sky and solitudes
> known only to God
> that only He can fathom.[3]
>
> Echeverría

Or he who has before him this adorned nature?

> From the bowels of America
> two torrents are unleashed:
> the Paraná, face of pearl,
> and the Uruguay, face of nacre.
>
> They both run through forests,
> or through flowering gardens,
> like two great mirrors
> framed by emeralds.
>
> They are greeted along their course
> by the melancholy peacock,
> the hummingbird and the linnet,
> the thrush and the wild dove.
>
> As if before kings, before them
> bow down bucares and palm trees,
> and toss them air flowers,
> myhrr and orange blossoms;
>
> then they meet in the Guazú,
> and uniting their waters,
> mixing nacre and pearl,
> spill into the Plata.[4]
>
> Domínguez

But this is learned poetry, the poetry of the city. There is another kind whose echoes are heard through the solitary fields: the popular poetry, innocent and disorderly, of the gaucho.

Ours is also a musical people. This is a national inclination that all our neighbors recognize. When an Argentine is presented at a home in Chile for the first time, he is invited to sit at the piano immediately, or they hand him a *vihuela,* and if he excuses himself, saying that he doesn't know how to play it, they are surprised and don't believe him, "because being an Argentine," they say, "he must be a musician."[5] This is a popular preconception that acknowledges our own national customs. Indeed: the cultivated young person of the cities plays the piano or the flute, the violin or the guitar; the mestizos devote themselves almost exclusively to music, and many talented composers and instrumentalists emerge from among them.[6] On summer nights guitars are heard ceaselessly at the shop doors, and late at night one's sleep is sweetly interrupted by serenades and strolling concerts.

The peasants have their own songs.

The *triste,* which predominates in the north, is a Phrygian, mournful song, natural to man in the primitive state of barbarism, according to Rousseau.

The *vidalita,* a popular song with a chorus, accompanied by a guitar and tambour, to whose refrain the multitude joins in as the number and noise of the voices grows. This type of song seems to me an inheritance from the indigenous people, because I have heard it at an Indian festival in Copiapó, celebrating Candlemas; being a religious song it must be very old, and the Chilean Indians could not have adopted it from the Argentine Spaniards. The *vidalita* is the popular meter used to sing about current events and for battle songs: the gaucho composes the verses he sings and popularizes them through the assemblies that his singing demands.

So then, among the coarseness of national customs, these two art forms, which beautify civilized life and give an outlet to so many generous passions, are honored and favored by the masses themselves, who exercise their rough muse in lyric and poetic compositions. The young Echeverría resided in the countryside for a few months in 1840, and the fame of his poetry about the Pampas had already preceded him: the gauchos crowded around him with respect and devotion, and when a recent arrival would show signs of disdain toward the "city slicker,"[7] someone would whisper into his ear, "He's a poet," and any hostile prejudices would cease upon hearing this privileged title.

It is well known, moreover, that the guitar is a popular instrument of the Spanish, and that it is common in America. In Buenos Aires above all, the *majo,* typical of the Spanish popular classes, is very much alive. He can be found in the *compadrito* of the city and the gaucho of the countryside. The Spanish *jaleo* survives in the *cielito:* the fingers substitute for castanets.[8] All the movements of the *compadrito* reveal the *majo:* the movement of his shoulders, the gestures, the placement of his hat, even the way he spits through his teeth; it is all still genuinely Andalusian.

From amid these customs and general tastes, noteworthy specialties emerge that someday will embellish our national drama and novel and give them an original hue. I only want to note a few that will serve to fill out the idea of these customs, in order then to trace the character, causes, and effects of the civil war.

The *Rastreador*

The most conspicuous one of all, the most extraordinary, is the *rastreador.*[9] All the gauchos of the interior provinces are rastreadors. In plains so spread out, where paths and roads cross in every direction and the animals graze or walk through open fields, it is necessary to know how to follow an animal's tracks and to distinguish them among a thousand others, to recognize whether the animal is going slowly or rapidly, loose or harnessed, loaded down or unburdened; this is popular, homegrown knowledge. I once got off a side road onto the main one leading to Buenos Aires, and the peon who was driving me looked down at the ground, as was his custom. "Here's a good little black-and-white mule," he said after a moment, " . . . this was Don N. Zapata's troop . . . she's real good in the saddle . . . she's saddled up . . . they went by yesterday. . . ." This man was from the sierra of San Luis, the troop was returning from Buenos Aires, and it had been a year since the last time he had seen the little black-and-white mule, whose tracks were mixed in with those of the whole troop in a two-foot-wide path. But this, which seems incredible, is simply common knowledge; this man was just a peon mule driver, not a professional rastreador.

The rastreador is a serious, circumspect person, whose pronouncements are accepted as evidence in the lower courts. The awareness of the knowledge he possesses gives him a certain reserved and mysterious dignity. Everyone treats him with consideration: the poor man, because the rastreador can do him harm by slandering or denouncing him; the landowner, because the rastreador's testimony can decide a judgment for or against him. A theft has been committed during the night: scarcely is it discovered, they run to search for a footprint made by the thief, and this found, cover it over with something so the wind will not fade it. The rastreador is called in immediately; he looks at the tracks and follows them, only looking at the ground from time to time, as if his eyes were seeing a relief of that footprint, imperceptible to others. He follows along the streets, crosses through gardens, enters a home, and coldly says, pointing out a man he finds there, "He's the one!" The crime is proven, and rare is the criminal who protests the accusation. For him, even more than for the judge, the testimony of the rastreador is absolute evidence: to deny it would be ridiculous, absurd. He submits, then, to this witness, whom he considers to be like the finger of God pointing at him. I myself have met Calíbar, who has been carrying out his work in one of the provinces for forty consecutive years. He is almost eighty years old now; bent over with age, he still retains a venerable appearance, full of dignity. When someone speaks of his fabulous reputation, he answers: "I'm no good anymore; the boys over there are the ones." The boys are his sons, who have learned in the school of this famous teacher. They say about him that once, while he was on a trip to Buenos Aires, his best saddle was stolen. His wife covered over the tracks with a wooden bowl. Two months later, Calíbar returned, saw the tracks, which by now were erased and unnoticeable to other eyes, and no more was said about the incident. A year and a half later, Calíbar went marching with his head down along a suburban street, went into a house, and found his saddle, blackened and nearly worn out from use. He had found the robber's tracks two years later! In 1830, a prisoner condemned to death had escaped from jail. Calíbar was given the job of finding him. The unlucky man, knowing he would be tracked, had taken all the precautions that the thought of the gallows suggested to him. Useless precautions! Perhaps they only served to bring him down, for since Calíbar's reputation was at stake, his slighted self-esteem made him carry out with greater passion a task that brought down a man but proved the marvel of his vision. The fugitive took advantage of every feature of the ground so as not to leave any traces; he had gone for whole blocks walking on his toes, suddenly jumping over low walls, crossing over a place, and walking backward; Calíbar followed him without losing the trail. If momentarily he went astray, upon finding it again he would exclaim: "You're not gettin' away from me!" Finally he arrived at a water canal in the suburbs, whose current the man had followed to fool the rastreador. . . . Useless! Calíbar went along the banks without distress, without hesitation. Finally he stopped, examined some grass, and said: "This is where he came out; there's no tracks, but these drops of water on the grass show where." He entered a vineyard: Calíbar scouted out the mud walls surrounding it, and said: "He's inside." The party of soldiers looked until they were tired, and returned to report the futility of their search. "He hasn't come out," was the brief answer the rastreador gave, without moving, or starting a new examination. In fact, he had not come out, and the next day he was executed. In 1831, some political prisoners planned an escape: everything was ready, their accomplices on the outside alerted. At the moment of the escape, one of them said: "What about Calíbar?" "That's right!" the others replied, terrified and stunned. "Calíbar!" Their families were able to arrange with Calíbar that he be sick for four days after the escape, and thus it could be carried out without difficulty.

What is this mystery of the rastreador? What microscopic power develops in the visual organs of these men? What a sublime creature God made in His image and likeness!

The *Baqueano*

After the rastreador comes the *baqueano,* an eminent personage who holds in his hands the fate of individuals and of provinces.[10] The baqueano is a reserved, serious gaucho, who knows twenty thousand square leagues of plains, forests, and mountains like the palm of his hand. He is the most complete topographer, the only map a general takes along to direct the movements of his campaign. The baqueano is always at his side. As modest and reserved as a mud wall, he is in on all the secrets of the campaign; the fate of the army, the success of the battle, the conquest of a province, all depend on him.

The baqueano is nearly always loyal to his duty, but the general does not always have total confidence in him. Imagine the position of a leader, condemned to take a traitor along beside him and to ask him for the knowledge indispensable to triumph. A baqueano comes upon a little path crossing the road he takes, and he knows to which remote water hole it leads; if he comes upon a thousand, and this happens in the space of a hundred leagues, he knows them all, he knows where they come from and where they go. He knows the hidden ford in the river, above or below the usual passage, and the same for a hundred rivers and streams; he knows of a path, in the extensive marshland, where it can be crossed without difficulty, and the same for a hundred different marshes.

In the darkest night, in the middle of the forests or limitless plains, his companions lost, losing their way, he goes in a circle around them, observing the trees; if there are none, he dismounts, bends down to the ground, examines some bushes, and figures out the altitude; then he mounts at once and says to reassure them: "We're straight across from such a place, so many leagues away from the settlement; the road must be to the south"; and he heads toward the direction he has indicated, calmly, with no hurry to find it and without responding to the objections that fear or fascination suggest to the others.

If even this is not enough, or if he finds himself in the Pampas and the darkness is impenetrable, then he pulls up grass from different spots, smells the roots and the soil, chews them, and after repeating this procedure various times confirms the proximity of some lake, or fresh or saltwater stream, and goes to look for it so as to firmly orient himself. General Rosas, they say, knows by its taste the grass of every *estancia* in southern Buenos Aires province.[11]

If the baqueano is from the Pampas, where there are no roads for crossing, and a traveler asks to be taken directly to a place fifty leagues distant, the baqueano stops for a moment, searches the horizon, examines the ground, fixes his gaze on a point, and takes off at a gallop as straight as an arrow, until he changes direction for reasons only he knows, and galloping day and night, he arrives at the designated place.

The baqueano also announces the closeness of the enemy—that is, at ten leagues away—and the direction from which he is approaching, through the movement of ostriches, deer, and guanacos that flee in a certain direction. When the enemy nears, he observes the dust and by its thickness counts the forces: "There are two thousand men," he says, "five hundred," "two hundred," and the leader operates on the basis of this data, almost always infallible. If the condors and the crows fly in a circle in the sky, he knows whether there are men hiding, or a recently abandoned camp, or simply a dead animal. The baqueano knows the distance between one place and another, the days and hours needed to get there, and even an unknown, lost path by which one can arrive by surprise in half the time; this is why parties of *montoneras* undertake surprise attacks on towns fifty leagues away, and are almost always successful. Do you think I exaggerate? No! General Rivera, from the Banda Oriental, is just a baqueano who knows every tree there is in the entire area of the Republic of Uruguay.[12] The Brazilians couldn't have occupied it without his assistance; without him, the Argentines couldn't have liberated it. Oribe, supported by Rosas, succumbed after three years of struggle with this baqueano general, and all the power of Buenos Aires today, with its numerous armies covering the whole Uruguayan countryside, can disappear, destroyed into pieces from a surprise attack today, from a force cut off tomorrow, from a victory that he will know how to turn into his advantage, from the knowledge of some little road that runs to the rear of the enemy, or from some other insignificant, unobservable feature.

General Rivera began his study of the terrain in 1804, and by waging war on the authorities then, as a smuggler, and afterward on the smugglers as a public servant; next on the king as a patriot, and later on the patriots as a *montonero;* on the Argentines as a Brazilian leader, and on the Brazilians as an Argentine general; on Lavalleja as president, and on President Oribe as a banished leader; and finally on Rosas, the ally of Oribe, as a Uruguayan general, he has had quite enough time to learn a little of the baqueano's knowledge.

The Bad Gaucho

This is a type in certain localities, an *outlaw,* a *squatter,* a particular sort of misanthrope.[13] He is Cooper's Hawkeye or Trapper, with all his knowledge of the desert, with all his aversion to white settlements, but without his natural morality and without his connection to the savages. They call him the *bad gaucho,* this epithet not totally disfavoring him. Justice has pursued him for many years; his name is feared, pronounced in a low voice, but without hatred and almost with respect. He is a mysterious person. He dwells in the Pampas, fields of thistle for his lodging, living on partridges and armadillos; once in a while, if he decides to treat himself to some tongue, he ropes a cow, throws her over by himself, kills her, pulls out his favorite morsel, and leaves the rest to carrion birds. Suddenly, a bad gaucho shows up in a place a posse has just left; he converses peacefully with the good gauchos, who surround and admire him; he stocks up on his "vices," and if he gets sight of the posse, he calmly mounts his horse and points it toward the desert, without haste, without show, disdaining even to look back.[14] The posse rarely follows him; they would kill their horses uselessly, because the one the bad gaucho rides is a bay racer as celebrated as its owner. If fate sometimes unexpectedly throws him into the claws of justice, he charges into the middle of the posse, and with four slashes that his knife opens in the soldiers' faces and bodies, makes his way through them, and stretching down low over the horse's back to elude the bullets that pursue him, he heads for the desert, until, putting a convenient distance between himself and his pursuers, he slows his trot to a tranquil walk. The poets of the surrounding region add this new deed to the biography of the hero of the desert, and his renown soars all across the vast countryside.

Sometimes, he shows up at the door of a country dance with a young girl he has abducted; he starts to dance with his partner, blends into the motions of the *cielito,* and disappears without anyone noticing. The next day he shows up at the home of the aggrieved family, makes the girl he has seduced get down from the horse's rump, and, disdaining the curses of the parents running after him, calmly goes on his way to his limitless abode.

This man, divorced from society, banished by the law, this white-skinned savage, at bottom is not a being more depraved than those who inhabit the settlements. The daring fugitive who charges an entire posse is inoffensive to travelers. The bad gaucho is not a bandit, or an ambusher; assaults on life do not enter his mind, as stealing did not enter the mind of the *churriador:* he steals, that is true, but it is his profession, his trade, his science.[15] He steals horses. One day he arrives at the camp of a cattle herd from the interior; the owner proposes to buy from him a horse of a certain extraordinary coat, a certain shape, certain features, with a white star on the shoulder. The gaucho hunches over, ponders for a moment, and after a short silence answers, "Right now there's no horse like that." What has the gaucho been thinking? In that moment, he has gone through a thousand *estancias* of the Pampas in his mind, he has seen and examined all the horses in the province, with their markings, color, particular traits, and has convinced himself that there is none with a white star on the shoulder; some have them on the forehead, others a white patch on the haunch. Is this memory surprising? No! Napoleon knew two hundred thousand soldiers by name, and recalled, upon seeing them, all the facts pertinent to each. If he isn't asked for the impossible, then, on the indicated day, at a certain point on the road, he will deliver a horse just as requested, payment in advance being no motive for missing the date. On this point, he has the same code of honor as do gamblers regarding their debts.

Sometimes he travels to the countryside of Córdoba or Santa Fe. Then he can be seen crossing the Pampas behind a troop of horses; anyone who encounters him continues on the path without approaching, unless asked to do so.

The *Cantor*

Here you have the ideal image of that life of revolt, civilization, barbarism, and danger. The gaucho *cantor* is the very same bard, poet, or troubadour of the Middle Ages, who moves in the same scenes, between the struggles of the city and the feudalism of the countryside, between the way of life that is ending and the one that is beginning. The cantor wanders from place to place, "from shacks to storehouses,"[16] singing of his heroes of the Pampas pursued by the law, the sobs of the widow whose children were carried off by wild Indians during a recent raid, the defeat and death of the valiant Rauch, the catastrophe of Facundo Quiroga, and the fate that befell Santos Pérez. The cantor, naively, is doing the same work of chronicle, customs, history, biography as the bard of the Middle Ages, and his verses would be collected later as the documents and data on which future historians would base their evidence, if alongside him there did not exist another, cultured society, with a knowledge of events superior to that which this poor fellow unfolds in his innocent rhapsodies. In the Argentine Republic we see at the same time two different societies on the same soil: one still nascent, which, with no knowledge of things over its head, repeats the naive, popular work of the Middle Ages; another which, with no regard for things beneath its feet, tries to attain the latest results of European civilization. The nineteenth and the twelfth centuries live together: one inside the cities, the other in the country.

The cantor has no permanent residence: his abode is wherever the night finds him; his assets are his verses and his voice. Wherever the *cielito* entwines its endless partners, wherever a glass of wine is drained, the cantor has his preferred place, his own role at the party. The Argentine gaucho does not drink unless the music and its verses excite him, and every *pulpería* has a guitar to put in the hands of the cantor, to whom the horses tied up at the door announce from afar that the assistance of his poetic art is needed.*

The cantor mixes in, among his heroic songs, the narration of his own deeds. Unfortunately, the cantor, despite being the Argentine bard, is not freed from having to deal with the law. He, too, has to own up to some stabbings he has dealt out, one or two *desgracias* (killings!) of his own, and some horse or girl he stole. In 1840, a cantor sat on the

---

*It is not beside the point to recall here the notable similarities with the Arabs shown by the Argentines. In Algiers, in Oran, in Mascara, and in desert villages, I always saw Arabs meeting in cafes, since they are completely prohibited from drinking liquor, grouped around a cantor—in general two—accompanying themselves on the *vihuela* as a duo, reciting national songs, mournful like our *tristes*. The reins used by Arabs are woven from leather, with little whips at the ends like ours; the bit we use is the Arab bit, and many of our customs reveal our parents' contact with the Moors of Andalusia. As for physical appearance, that goes without saying: I have met some Arabs whom I would swear I had seen in my own country. (Author's note to the second edition.)

ground with his legs crossed among a group of gauchos on the banks of the majestic Paraná, keeping his audience amused and terrified with the long and animated story of his hardships and adventures. He had already told about the abduction of his love, and the hardship he suffered; about his *desgracia* and the argument that caused it; he was relating his encounter with a posse, and the stabbings he had dealt out in self-defense, when the clatter and shouts of soldiers informed him that this time he was surrounded. The posse, in fact, had formed a horseshoe, with the open side toward the Paraná, which ran twenty yards down below; the banks were that high. The cantor heard the shouting, without getting upset; suddenly they saw him on his horse, and, taking a searching glance at the circle of soldiers with carbines at the ready, he turned the horse toward the bank, put his poncho over its eyes, and dug in his spurs. A few instants later they saw the horse emerging from the depths of the Paraná, without a bit so he could swim more freely, and the cantor holding onto his tail, looking back calmly at the scene he had left on the bank, just as if he were in a rowboat. A few bullets fired by the posse didn't stop him from arriving, safe and sound, at the first small island he lay eyes on.

Otherwise, the original poetry of the cantor is tedious, monotonous, and irregular, as he abandons himself to the inspiration of the moment. More narrative than sentimental, full of images taken from rural life, of horses and scenes of the desert, which make it metaphorical and pompous. When he relates his feats or those of some famous villain, he resembles a Neapolitan improviser, disordered and usually prosaic, elevating himself to poetic heights at moments, then falling again into an insipid, almost meterless recitation. Beyond this, the cantor possesses a repertory of popular poetry: different types of octosyllabic verse in five-, ten-, or eight-line stanzas. Among these are many compositions of merit, which show inspiration and feeling.

I could add to these original character types many others equally curious, equally local, if they had, like these do, a peculiar quality for revealing national customs, without which it is impossible to understand our political personages, or the primordial, American character of the bloody struggle that tears apart the Argentine Republic. As this story goes on, the reader will discover for himself where the rastreador, the baqueano, the bad gaucho, or the cantor are to be found. He will see, in the caudillos whose names have gone beyond Argentine borders, and even in those who fill the world with the horror of their name, the living reflection of the country's internal conditions, customs, and organization.

CHAPTER III

Association

Le Gaucho vit de privation, mais son luxe est la liberté. Fier d'une indépendance sans bornes, ses sentiments, sauvages comme sa vie, sont pourtant nobles e bons.

Head[1]

The *Pulpería*

In the first chapter, we left the Argentine peasant at the moment when he reaches manhood, exactly as nature and the lack of a true society have shaped him. We have seen him as a man independent of all need, free of all subjection, with no idea of government, since all regular and systematic order becomes wholly impossible. With these habits of indolence, of independence, he enters another phase of rural life, which, though common and ordinary, is the starting point for all the great events we will see develop very shortly.

It should not be forgotten that I am speaking of an essentially pastoral people; that I take up their fundamental physiognomy, leaving aside the lesser modifications they experience, to indicate these partial effects at the proper time. I am speaking here of the association among *estancias,* which, distributed more or less four leagues apart, cover the area of a province.

The agricultural countryside also subdivides and spreads out society, but on a greatly reduced scale: one farmer lives next to another, next to the farm tools and the multitude of instruments, harnesses, animals that he uses. The variety of products and the different skills that agriculture calls to its aid establish a necessary relationship between the inhabitants of a valley and make indispensable a rudimentary town to serve as their center. Moreover, the attention and daily chores that farmwork demands require so many hands that leisure becomes impossible, and the men are compelled to remain on their own inherited land. The exact opposite happens in this singular kind of association. Property limits are not marked; the more livestock there is, the fewer hands it occupies; the women take care of all the domestic chores and crafts; the men are left unemployed, without pleasures, without ideas, without business to attend to; domestic home life annoys them, or let us say they reject it. There is a need, then, for a fictitious society to remedy this norm of dissociation. The habit of riding on horseback, acquired since early childhood, is one more stimulus for leaving the home.

Boys have the job of driving the horses out of the corral scarcely has the sun come up, and all the males, even the little ones, saddle up their horses, even if they don't know what to do next. The horse is an integral part of the rural Argentine; it is for him what the cravat is for those who live in the bosom of the cities. In 1841, El Chacho, a caudillo of the plains, emigrated to Chile.[2] "How's it going, friend?" someone asked him. "How do you think it's going?" he answered, with a pained, melancholy tone. "In Chile! And on foot!" Only an Argentine gaucho can appreciate all the misfortune and all the anguish that those two phrases express.

Here, the Arabic, Tartar life appears once again. The following words of Victor Hugo could have been written in the Pampas: "He could not fight on foot; he and his horse are but one person. He lives on horseback; trades, buys, and sells on horseback; drinks, eats, sleeps, and dreams on horseback" (Le Rhin).[3]

The males, then, leave without knowing exactly where they are going. A turn around the herds, a visit to some newborn or to the haunt of a favorite horse, takes up a small part of the day; the rest is absorbed in gatherings at a tavern or a pulpería. There, a certain number of inhabitants from the surrounding parishes assemble; there, news concerning stray animals is given and received; the markings of cattle are traced on the floor; one learns where the tiger hunts, where the lion's tracks have been seen; there, races are set up, the best horses decided; there, finally, is the cantor; there they fraternize by means of drinks passed around the circle and the extravagance of those who can pay.

In this life so without emotion, gambling brings out enervated spirits, liquor lights up slumbering imaginations. This accidental, everyday association, through its repetition, comes to form a closer society than that from which each individual came, and in this assembly without public objective, without any social purpose, begin to grow the rudiments of reputations that later, after years have passed, will appear on the political scene. Let's see how this happens.

The gaucho esteems, above all things, physical strength, skill in handling a horse, and also valor. This meeting, this daily club, is truly an Olympic circus, in which the points each man merits are tested and proven.

The gaucho goes armed with the knife he has inherited from the Spanish. This peculiarity of the Iberian peninsula, this characteristic Saragossan yell of *"Guerra a cuchillo!"* [4] is more real here than in Spain. The knife, more than just a weapon, is an instrument that serves him in all his work. He can't live without it; it is like an elephant's trunk, his arm, his hand, his finger, his everything. The gaucho, as a horseman, boasts of his valor, and at any moment, at the slightest provocation or with no provocation at all, with no purpose other than sizing up a stranger, his knife gleams, describing circles in the air; he plays at stabbing just as he would play at dice. These quarrelsome habits have entered the inner life of the Argentine gaucho so profoundly that custom has created an honor code and rules for knifeplay that guarantee the saving of life. The common man of other countries takes up a knife to kill, and he kills; the Argentine gaucho unsheaths his to fight, and he only wounds. He must be very drunk, he must have truly evil instincts or very deep resentments, for him to make an attempt on the life of his adversary. His object is only to mark him, give him a slash on the face, leave an indelible sign on him. This is why one sees gauchos full of scars that are rarely deep. A fight, then, is joined so one may shine, for the glory of victory, for the love of fame. A wide circle forms around the combatants, and all eyes follow, with passion and fervor, the flash of knives which don't cease waving for a moment. When blood flows in torrents, the spectators, in good conscience, feel obligated to separate them. If a *desgracia* occurs, their sympathies are with the one who has killed; the best horse is offered so he may escape to a faraway place, and there he is received with respect or compassion.[5] If justice catches up with him, it is not unusual for him to face off with the posse, and if he charges them, he acquires from then on a widespread renown. Time goes by, the judge has been replaced, and he may once again show up in his own region, with no steps taken toward further prosecution; he has been absolved.

To kill is a misfortune, unless the deed is repeated so many times that contact with the murderer inspires horror. The rancher Don Juan Manuel Rosas, before entering public life, had made his residence into a kind of asylum for killers, without ever consenting to its use by thieves. This is a preference that could be explained simply by his being a gaucho landowner, if his later conduct hadn't revealed affinities that have appalled the world.

As for the equestrian games, it will suffice to indicate just one of the many that are practiced, to judge the daring required to take part in them. One gaucho rides by his companions at full speed. Another one throws a set of bolas that, in midcourse, manacle his horse. From the whirl of dust stirred up by the latter as he falls, the rider emerges at a run, followed by the horse, who, obeying the laws of physics, is pushed forward by the impulse of his interrupted course. Life is gambled in this pastime, and sometimes is lost.

Would anyone believe that this prowess, skill, and audacity in handling a horse serve as the basis for the great exemplars who have filled the Argentine Republic with their names and changed the face of the country? Yet nothing is more certain. I don't mean to argue that murder and crime have always provided a ladder up. Thousands of bold men have remained obscure bandits, but those who owe their position to these deeds pass the hundreds. In all despotic societies, great natural gifts will be lost to crime; the Roman genius that conquered the world today is the terror of the Pontine Marshes, and the Zumalacárreguis and Minas of Spain are found by the hundreds in Sierra Leone.[6] Man has a need to develop his strength, his capacity, and ambition, so that when legitimate means are lacking, he forges a world with its own laws and morality, and there takes pleasure in showing how he was born a Napoleon or a Caesar.

Within this society, then, in which a culture of the spirit is useless and impossible; where municipal affairs do not exist; where the public good is a word without meaning, because there is no public, the eminently gifted man struggles to realize himself and adopts for that purpose the means and ways he can find. The gaucho will be an evildoer or a caudillo, according to the direction in which things go at the moment when he becomes famous.

Customs of this kind require vigorous means of repression, and to repress merciless men even more merciless judges are needed. What I said in the beginning about the foreman of a wagon train can be applied exactly to the country judge. Before all else, he needs courage: the terror of his name is more powerful than the punishments he applies. The judge, naturally, is some man who was famous years ago, called up by age and his family to an orderly life. Of course, the justice he administers is arbitrary on every point; his conscience or his passions guide him, and his sentences cannot be appealed. Sometimes, there are judges of the lifelong sort, and they are remembered respectfully. But the combination of these executive methods with the arbitrariness of the penalty forms ideas among the people about the power of "authority" that later on have their effect. The judge makes others obey him by his reputation for fearful audacity, his authority, his unpredictable judgments, his sentences, the phrase "I so order," and his punishments, which he himself invents. From this disorder, perhaps long inevitable, it follows that the caudillo who reaches a high position during a revolt possesses, without contradiction and without doubt on the part of his followers, the broad and terrible power that today is found only among Asian peoples. The Argentine caudillo is a Mohammed, who could change at a whim the dominant religion and forge a new one. He has all the powers: his injustice is a misfortune for his victim but not an abuse on his part. Because he may be unjust, and even more, inevitably must be unjust; he always has been.

What I am saying about the judge is applicable to the campaign commander.[7] The latter is a person of higher category than the former, and in whom the qualities of reputation and background must be combined to a higher degree. Still, far from lessening the evil, a new circumstance here aggravates it. The government of the cities gives the title of campaign commander, but, as the city is weak in the countryside, without influence or supporters, the government picks the men who scare it the most, conferring this position on them so as to keep them obedient— a well-known way in which all weak governments proceed, pushing away the evil of the present moment so that later on it reappears in colossal dimensions. Thus the papal government transacts with bandits, to whom it gives jobs in Rome, encouraging banditry and creating for it a secure future. Thus the sultan granted to Mehemet Ali investiture as pasha of Egypt, only to have to recognize him later on as hereditary king, in exchange for not dethroning the sultan himself. It is significant that all the caudillos of the Argentine Revolution have been campaign commanders: López and Ibarra, Artigas and Güemes, Facundo and Rosas. It is the starting point for all ambitions. Rosas, after taking control of the city, exterminated all the commanders who had promoted him, turning this influential post over to vulgar men who would not have been able to follow the path he took: Pajarito, Celarrayán, Arbolito, Pancho el Ñato, and Molina were some of the commanders Rosas purged from the country.

I give much importance to these small details because they will serve to explain all our social phenomena and the revolution that has been happening in the Argentine Republic, a revolution disfigured by the words of the civil government's dictionary, which disguise and hide it, creating erroneous ideas. In this same way the Spanish, upon disembarking in America, gave a familiar European name to the new animals they encountered, saluting with the terrible name lion, which brings to mind an image of the magnanimity and strength of the king of beasts, the miserable cat called a puma that runs away from the sight of a dog, and with the name tiger the jaguar of our forests. As slight and petty as this foundation I wish to give the civil war may seem, the evidence will come to show just how solid and indestructible it is.

Life in the Argentine countryside, as I have shown it, is not just any accident. It is the order of things, a system of association that is characteristic, normal, in my view unique in the world, and it alone suffices to explain our revolution. In the Argentine Republic before 1810, there were two distinct, rival, and incompatible societies, two diverse civilizations: one Spanish, European, cultured, and the other barbarous, American, almost indigenous. The revolution in the cities would serve only as a cause, as a driving force, whereby these two distinct ways of being in one people would be brought together, would collide, and after long years of struggle, one would absorb the other. I have indicated the normal association of the countryside, the lack of association a thousand times worse than that of a nomad tribe. I have shown the fictitious association of idleness, the shaping of gaucho reputations—valor, daring, skill, violence, and opposition to regular justice, the civil justice of the city. This phenomenon of social organization existed in 1810, and it still exists, modified on many points, modifying slowly on others, and on many still intact. These meeting places of the valiant, ignorant, free, and unemployed gauchos were disseminated by the thousands over the countryside. The revolution of 1810 brought uprisings and the sound of arms everywhere. Public life, until then lacking from this Arab-Roman association, began to happen in all the taverns, and the revolutionary movement finally brought military association in the form of the provincial *montonera*, legitimate child of the tavern and the *estancia*, enemy of the city and the revolutionary patriot army. As events unfold, we will see the provincial *montoneras* with their caudillos in the lead; in

Facundo Quiroga, the ultimate triumph everywhere of the countryside over the cities; and with the spirit, government, and civilization of the cities dominated, the final formation of the central, unitarist, despotic government of the rancher Don Juan Manuel Rosas, who sticks the gaucho's knife into cultured Buenos Aires and destroys the work of centuries, of civilization, law, and liberty.

CHAPTER IV

The Revolution of 1810

Cuando la batalla empieza, el tártaro da un grito terrible, llega,
hiere, desaparece, y vuelve como el rayo.

Victor Hugo[1]

I have had to trod this whole path I have covered, so as to arrive at the
place where our drama commences. It is pointless to spend time on the
character, objective, and ends of the Revolution of Independence. They
were the same all over America, born from the same origin: that is, the
circulation of European ideas. America acted like this because this was
the way all peoples were acting. Books, events, everything brought
America to associate itself with the impulse given to France by North
America, and by its own writers; to Spain, by France and its books. But
what I need note for my purposes is that the revolution, except for its
exterior symbol of independence from the king, was of interest and intelligible for the Argentine cities only, while foreign and without importance for the countryside. In the cities, there were books, ideas, civil
spirit, courts, rights, laws, education: all the points of contact and alliance that we have with Europeans. There was a base of organization,
incomplete, backward if you will; but precisely because it was incomplete, because it was not at the level that, by then, one knew it could
attain, the revolution was enthusiastically adopted. For the countryside, the revolution was a problem; to remove itself from the king's authority was fine, insofar as it meant a removal of authority. The pastoral
countryside could not see other aspects of the question. Liberty, the

responsibility of power, all the questions that the revolution proposed to resolve, were foreign to its way of life, to its needs. But the revolution was useful to it in this sense: it would give an object and an outlet to that excess vitality we have indicated, and it would add a new meeting place, greater than the very circumscribed one where men had been assembling daily throughout the countryside.

Those Spartan constitutions and physical strength, so very developed; those warlike dispositions, wasted on stabbing and slashing each other; that Roman idleness, only lacking a battlefield to go into active maneuvers; that antipathy for the authority with which they lived in constant struggle: all this finally found a channel to make its way and emerge into daylight, to flourish and develop.

The revolutionary movements, then, began in Buenos Aires, and all the cities of the interior provinces responded decisively to the call. The pastoral countryside became restless and joined the initiative. In Buenos Aires, passably disciplined armies began to form and to move into Upper Peru and Montevideo, where the Spanish troops sent by General Vigodet were located. General Rondeau laid siege to Montevideo with a disciplined army: Artigas, the celebrated caudillo, met him there with a few thousand gauchos. Artigas had been a fearsome smuggler until 1804, when the civil authorities of Buenos Aires were able to catch him and force him to serve as a campaign commander, in support of those same authorities on whom he had been waging war until then. If the reader has not forgotten the *baqueano,* and the general qualities that constitute a candidate for a campaign command, he will easily understand the character and instincts of Artigas.

One day Artigas, with his gauchos, split off from General Rondeau and began to wage war on him. The general's position was the same as that of Oribe today, laying siege to Montevideo and facing another enemy at the rear. The only difference was that Artigas was an enemy of both the patriots and the royalists at the same time. I don't want to get into an evaluation of the causes and pretexts that motivated this break; neither do I want to give it any of the names consecrated by political language, since none of them fit. When a people begins a revolution, two opposing interests struggle at first: the revolutionary and the conservative. Among us, the parties that supported these interests have been designated patriot and royalist. Naturally, after its triumph, the victorious party divides into factions of moderates and radicals; those who would carry out the revolution in all its consequences and those who would keep it within certain limits. It is also the character of revolutions that the originally defeated party reorganizes and triumphs, thanks to the division of the victors. But when, in a revolution, one of the forces called in to help immediately breaks away, forms a third entity, shows itself to be equally hostile to both the combatants (to royalists and to patriots), this force that splits off is heterogeneous. The society surrounding it hasn't known, until then, of its existence, and the revolution has merely caused it to show itself and develop.

This was the element the celebrated Artigas put into motion, a blind instrument, but one full of life, of instincts hostile to European civilization and to all regular organization; adverse to the monarchy as to the republic, because both came from the city and brought a readied order and the consecration of authority. This then was the instrument used by the different parties of the cultured cities, particularly the least revolutionary party, until, as time went by, the very ones who had called upon it for help succumbed, and with them the city, its ideas, its literature, its academies, its tribunals, its civilization!

This spontaneous movement in the pastoral countryside was so innocent in its primitive manifestations, so open and so expressive in its spirit and tendencies, that today it puts to shame the sincerity of the parties in the cities that assimilated it into their cause and baptized it with the political names that divided them. The force that sustained Artigas, in Entre Ríos, was the same one of López, in Santa Fe; of Ibarra, in Santiago; of Facundo, in the Llanos. Individualism constituted its essence, the horse its exclusive weapon, the immense Pampas its theater. The Bedouin hordes that today harass the Algerian border with their shouts and depredations give an exact idea of the Argentine *montonera,* which both wise men and notable villains have put to use. The same struggle of civilization and barbarism, of the cities and the desert, exists today in Africa; the same personages, the same spirit, the same undisciplined strategy, of the hordes and the *montonera.* Immense masses of horsemen that wander through the desert, engaging in combat with the disciplined forces of the city if they feel themselves superior in strength, dispersing like swarms of Cossacks in all directions if the combat is merely equal, so as to regroup, fall suddenly upon those who sleep, snatch away their horses, kill their stragglers and advance parties. Always present, intangible because of their lack of cohesion, weak in combat but strong and invincible in a long campaign—in which the organized force, the army, in the end succumbs, decimated by limited encounters, surprise attacks, fatigue, exhaustion.

The *montonera,* just as it appeared in the first days of the Republic under Artigas's command, already presented that character of brutal ferocity and that terrorist spirit whose transformation into a legislative system applied to a cultured society, and presentation in the name of an abashed America for Europe to contemplate, was reserved for the immortal bandit, the rancher from Buenos Aires.[2] Rosas has not invented anything; his talent has consisted solely in plagiarizing his predecessors and in making the brutal instincts of the ignorant masses into a coldly planned and coordinated system. The strip of skin taken from Colonel Maciel, out of which Rosas has made himself a horse hobble that has been seen by foreign representatives, has its background in Artigas and in the other barbarous, Tartar caudillos. Artigas's *montonera* would "straitjacket" its enemies—that is, sew them up inside a covering of fresh hides—and leave them like that, abandoned in the fields.[3] The reader will fill in all the horrors of this slow death. In 1836, this horrible punishment was repeated on an army colonel. Execution by the knife, throat slashing rather than shooting, is an instinct for butchery that Rosas has known how to take advantage of so as to even give death a gaucho form, and to the murderer, horrible pleasures; above all, to change the legal form accepted by cultured societies into another that he calls American and in the name of which he asks America to come to his defense, while the suffering in Brazil, in Paraguay, in Uruguay, invokes an alliance of the European powers, with whose help they might free themselves from this cannibal already invading them with his bloody hordes. It is impossible to maintain the calmness of spirit needed to research historical truth, when, at every step, one stumbles over the idea that he has been able to deceive America and Europe for so long, with a system of murders and cruelty only tolerable in Ashanti or Dahomey, in the African interior!

This is the character presented by the *montonera* since its first appearance; a singular sort of war and justice that has antecedents only in the Asiatic peoples inhabiting the plains, and that should never have been confused with the ways, ideas, and customs of Argentine cities, which were, like all American cities, a continuation of Europe and Spain. The *montonera* can only be explained by examining the inner organization of the society from which it proceeds. Artigas, a *baqueano,* a smuggler, that is, waging war on civil society, on the city, a campaign commander because of a deal, the caudillo of masses on horseback, is the same type who, with slight variation, continues to reproduce himself in every campaign commander who has become a caudillo. Like all civil wars, in which profound differences in education, beliefs, and objectives divide the parties, the internal war of the Argentine Republic has been long and obstinate, until one of the elements won. The Argentine Revolution's war has been double: first, a war of the cities, initiated into European culture, against the Spanish, in order to further broaden that culture; and second, a war of the caudillos against the cities, in order to free themselves from all civil control, to develop their character and their hate for civilization. The cities triumph over the Spanish, and the countryside over the cities. Thus is explained the enigma of the Argentine Revolution, whose first shot was fired in 1810 and whose last has not yet sounded.

I won't go into all the details this matter would require: the struggle is more or less lengthy; some cities succumb first, others later. The life of Facundo Quiroga will provide us with occasion to show these details in all their nakedness. What I must note now is that with the triumph of these caudillos, every form of civil life—even the way the Spanish practiced it—has disappeared, totally from some areas, in a partial way from others, but visibly moving toward its destruction. The masses aren't capable of distinguishing some eras from others; for them, the present moment is the only one over which they cast their gaze. This is why no one has observed, until now, the destruction of the cities and their decadence, in the same way that the peoples of the Argentine interior do not foresee the total barbarity toward which they visibly are marching. Buenos Aires is so powerful with elements of European civilization, that in the end it will educate Rosas and contain his bloody and barbarous instincts. The high position he occupies, his relations with European governments, the need he has experienced to respect foreigners, the need to lie in the press and deny the atrocities he has committed so as to save himself from the universal reproach that pursues him, all this, finally, will contribute to the containment of his outrages, as is already happening. But this is not preventing Buenos Aires from becoming, like Havana, the richest town in America but also the most subjugated and most degraded.

Four are the cities that already have been annihilated by the domination of the caudillos who support Rosas today: Santa Fe, Santiago del Estero, San Luis, and La Rioja. Santa Fe, situated at the convergence of the Paraná and another navigable river that flows into it, is one of the most favored spots in America, but nevertheless, today it does not count even two thousand souls; San Luis, capital of a province of fifty thousand inhabitants where there is no other city but the capital, does not have fifteen hundred.

To make perceptible the ruin and decadence of civilization in the interior, and the rapid progress made by barbarism, I need to take two cities, one already annihilated, the other moving toward barbarism without perceiving it: La Rioja and San Juan. La Rioja, in other times, had not been a city of the first order, but in comparison with its present state its own sons would not recognize it. When the 1810 revolution began, it counted a large number of capitalists and notable persons who had figured in a distinguished way in the military, at the bar, on the bench, in the pulpit. From La Rioja came Dr. Castro Barros, a representative to the Tucumán Congress and a celebrated canonist; General Dávila, who liberated Copiapó from Spanish power in 1817; General Ocampo, the president of Charcas; Dr. Gabriel Ocampo, one of the most celebrated lawyers of the Argentine bar; a large number of lawyers of the Ocampo, Dávila, and García families, who today live scattered over Chilean territory, as do various learned priests, among them Dr. Gordillo, residing in Huasco.

For a province to have produced so many eminent and enlightened men in a given period, knowledge must have been diffused over a great number of individuals and have been respected and eagerly pursued. If this was happening in the first days of the revolution, what increases in knowledge, wealth, and population should we not be seeing today, if a frightful retrogression toward barbarism hadn't impeded that poor people from continuing its development? What Chilean city, insignificant as it may be, could not enumerate the kinds of progress it has made over ten years in knowledge, growth of wealth, and adornment, even without excluding from this figure the cities destroyed by earthquakes?

Very well then: let us look at the state of La Rioja, according to the answers given in one of the many interviews I have conducted to learn in depth about the facts on which I base my theories. Here, a respectable person speaks, without even knowing the objective of my inquiry into his recent memories, because he had left La Rioja only four months earlier.*

Q1   Approximately what does the current population of the city of La Rioja number?

A   Scarcely fifteen hundred souls. It is said that only fifteen males live in the city.

Q2   How many noteworthy citizens live there?

---

*Dr. Don Manuel Ignacio Castro Barros, canon of the Cathedral of Córdoba. (Author's note to the second edition.)

A   In the city, there are probably six or eight.

Q3 How many lawyers' offices are open?

A   None.

Q4 How many doctors attend to the sick?

A   None.

Q5 How many judges with law degrees?

A   None.

Q6 How many men wear tailcoats?

A   None.

Q7 How many young men from La Rioja are studying in Córdoba or Buenos Aires?

A   I know of only one.

Q8 How many schools are there, and how many children attend them?

A   None.

Q9 Are there any public charitable institutions?

A   None, not even a primary school. The one Franciscan brother who is in the monastery there keeps a few children.

Q10 How many ruined churches are there?

A   Five: only the Mother Church can be used at all.

Q11 Are new houses being built?

A   None, nor are the damaged ones being repaired.

Q12 Are existing ones going to ruin?

A   Almost all, because the streets are so often flooded.

Q13 How many priests have been ordained?

A   In the city, only two young fellows: one is a presbyter, the other is a friar from Catamarca. In the province, four more.

Q14 Are there any large fortunes of fifty thousand pesos? How many of twenty thousand?

A   None; everyone is very poor.

Q15 Has the population increased or decreased?

A   It has decreased by more than half.

Q16 Is some feeling of terror prevalent among the people?

A   To the maximum degree. One fears to speak of even innocent things.

Q17 Is the money coined worth its full value?

A   That of the province is counterfeit.

Here the facts speak in all their sad and frightening severity. Only the history of the conquest of Greece by the Muslims offers examples of such rapid destruction and barbarization. And this is happening in

America in the nineteenth century! It is nevertheless the work of only twenty years! What is true of La Rioja is exactly applicable to Santa Fe, to San Luis, to Santiago del Estero, skeletons of cities, decrepit and devastated little hamlets. In San Luis, for the past ten years there has been only one priest, and there is no school or even one person who wears a tailcoat. Let us judge in San Juan, though, the fate of cities that have escaped destruction but are becoming imperceptibly barbarized.

San Juan is an exclusively agricultural and commercial province; not having an open countryside had kept it free, for a long time, from domination by the caudillos. Whatever the dominant party, the governor and public servants came from the educated sector of the populace—until 1833, when Facundo Quiroga placed a coarse man as governor.[4] The latter, unable to pull away from the influence of civilized customs, which prevailed in spite of those in power, let the cultured sector guide him until he was defeated by Brizuela, military leader of La Rioja. He was succeeded by General Benavides, who has held command for the past nine years, no longer as a term magistracy but as his personal property. San Juan has grown in population due to the progress of agriculture and emigrants from La Rioja and San Luis, who flee hunger and misery. Its buildings have grown perceptibly in number, proving the wealth of those areas of the country, and how much they could progress if the government would concern itself with fomenting education and culture, the only means of raising the level of a people.

Benavides's despotism is mild and pacific, which keeps people's spirits quiet and calm. He is the only one of Rosas's caudillos who hasn't sated himself with blood, but this doesn't make one feel any less the barbarizing influence of the current system.

In a population of forty thousand inhabitants grouped into a city, today there is not one single lawyer native to the area or to the other provinces.

All the judgeships are held by men who do not have the slightest knowledge of the law, and who are, in addition, unfit men in every sense of the word. There is no institution of public education. A school for ladies was closed in 1840; three for men have been opened and closed in succession between 1840 and 1843, because of the indifference and even hostility of the government.

Only three young people are studying outside the province.

There is only one doctor native to San Juan.

There are not three young people who know English, or four who know French.

Only one has studied mathematics.

There is only one young man who has an education worthy of a cultured people: Señor Rawson, already distinguished by his extraordinary talents. His father is North American, and he has received an education owing to that.

There are not ten citizens who know more than how to read and write.

There is not one military officer who has served in regular armies outside the Republic.*

Might you think that such mediocrity is normal for a city of the interior? No! Past tradition there proves the opposite. Twenty years ago, San Juan was one of the most cultured towns of the interior, and just what must the decadence and prostration of an American city be, to have to search back twenty years for its era of brilliance?

In 1831, two hundred citizens, heads of household, youths, men of letters, lawyers, military officers, and so on immigrated to Chile. Copiapó, Coquimbo, Valparaíso, and the rest of the Chilean Republic are still filled with these noble outlaws, some capitalists, others intelligent miners, many merchants and farmers, several lawyers, doctors. As with the Babylonian dispersion, none of them saw the promised land again. Another group of emigrants left, never to return, in 1840!

San Juan had been, until then, sufficiently rich in civilized men to give the celebrated Tucumán Congress a president of the capability and stature of Dr. Laprida, who later died, assassinated by the Aldaos; a prior to Chile's Dominican Recollect monastery in the distinguished, wise, and patriotic Oro, later bishop of San Juan; an illustrious patriot, Don Ignacio de la Roza, who planned the expedition into Chile with San Martín, and who scattered in his country the seeds of class equality promised by the revolution; a minister of Rivadavia's government; a minister of the Argentine Legation in Don Domingo Oro, whose dip-

---

*From 1845, when this book was written, to the present time, there has been a healthy reaction in the province of San Juan. Today there is a school for men, another for ladies, and the honorable Council of Representatives has just declared primary education for both sexes to be a public institution in the province. More than twenty young people are studying in Buenos Aires, Córdoba, and Chile, in order to devote themselves to careers in law and medicine. Music and drawing have become noticeably generalized among both sexes, and the artisans and other classes of society enjoy wearing frock coats and other garments, indicating that public spirit has been well educated to better its condition. Men of action have been annulled by time and their own ineptitude, and the government has found itself obligated to put into place persons of higher vision who, without being "savages," have an aversion to violence and vassalage. (Author's note to the second edition.)

lomatic talents are not yet justly appreciated; a representative to the 1826 Congress in the learned priest Vera; a representative to the Santa Fe Convention in the presbyter Oro, an orator of note; another to the Córdoba Convention in Don Rudecindo Rojo, as eminent for his talents and genius in industry as for his great learning; a military officer to the army, among others, in Colonel Rojo, who saved two provinces by snuffing out riots with just his serene audacity, and of whom General Paz, a competent judge on the subject, said that he would be one of the first generals of the Republic. San Juan possessed, at that time, a theater and a permanent acting company.

There still exist the remains of six or seven private libraries, in which the principal works of the eighteenth century and translations of the best Greek and Latin works were collected. I had no instruction before 1836 other than the one those rich, though incomplete, libraries could provide me. San Juan, in 1825, was so rich in learned men that the House of Representatives counted six orators of note. The miserable villagers who today* dishonor the San Juan House of Representatives— in whose precinct such eloquent speeches and such elevated thoughts were heard—should shake the dust off the proceedings of those days and flee in shame from profaning that august sanctuary with their diatribes!

The judicial courts, the ministries, were served by educated lawyers, and there remained a sufficient number to defend the interests of all sides.

The cultured manners, the refined customs, the cultivation of literature, the great commercial enterprises, the public spirit that animated the residents, everything announced to the outside world the existence of a cultured society that was moving rapidly in its rise to a distinguished rank, giving the London press cause to spread this honorable idea through America and Europe: "they show the best disposition for making progress in civilization; today that town is thought to be the one immediately following Buenos Aires in the pace of social reform; several of the newly established institutions of Buenos Aires have been adopted there, in relative proportion; and in ecclesiastical reform, the people of San Juan have made extraordinary progress, incorporating all the regular clergy into the secular clergy, and wiping out the convents and monasteries of the former . . . "

---

*1845. (Author's note to the second edition.)

But the state of primary education is what gives the most complete idea of the culture of that time. No city of the Argentine Republic has distinguished itself more than San Juan in its diligence to expand education, nor has any other obtained more complete results. The government, not satisfied with the capability of the province's men to carry out such an important duty, in 1815 ordered that a person combining competent training with great morality be brought from Buenos Aires. The Señores Rodríguez came, three brothers worthy of mingling with the first families of the area, into which they married; such was their merit and the distinction bestowed on them. I, who today make my profession in primary education, who have studied the subject, can say that if ever in America something similar to the famous Dutch schools described by M. Cousin has been achieved, it is in San Juan. The moral and religious education was perhaps even superior to the elementary instruction given there; and I do not attribute the fact that so few crimes have been committed in San Juan, or the moderate conduct of Benavides himself, to any cause other than that a majority of San Juan residents, including him, have been educated in this famous school, in which moral precepts were inculcated in students with special diligence. If these pages reach the hands of Don Ignacio and Don Roque Rodríguez, may they receive this feeble homage that I believe is owed for their eminent service, in association with their deceased brother Don José, to the culture and morality of an entire people.*

This is the history of Argentina's cities. All of them must reclaim their past glory, civilization, and noteworthiness. Now, a barbarizing level weighs them all down. The barbarism of the interior has even come to penetrate the streets of Buenos Aires. From 1810 to 1840, however, the provinces that used to hold so much civilization in their cities were barbaric enough to destroy, with their impetus, the colossal work of the Revolution of Independence. Now that they have nothing left of the men, learning, and institutions they had, what will become of them? Ignorance and poverty, which is its result, are like carrion birds, waiting for the cities of the interior to take their last gasp in order to devour their prey, to make them into fields, *estancias*. Buenos Aires can again

---

*Details about the system and organization of this establishment of public education may be found in *Educación Popular,* a work especially devoted to the subject and the fruit of a trip to Europe and the United States commissioned by the government of Chile. (Author's note to the second edition.) [Translator's note: Sarmiento published *La educación popular* in 1849.]

be what it was, because European civilization is so strong there that, despite the brutality of the government, it will be sustained. But what will support it in the provinces? Two centuries would not be enough to put them back on the path they have abandoned, since the present generation educates its children in the barbarism that has overtaken it. Now ask us, why do we fight? We fight to give the cities back their very life.

CHAPTER V

Life of Juan Facundo Quiroga

Au surplus, ces traits appartiennent au caractère original du genre humain. L'homme de la nature, et qui n'a pas encore appris à contenir ou déguiser ses passions, les montre dans toute leur énergie, et se livre à toute leur impétuosité.

Alix, Histoire de l'Empire Ottoman[1]

Childhood and Youth

Between the cities of San Luis and San Juan there lies a vast desert, which because of its complete lack of water is given the name *travesía.* In general, those solitudes have a sad and abandoned aspect, and no traveler coming from the east passes the last reservoir or cistern of the countryside without supplying his *chifles* with a sufficient quantity of water.[2] In this *travesía,* there once took place the following strange scene. The knife fights so common among our gauchos had forced one of them to abandon the city of San Luis precipitously and to gain the *travesía* on foot, with his saddle over his shoulder, in order to escape the pursuit of the law. Two companions were to catch up with him as soon as they could rob horses for all three.

At that time, hunger and thirst were not the only dangers awaiting him in that desert, where a "ravening" tiger had been roaming for a year, following travelers' tracks, and by then more than eight were those who had become victims to his predilection for human flesh.[3] It sometimes happens, in those areas where man and beast dispute the dominance of nature, that the former falls beneath the bloody claw of the latter; then the tiger begins to prefer the taste of his flesh, and is called "ravening" when it is given to this new sort of hunt, the manhunt. The country judge of the area immediate to the scene of this devastation summons able men to the chase, and under his authority and direction they pursue the "ravening" tiger, who rarely escapes the sentence that declares it outside the law.

When our fugitive had walked some six leagues, he thought he heard the tiger roar in the distance, and his fibers shuddered. The tiger's roar is a grunt like that of a hog, but sharp, prolonged, strident, and even with no reason to fear, it causes an involuntary shaking of the nerves, as if the flesh all by itself were trembling at the announcement of death.

Some minutes later, he heard the roar more distinctly and more near; the tiger was on his track now, and only at a great distance could he sight a small carob tree. He needed to hurry his pace, even to run, because the roars were following each other with increasing frequency, and each was more distinct, more vibrant than the last.

Finally, throwing his saddle down by the side of the road, the gaucho headed for the tree he had sighted, and despite its weak trunk, luckily quite a tall one, he was able to climb up to the top and sway continuously, half-hidden among the branches. From there, he could observe the scene taking place on the road. The tiger marched at a hurried pace, sniffing the ground and roaring more frequently as it sensed the proximity of its prey. It passed the point where the latter had left the road and lost the track; the tiger became infuriated, whirled around until it sighted the saddle, which it tore to pieces with a slap of the paw, scattering all the gear in the air. Irritated all the more by this disappointment, it went back to search for the track, finally finding the direction in which it went, and lifting its gaze, perceived its prey using his weight to keep the little carob tree swaying, as does the fragile reed when birds perch on its tip.

From that moment, the tiger roared no more: it bounded over, and in the blink of an eye its enormous paws were bearing on the slender trunk two yards above the ground, sending it a convulsive tremor that worked its way into the nerves of the badly secured gaucho. The beast tried to make a leap, in vain; it took a turn around the tree, measuring its height with eyes reddened by the thirst for blood, and finally, roaring with rage, lay down on the ground, ceaselessly switching its tail, eyes fixed on its prey, mouth partly open and parched. This horrible scene had now lasted two deadly hours; the strained pose of the gaucho and the terrifying fascination exerted over him by the bloody, immobile gaze of the tiger—from which, owing to an invincible force of attraction, he could not avert his eyes—had begun to weaken his strength, and he could feel the moment coming in which his exhausted body would fall into the tiger's wide mouth, when the far-off sound of galloping horses gave him hope for salvation.

In fact, his friends had seen the tiger's tracks and had raced forward with no hope of saving him. The scattered saddle gear showed them the place, and to fly there, unroll their lassos, throw them over the tiger, heels dug in and blind with fury, was but the work of a moment. The beast, stretched between two ropes, could not escape the repeated blows of the knife with which, in vengeance for his prolonged agony, the one who would have been its victim ran it through. "That was when I found out what being afraid means," General Juan Facundo Quiroga used to say, telling a group of officers this story.

He too was called the "Tiger of the Plains,"[4] and in truth, the designation was not a bad fit. Phrenology and comparative anatomy have, in fact, demonstrated the relationship that exists between external form and moral disposition, between the physiognomy of man and that of some animals similar to him in character. Facundo—because that was what the people of the interior provinces long had called him; General Don Facundo Quiroga, most excellent Brigadier General Don Juan Facundo Quiroga, all of that came later, when he was received in the bosom of society and crowned with the laurels of victory—Facundo, then, was of short and well-built stature; his broad shoulders supported, on a short neck, a well-formed head covered with very thick, black, and curly hair. His face, slightly oval-shaped, was sunk in the middle of a forest of hair, matched by an equally thick, equally curly and black beard that went up to his rather pronounced cheekbones, to disclose a firm, tenacious will.

His black eyes, full of fire and shadowed by heavy eyebrows, caused an involuntary feeling of terror in those on whom, at some moment, they fixed; because Facundo never looked straight ahead, and by habit, by design, because of a wish to make himself always fearsome, he ordinarily had his head down and looked up through his eyebrows, like the Ali Pasha of Monvoisin.[5] The Cain represented on stage by the famous Ravel Company reminds me of the image of Quiroga, except for the artistic, statuelike positions that don't fit him. In other ways his physiognomy was normal, and his slightly dark complexion went well with the thick shadows among which it was enclosed.

The structure of his head, however, revealed beneath this junglelike covering the privileged order of men born to lead. Quiroga possessed those natural qualities that made a Brienne student into the genius of France, and an obscure Mameluke who fought the French at the Pyramids into the viceroy of Egypt. The society into which they are born gives these characters their particular manifestation: noble, one could say classic, they lead civilized humanity in some places; terrible, bloody, and evil, they are in others their stain, their shame.

Facundo Quiroga was the son of a San Juan native of humble origins, who, settled in the Llanos of La Rioja, had acquired a moderate fortune from pasturage. In 1799, Facundo was sent to his father's hometown to receive the limited education that could be had in its schools: reading and writing. When a man comes to fill the hundred trumpets of fame with the noise of his deeds, curiosity or an investigative spirit will track down even his insignificant childhood, in order to tie it to the hero's biography; and more than a few times, among the fables invented by adulation, the germ of the historical personage's characteristic features can already be found there.

They say of Alcibiades that while playing in the street he lay down across the pavement in order to defy a coachman who had warned him to move out of the way or be run over; of Napoleon, that he dominated his fellow students and entrenched himself in his room to resist offensive attacks. Of Facundo, various anecdotes are told today, many of which reveal him completely.

In the boarding house, he could never be made to sit at the common table; in school, he was arrogant, disdainful, and solitary; he didn't mix with the other children, except to lead them in rebellious acts and to beat them up. The schoolmaster, tired of struggling with this indomitable character, one day got himself a new, hard whip, and, showing it to the terrified children, "this," he said, "is going to be broken in on Facundo." Facundo, eleven years of age, heard this threat, and the next day put it to the test. He didn't know the lesson, but asked the master to examine him personally, since the tutor disliked him. The master complied; Facundo made one error, made two, three, four; then the master brandished his whip, and Facundo, who had calculated everything down to the weakness of the chair where the master sat, punched him in the face, lay him flat on his back, and amid the uproar aroused by this scene, took to the street and went to hide in the grapevines of some vineyard, from which they couldn't pull him out until three days later. Is this not the caudillo who, later on, will challenge society as a whole?

When he reached puberty, his character took on a more pronounced hue. More and more somber, more imperious, more savage; a passion for gambling, the passion of coarse souls that need a strong shaking to come out of their heavy sleep, irresistibly dominated him from the age of fifteen. Because of it he acquired a reputation in the city; because of it he could no longer be tolerated in the house where he boarded; because of it, finally, with a shot fired at one Jorge Peña, he spilled the first rivulet of blood that would become the broad torrent that has marked his passage through the world.

At the point when he reaches adulthood, the thread of his life becomes lost in an intricate labyrinth of twists and turns through different neighboring towns; at times in hiding, always pursued, gambling, working as a peon, dominating everything that got near him and dealing out stabbings. Today in San Juan, on the Godoy farm, they show the mud walls Quiroga stamped with his feet; in La Rioja there are some he made by hand, in Fiambalá. He himself pointed out others in Mendoza, in the very same place where one afternoon he had twenty-six of the officials who surrendered at Chacón brought from their houses and shot, to expiate the ghost of Villafañe.[6] In the countryside of Buenos Aires, he also showed some of the monuments of his life as an errant peon. What caused this man, reared in a decent home, son of a wealthy and virtuous man, to descend to the level of a day laborer, and to choose the stupidest, most brutal job, in which only tenacity and physical strength matter? Could it be because a mud-wall builder earns double wages and he was in a hurry to get together a bit of money?

The most orderly account that I have been able to put together from this obscure, errant life is the following. Toward 1806 he came to Chile with a shipment of cochineal, sent by his parents. He gambled it away, along with the mule train and its drivers, who were family slaves. He would often take herds of cattle from his father's estate to San Juan and Mendoza, and they always met the same fate, because for Facundo gambling was a fierce, ardent passion burning in his belly. These successive acquisitions and losses must have worn down his father's largesse, because Facundo finally broke off all friendly relations with his family. When he had become the terror of the Republic, one of his courtiers asked him: "General, what's the largest bet you've ever made in your life?" "Seventy pesos," answered Quiroga indifferently; however, he had just won one of two hundred ounces. What happened, as he later explained it, was that in his youth, having only seventy pesos, he had lost it all on a jack.

But this fact has its characteristic history. He was working as a peon in Mendoza, on the hacienda of a *señora* in the Plumerillo area. Facundo, for a year, had stood out for his punctuality at work, and for the influence and control he exercised over the other peons. When they wanted to skip work and spend the day getting drunk, they would discuss it with Facundo, who would inform the *señora*, promising her that he would be responsible the following day for everyone's attendance, which was always punctual. Because of this intercession, the peons called him "the Padre."

At the end of a year of assiduous work, Facundo asked for his wages, which amounted to seventy pesos; mounted his horse without knowing where he was going; saw some people in a *pulpería;* dismounted; and reaching his hand over the group surrounding the dealer, put his seventy pesos on one card; lost them; and remounted, going off in no fixed direction, until shortly down the road one Judge Toledo, who happened to pass by at that moment, stopped him to ask for his working papers.

Facundo rode up as if he were going to hand the papers over, pretended to be looking for something in his pocket, and with one blow of his knife left the judge lying flat. Was he avenging his recent loss on the judge? Did he only want to satiate the rancor of a bad gaucho for civil authority, and add this new deed to the luster of his growing fame? Both. These acts of vengeance on the first object to appear were frequent in his life. When he was being addressed as General and had colonels at his command, he had one of them given two hundred lashes in his house in San Juan, for having beaten him by cheating, Facundo said; to a young man, two hundred lashes, for having permitted himself a joke at a moment when Facundo was not in the mood for jokes; two hundred lashes, to a woman in Mendoza who had said "Adios, mi General" to him in passing, when he was fuming because he hadn't been able to intimidate a citizen as peaceful and judicious as he himself was a gaucho and bold.

Facundo reappears later in Buenos Aires, where in 1810 he enrolled as a recruit in the Arribeños Regiment under the command of his compatriot General Ocampo, later the president of Charcas.[7] A glorious career at arms was opening up for him, with the first rays of the May sun; and there is no doubt that, with the temperament with which he had been endowed, with his instincts for destruction and butchery, Facundo, made moral by discipline and ennobled by the lofty goal of the struggle, would have one day returned from Peru, Chile, or Bolivia a general of the Argentine Republic, like so many other bold gauchos who began their careers in the humble position of soldier. But Quiroga's re-

bellious soul could not stand the yoke of discipline, the order of the barracks, or delays in promotion. He felt himself called to lead, to rise in
one jump, to create for himself, in spite of civilized society and with
hostility toward it, his own kind of career, combining valor and crime,
government and disorganization. After this, he was recruited into the
Army of the Andes and enrolled in the Granaderos cavalry; a Lieutenant
García took him as an assistant, and soon enough, desertion left a va-
cant place in those glorious ranks.[8] Later, Quiroga, like Rosas, like all
those vipers who have prospered in the shade of the laurels of the homeland, became known for his hatred of the soldiers of the Wars of Independence, on whom both men have carried out a horrible slaughter.

Facundo, deserting in Buenos Aires, set out for the provinces with
three companions. A party of soldiers caught up with him; he faced off
with them, waging a true battle that remained undecided for a while until, killing four or five, he could continue on his way, still clearing a path
with blows of his knife through the other parties that came after him as
far as San Luis. Later, he would travel this same road with a handful of
men, dissolve armies rather than parties of soldiers, and go all the way
to the famous Ciudadela of Tucumán to wipe out the last remains of the
Republic and of civil order.

Facundo reappeared in the Llanos, at his father's house. An event is
recounted from this time that is quite valid, and which no one doubts.
Nevertheless, in one of the manuscripts I am consulting, the author,
questioned about this same fact, answers "that to his knowledge Quiroga never tried to take money away from his parents by force"; and
against a proven tradition, against general agreement, I want to go by
this contradictory opinion. The contrary is horrible! It is said that, his
father having refused to give him the sum of money he had asked for,
he lay waiting for the moment when both his father and mother were
sleeping the siesta, so as to bar the door of their room and set fire to the
thatched roof that generally covers the dwellings of the Llanos.*

But what has been proven is that one time his father requested the
government of La Rioja to arrest him in order to contain his outrages;

---

*After writing this, I received from a reliable person a statement that Quiroga himself, in
Tucumán, in front of ladies who are still living, had told the story of the burning of the
house. All doubt disappears before depositions of this kind. Later, I obtained the cir-
cumstantiated account of an eyewitness and childhood companion of Facundo, who saw
him punch his father in the face and run away. But these details just sadden us, without
instructing, and it is a duty imposed by decorum to avert our eyes from them. (Author's
note to the first edition and expanded in the second.)

that Facundo, before fleeing to the Llanos, went to the city of La Rioja where his father was at that time, and suddenly falling upon him, punched him in the face, saying: "You ordered them to arrest me? Go on, order them to arrest me now!" with which he mounted his horse and took off at a gallop for the countryside. A year later, he showed up again at his father's house, threw himself at the feet of the abused old man, their sobs combined, and amid the protests of the son to mend his ways and the reproaches of the father, peace was restored, though on such a slight and ephemeral basis.

But his character and unruly habits did not change, and the racing, the gambling, the flights into the countryside, were the scenes of new violence, of new knife fights and aggression, until finally no one could tolerate him and his position became insecure. Then a great thought took hold in his mind, and he announced it without embarrassment. The deserter of the Arribeños, the soldier of the Granaderos cavalry who refused to immortalize himself at Chacabuco and Maipú, resolved to go join Ramírez's *montonera,* the offspring of Artigas's, whose reputation for crime and for hatred of the cities on which it was waging war had reached even the Llanos, filling governments with fear.[9] Facundo went off to join those filibusters of the Pampas, and perhaps the awareness he left behind of his character and instincts, and of the importance of the reinforcement he would give those destroyers, alarmed his compatriots, who informed the authorities in San Luis, where he would be passing through, of the infernal design that was guiding him. Dupuy, governor at the time (1818), had him arrested, and for a while he remained blended in among the criminals held in the prison. This San Luis prison, however, was to be the first step that would take him to the heights he later reached. San Martín had ordered a large number of Spanish officers of all ranks, from those who had been taken prisoner in Chile, transported to San Luis. Perhaps because they felt galled by their humiliation and suffering, perhaps because they foresaw the possibility of rejoining the Spanish armies, this group of prisoners one day revolted and opened the cell doors of common prisoners to get them to help with a general escape. Facundo was one of those prisoners, and as soon as he found himself disencumbered of his chains, raising high the *macho,* the iron bar from his shackles, he split open the head of the same Spaniard who had taken them off him, and going along through the group of rioters, left a broad swath sown with cadavers as he moved along the way. It is said that the weapon he used was a bayonet, and that no more than three were killed. Quiroga, however, always spoke of the *macho* from the shackles and of fourteen killed. Perhaps this is one of those idealizations with which a people's poetic imagination embellishes the kind of brutal force it so admires; perhaps the story of the shackles is an Argentine translation of Samson's jawbone, the Hebrew Hercules. But Facundo accepted it as a mark of glory, according to his own ideal, and with *macho* or bayonet, joining other soldiers and prisoners encouraged by his example, he was able to snuff out the uprising, reconciling with society through this act of valor, and to place himself under the protection of the homeland, getting his name to soar everywhere, ennobled and cleansed, though with the blood of the stains that marred it. Facundo, covered in glory, worthy of the homeland and with a credential attesting to his conduct, returned to La Rioja and flaunted among the gauchos of the Llanos the new titles that justified the terror his name already was beginning to inspire; because there is something imposing, something dominant and subjugating, in the honored murderer of fourteen men at once.

Here ends Quiroga's private life, from which I have omitted a long series of facts that only portray the bad nature, the bad manners, and the fierce and bloody instincts with which he was endowed. I have made use only of those that explain the character of the struggle, of those that are present in different proportions, although composed of analogous elements, in the pattern of the caudillos of the countryside, who have at last succeeded in suffocating the civilization of the cities and finally have reached their consummation in Rosas, the legislator of this Tartar civilization, who has flaunted all his antipathy for European civilization through atrocities and turpitude still without name in history.

But there is still something left for me to note about the character and spirit of this pillar of the federation. An uneducated man, a companion of Quiroga's childhood and youth who has furnished me with many of the facts to which I refer, includes these curious facts for me in his manuscript, speaking of Quiroga's early years: "that he was not a thief before he became a public figure; that he never stole, even when he was most in need; that not only did he like to fight, but he would pay to do so and to insult the most well-known opponent; *that he had a great aversion for decent men;* that he could never hold his liquor; that in his youth he was very reserved, and not only wanted to inspire fear but to terrorize, so he led the men closest to him to believe that he could tell fortunes or was a soothsayer; that he treated those around him like slaves; that he never has been to confession, prayed, or heard Mass; that as a general, once he was seen in Mass; that he himself said he didn't believe in anything." The sincerity with which these words are written reveals their truthfulness.

Quiroga's entire public life seems to me to be summed up in these facts. I see in them a great man, a man of genius in spite of himself and without knowing it, a Caesar, a Tamerlane, a Mohammed. He was born this way, and it wasn't his fault; he descended the social scale in order to command, to dominate, to fight the power of the city, the authority of the police. If they offered him a position in the army, he disdained it, because he didn't have the patience to wait for promotion; because there was too much subjection, too many fetters placed on personal independence, there were generals that weighed him down, there was a coat that oppressed the body and tactics that regulated movement; all of that was insufferable! A life on horseback, a life of danger and strong emotions, had steeled his spirit and hardened his heart; he had an invincible, instinctive hatred for the laws that had persecuted him, for the judges who had condemned him, for all that society and organization from which he had withdrawn since childhood and which regarded him with prejudice and contempt. Here the epigraph of this chapter forms an imperceptible link: "It is the natural man who has not yet learned to contain or disguise his passions, who shows them in all their energy, giving himself over to all their impetuousness. This is the original character of humankind"; and this is how he appears in the pastoral countryside of the Argentine Republic.[10] Facundo is a figure of primitive barbarism; he never knew any kind of subjection. His anger was like that of beasts: the mass of his very black, curly hair would fall forward over his forehead and eyes in locks like the serpents of Medusa's head, his voice would grow hoarse, and his gaze would turn into daggers. Overcome by anger, he kicked N. to death, splattering his brains out over a gambling argument; he tore off both his lover's ears because she once asked him for thirty pesos, to celebrate a marriage to which he himself had consented; he split open his son Juan's head with an ax, because there was no way to quiet him; in Tucumán, he beat up a pretty lady whom he could neither seduce nor take by force. In all these acts, the man showed himself to be still a beast, although not stupid and not lacking in lofty goals. Incapable of making himself admired or esteemed, he had a taste for being feared; but this was an exclusive taste, dominant to the point that he arranged all the actions of his life in order to produce terror around him, over towns as well as soldiers, over the victim about to be executed as well as his wife and children. Incapable of managing the mechanisms of civil government, he used terror as a method to take the place of patriotism and abnegation; ignorant, he surrounded himself with mystery; and by making himself impenetrable, availing himself of a natural sagacity, an uncommon capacity for observation, and the credulity of the populace, he pretended to have a foreknowledge of events that gave him prestige and fame among the common people.

The repertory of anecdotes about Quiroga that fill popular memory is inexhaustible: his sayings, his methods, have a stamp of originality that gave him a certain Oriental aspect, a certain tint of Solomonic wisdom in the mind of the common class. What difference, in fact, is there between that famous method of ordering a disputed child to be cut in half so as to discover the real mother, and the following one for finding a thief? Among the individuals forming a company of soldiers, someone had stolen an object, and every procedure carried out to discover the thief had been fruitless. Quiroga formed the troop, ordered that as many short, equal-length sticks be cut as the number of soldiers, immediately had them distributed to everyone, and then, with a sure voice, said: "The one whose stick is longer than all the others tomorrow morning, that's the thief." The next day, the troop re-formed, and Quiroga proceeded to inspect and compare the sticks. There was one soldier, however, whose stick turned up shorter than the rest. "Wretch!" Facundo shouted at him, with a terrifying voice. "You're the one!" And, in fact, he was: his bewilderment made this all too clear. The method was simple: the credulous gaucho, fearing that his little stick in fact would grow, had cut a piece of it off. But a certain superiority and a certain knowledge of human nature are necessary to avail oneself of these measures.

Some gear from a soldier's saddle had been stolen, and all efforts to uncover the thief had been useless. Facundo had the troop form and march past him, there with his arms folded, his gaze fixed, scrutinizing, terrible. Before this he had said: "I know who it is," with a confidence belied by nothing. They began to march, many marched past, and Quiroga remained motionless; he was a statue of the thundering Jupiter, an image of the God of the final judgment. Suddenly, he pounced on one man, grabbed him by the arm and said to him in a dry, curt voice: "Where's the saddle gear?" "Over there, sir," he answered, pointing to a wooded area. "Firing squad!" shouted Quiroga.

What sort of revelation was this? One of terror and one of crime, made before a prescient man. On another occasion, a gaucho was responding to the charges being made against him for a robbery; Facundo interrupted him, saying, "This rogue is lying; take him away . . . one hundred lashes!" When the prisoner was gone, Quiroga said to one of those present: "You see, *patrón,* when a gaucho makes marks in the ground with his foot while he talks, it's a sign that he's lying." With the lashes, the gaucho told the real story, that is, that he had stolen a yoke of oxen.

Another time he needed and had asked for a bold, resolute man with whom he could entrust a dangerous mission. Quiroga was writing when they brought him the man; he lifted his head after they had announced him several times, looked at him, and said while continuing to write, "Ugh! . . . That one's a wretch! I want a man who's brave and fearless!" It was later learned that, in fact, he was a fool.

There are deeds like these by the hundreds in Facundo's life, which, while revealing a superior man, also effectively built his mysterious reputation among vulgar men, who came to attribute him with supernatural powers.

CHAPTER VI

La Rioja

The sides of the mountains enlarge and assume an aspect at
once more grand and more barren. By little and little the scanty
vegetation languishes and dies; and mosses disappear, and a red-
burning hue succeeds.

Roussel, Palestine[1]

The Campaign Commander

In a document as old as 1560, I have seen consigned the name Mendoza,
with this added to it: "Mendoza, in the valley of La Rioja." But present-
day La Rioja is an Argentine province to the north of San Juan, from
which it is separated by several *travesías,* although these are interrupted
by populated valleys. Branches of the Andes break off and cut into its
western part with parallel lines, in whose valleys are Los Pueblos and
Chilecito, named for the Chilean miners who went there because of
the fame of the rich Famatina mines. Further to the east extends a sandy
plain, deserted, parched by the heat of the sun, at whose northern extreme, alongside a mountain covered to the summit with luxuriant,
high vegetation, lies the skeleton of La Rioja, a solitary city with no surrounding areas, withered like Jerusalem at the foot of the Mount of
Olives. To the south, at a far distance, this sandy plain is bordered by the
Colorados, mountains of petrified chalk, whose regular outline takes on
the most picturesque and fantastic of forms: sometimes it is a smooth
wall with projecting bastions, sometimes one can see towers and the
battlements of castles in ruins. Finally, to the southeast and surrounded

by extensive *travesías,* are the Llanos, broken and mountainous country in spite of its name, an oasis of pasturage that in other times fed thousands of flocks.[2]

The aspect of this countryside is, in general, desolate; the climate, burning hot; the earth, dry and without flowing water. The peasant makes reservoirs to collect rainwater and give drink to his livestock. I have always had the idea that Palestine is similar in aspect to La Rioja, down to the reddish or ocher color of the earth, the dryness of some areas, and their cisterns; down to the orange and fig trees and grapevines with exquisite, massive fruit, grown where some muddy, narrow Jordan flows. There is a strange combination of mountains and plains, fertility and aridness, gloomy, bristling mountains and gray-green hills carpeted with vegetation as colossal as the cedars of Lebanon. What most brings this Oriental reminiscence to my mind is the truly patriarchal aspect of the peasants in La Rioja. Today, thanks to the whims of fashion, it isn't a novelty to see men with full beards, in the immemorial style of the Oriental peoples. But even so, the vision of a people that speaks Spanish and wears, and always has worn, complete beards often falling to the chest, still would not fail to surprise; a people of sad, taciturn, grave, and sly aspect, Arab-like, riding on donkeys and sometimes dressed in goatskins, like the hermit of Engedi. There exist places where the population eats only wild honey and carob beans, as John the Baptist ate locusts in the desert. The *llanista* is the only one unaware that he is the most unfortunate, most wretched, and most barbarous of beings; and thanks to this, he lives contented and happy when not beset by hunger.

I said before that there were reddish mountains that from a distance had the aspect of feudal towers and castles in ruins; and so that such reminders of the Middle Ages might blend in with those other, Oriental shadings, La Rioja has offered for more than a century the struggle of two families, no less hostile, lordly, and illustrious than the Italian fiefs in which figure the Ursinos, Colonnas, and Medicis. The quarrels of the Ocampos and the Dávilas shape the whole written history of La Rioja. Both families, old, rich, titled, fought for power during a long period, dividing the population into bands like the Guelphs and the Ghibellines even much before the Revolution of Independence. From these two families have emerged a multitude of men noteworthy in the military, at the bar, and in industry, because the Dávilas and the Ocampos have always tried to surpass each other in all the influential areas consecrated by civilization. More than a few times, snuffing out these hereditary rancors was part of the politics of the Buenos Aires patriots. The Lautaro

Lodge got the two families to marry an Ocampo to a Doria y Dávila, in order to reconcile them.³ Everyone knows that this was the practice in Italy, but here Romeo and Juliet were happier. Around the year 1817, the government of Buenos Aires, also in order to end the hatred between these houses, sent in a governor from outside the province, a Señor Barnachea, who didn't take long to fall under the influence of the Dávila party, which counted among its supporters Don Prudencio Quiroga, a resident of the Llanos much loved by the inhabitants there, and who because of this was summoned to the city and made its treasurer and mayor. Note that—although it happened in a legitimate, noble manner—through Don Prudencio Quiroga, Facundo's father, the pastoral countryside came to figure as a political element in the civil parties. The Llanos, as I have already said, are a mountainous oasis of pasture, buried deep in the middle of an extensive *travesía;* their inhabitants, exclusively shepherds, lead the patriarchal, primitive life that isolation has preserved in all its purity, barbarous and hostile to the cities. There, hospitality is a common duty, and among the duties of the peon is that of defending his *patrón* against any danger, even at the risk of his own life. These customs, then, will explain a bit the phenomena we are about to witness.

After the events in San Luis, Facundo appeared in the Llanos, strengthened by the prestige of his recent deeds and armed with a recommendation from the government. The parties that divided La Rioja didn't take long to solicit the adherence of a man looked at by all with the respect and awe that daring acts always inspire. The Ocampos, who won the government in 1820, gave him the title of sergeant major of the Llanos Militia, with the influence and authority of campaign commander.

From this moment on, Facundo's public life began. The pastoral, barbarous elements of that province, that third entity which appeared at the siege of Montevideo in Artigas, will show up at La Rioja in Quiroga, called on for support by one of the parties of the city. This is a solemn and critical moment in the history of all the pastoral peoples of the Argentine Republic: for all of them, there comes a day when, whether because of need for outside support or because of the fear already inspired by some bold man, he is chosen as campaign commander. This is the Greek horse that the Trojans hurried to introduce into the city.

Around this time in San Juan, there occurred the disgraceful uprising of the First Regiment of the Andes, which had returned from Chile to regroup. Frustrated in the riot's objectives, Francisco Aldao and

Corro undertook a disastrous retreat to the north to join Güemes, the caudillo of Salta. General Ocampo, governor of La Rioja, resolved to cut off their march, and to this end summoned all the forces of the province and prepared to give battle. Facundo appeared with his *llanistas*. These forces came to blows, and the First only needed a few minutes to show that despite the rebellion, it hadn't lost any of its old brilliance on the field of battle. Corro and Aldao headed for the city, and the defeated attempted to regroup, heading for the Llanos where they could await the forces coming from San Juan and Mendoza in pursuit of the fugitives. Facundo, meanwhile, left the place where they had met, fell upon the rear guard of the victors, shot at them, harassed them, killed them, and took the stragglers prisoner. Facundo was the only one with a life of his own, who didn't wait for orders, who operated by his own will. He felt called to action, and didn't wait to be pushed. Even more, he spoke with scorn of the government and the general, and announced his intention to work, from this point on, according to his own dictates, and to overthrow the government. It is said that a council of army leaders urged General Ocampo to arrest, try, and execute him; but the general did not consent to this, perhaps less from a desire for moderation, than from a feeling that Quiroga was now not so much a subordinate as a fearsome ally.

A definitive accord between Aldao and the government agreed that the former, not wishing to follow Corro, would go back to San Luis, the government providing him with the means to leave the provincial territory by an itinerary passing through the Llanos. Facundo was given the duty of carrying out this part of the stipulated terms, and returned to the Llanos with Aldao. Quiroga was now aware of his strength, and when he turned his back on La Rioja had been able to say to it, as a farewell: "Woe to you, city! Truly, I say to you that soon there will not be left one stone upon another."[4]

Aldao arrived at the Llanos and, aware of Quiroga's discontent, offered him one hundred men from his ranks in order to take control of La Rioja, in return for his alliance in future enterprises. Quiroga accepted eagerly, set out for the city, took it, arrested the government officials, had confessors brought in for them, and ordered them to prepare to die. What was his objective in this revolution? None at all; he felt himself strong; he flexed his arms and knocked down the city. Was it his fault?

Former Chilean patriots doubtless haven't forgotten the prowess of Sergeant Araya, of the Granaderos cavalry, because from among those veterans the aura of glory often would fall upon even a simple soldier. Presbyter Meneses, who was the priest of Los Andes, told me how after the defeat at Cancha Rayada, Sergeant Araya was setting out on the road to Mendoza with seven Granaderos. The patriots were heartbroken to see the bravest soldiers of their army leave across the Andes while Las Heras still had a regiment under his command, ready to face the Spanish. They needed to detain Sergeant Araya, but there was a difficulty. Who would go after him? A party of sixty militia men was at hand, but all the soldiers knew that the fugitive was Sergeant Araya, and they would have preferred a thousand times over to attack the Spanish rather than this lion of the Granaderos. Don José María Meneses, at that point, went forward alone and unarmed, caught up with Araya, cut off his path, reminded him of his past glories and of the shame in fleeing with no motive; Araya allowed himself to be moved, and didn't resist the pleas and orders of a good countryman. He immediately became enthused, ran to detain other groups of Granaderos that had preceded him in flight, and thanks to his diligence and reputation, returned to rejoin the army with sixty comrades-at-arms, who cleansed themselves at Maipú of the momentary stain that had fallen upon their laurels.

This Sergeant Araya, and one Lorca, also a brave man known in Chile, commanded the forces that Aldao had put at Facundo's command. The prisoners of La Rioja, among whom was Dr. Gabriel Ocampo, an ex–government minister, solicited Lorca's protection in order that he might intercede on their behalf. Facundo, still not secure in his sudden rise, consented in granting them their lives; but this limit on his power made him feel another need. He had to take over those veteran forces, so as not to meet resistance afterward. Upon returning to the Llanos he came to terms with Araya, and with both in agreement, they fell upon the rest of Aldao's forces, surprised them, and Facundo immediately found himself the chief of four hundred men, from whose ranks later emerged the officers of his first armies.

Facundo remembered that Don Nicolás Dávila was in exile in Tucumán, and had him come back to take charge of the bothersome details of governing La Rioja, reserving for himself alone the real power that went with him to the Llanos. The abyss that lay between him and the Ocampos and Dávilas was so wide, the transition so abrupt, that it was impossible for it to happen all at once. The spirit of the city was still too powerful to be overcome by that of the country; a doctor of laws was still worth more to the government than just any peon. Later, all this changed.

Dávila took charge of the government under Facundo's patronage, and during that time any motive for unease seemed far off. The haciendas and properties of the Dávilas were located around Chilecito, so that there, among his friends and relations, was concentrated the physical and moral force that would support his government. Moreover, the population of Chilecito having increased with the profitable exploitation of the mines and large fortunes amassed, the government established a provincial palace and transferred its residence to that little town, perhaps to carry out the enterprise, perhaps to get away from the Llanos and elude the uncomfortable subjection that Quiroga wanted to exercise over it. Dávila didn't take long to move from these purely defensive measures to a more decisive attitude, and taking advantage of the temporary absence of Facundo, who was in San Juan, he contrived with Captain Araya to arrest him upon his return. Facundo was informed of the measures being prepared against him, and secretly entering the Llanos, ordered Araya's murder. The government, whose authority was being contested in such an insulting manner, summoned Facundo to appear in order to respond to the charges being made against him for the murder. A ridiculous parody! The only recourse left was a call to arms, and an incitement to civil war between the government and Quiroga, between the city and the Llanos. Facundo, in turn, sent a commission to the Representative Assembly, asking that Dávila be deposed. The Assembly had persistently called for the governor to invade the Llanos and to disarm Quiroga, with the support of all the citizens. They had a local interest in this, which was to have the government palace moved to the city of La Rioja; but, since Dávila persisted in residing in Chilecito, the Assembly, acceding to Quiroga's request, declared him deposed. Governor Dávila had gathered many of Aldao's soldiers together under the orders of Don Miguel Dávila; he had a good stockpile of weapons, many followers who wanted to save the province from domination by the caudillo rising up in the Llanos, and several trained officers to lead the forces. Preparations for war began, then, with equal ardor in Chilecito and the Llanos; and rumor of the disastrous events being planned reached all the way to San Juan and Mendoza, whose governments sent a commissioner to procure an agreement between the belligerent parties, who were at the point of coming to blows.

Corbalán, that same man who today serves as Rosas's aide-de-camp, showed up at Quiroga's camp to carry out the mediation with which he had been entrusted, and which was accepted by the caudillo; he immediately went to the enemy camp, where he received the same cordial welcome. He returned to Quiroga's camp to arrange a definitive agreement; but Quiroga, leaving him there, moved against his enemy, whose forces, unprepared because of the assurances given them by the envoy, were easily routed and scattered. Don Miguel Dávila, pulling together some of his men, resolutely attacked Quiroga, whom he managed to wound in the thigh before a bullet took away his own wrist; he was immediately surrounded and killed by the soldiers. There is, in this incident, a detail very characteristic of the gaucho spirit. A soldier takes pleasure in showing his scars; a gaucho hides and conceals them when they come from a blade, because they prove his lack of skill, and Facundo, loyal to these ideas of honor, never reminded anyone of the wound that Dávila had opened in him before dying.

Here ends the history of the Ocampos and the Dávilas, and also that of La Rioja. What follows is the history of Quiroga. This day was also a fatal one for the pastoral cities, a disastrous day that finally had arrived. In the history of Buenos Aires, this day corresponds to the one in April 1835 when its campaign commander, its Hero of the Desert, took power over the city.[5]

There is a curious circumstance (1823) that I shouldn't omit, because it brings honor to Quiroga. In this black night we are going to cross, the weakest little light shouldn't be lost. Facundo, upon entering La Rioja in triumph, had the bells cease tolling, and after sending his condolences to the widow of the dead general, ordered pompous funeral rites to honor his ashes. He named or had named as governor a vulgar Spaniard, one Blanco, and with him began the new order of things that the ideal government, as conceived by Quiroga, was going to realize; because Quiroga, in his long career, in all the different towns he conquered, never took charge of organized government, which he always left to others. An important moment for a town, deserving of notice, is the one when a vigorous hand takes power over its destiny. Institutions are affirmed, or cede their place to other, new ones more productive in results or more in conformity with prevailing ideas. From that central focus often go forth the threads that, interweaving over time, come to change the fabric that composes History.

Not so when a force foreign to civilization prevails, when Attila takes power over Rome, or Tamerlane runs over the Asiatic plains. The ruins remain, but in vain would the hand of Philosophy dig through them afterward, looking underneath for the vigorous plants born from the nutritious fertilizer of human blood. Facundo, a barbaric genius, took power over his region; the traditions of government disappeared, form was degraded, laws were toys in his rough hands; and in the midst of this destruction carried out by the hoofbeats of horses, nothing was replaced, nothing was established. Lack of restraint, idleness, and indolence are the highest good for the gaucho. If La Rioja had had as many statues as it did doctors, they would have served as hitching posts.

Facundo's desire was to possess, and, incapable of creating a system of revenue, he resorted to what rough, imbecile governments always resort to; but here, the monopoly will bear the stamp of pastoral life, spoliation, and violence. The tithes of La Rioja, at that time, were auctioned off for ten thousand pesos annually; that, at least, was the average.[6] Facundo appeared before the auction board, and his attendance alone, up to then rare, was enough to impose respect on the other bidders. "I give two thousand pesos," he said, "and one more, above the best bid." The scribe repeated the proposal three times, and no one outbid it. For all those present had crept away, one by one, upon reading in Quiroga's sinister gaze that that bid was the last one. The following year, he merely sent in a little scrap of paper to the auction, expressing these terms: "I give two thousand pesos, and one more, above the best bid.—Facundo Quiroga."

The third year the auction ceremony was suspended, and in 1831, Quiroga was still sending two thousand pesos to La Rioja, the value he had set for the tithes.

But he needed to take one more step in order to have the tithes yield a hundred for one, and Facundo, after the second year, refused to accept the animals, but instead distributed his brand to all the property owners, in order that they might brand the animals of the tithe and keep them on their *estancias* until he claimed them. The broods increased, new tithes added on to the herd of livestock, and within ten years it could be calculated that half the livestock on the *estancias* of this pastoral province belonged to the commander general-at-arms and bore his brand.

A custom of time immemorial in La Rioja had it that the livestock called *mostrencos*—that is unbranded by a certain age—belonged by rights to the treasury, which sent out its agents to round up these lost head and obtained from this levy a not insignificant revenue, even though the property owners felt its collection to be intolerable. Facundo asked that this livestock be awarded to him, as compensation for the expenses that the invasion of the city had required; expenses that boiled down to a convocation of the militias, who show up on their own horses and always live on whatever they find. Now possessing a new batch of six thousand young bulls per year, he sent his own suppliers to the cities, and woe to the one who tried to compete with him! This business of supplying the meat markets is one he practiced wherever his forces appeared, in San Juan, Mendoza, Tucumán—always being careful to monopolize it to his favor with some proclamation or just a simple announcement. It is sickening and shameful, without a doubt, to have to descend to the level of these details, unworthy of remembrance. But what choice do I have? Immediately after the bloody battle that had cleared the way for his entry into some city, the first thing the general ordered was that no one could supply meat for the market! . . . In Tucumán he learned that a resident, going against the order, slaughtered cattle at his house. The general of the Army of the Andes, the victor of the Ciudadela, felt he could not entrust anyone with the investigation of such an enormous crime. He himself went in person, knocked loudly on the door to the house, which remained closed and which those inside, astonished, couldn't manage to open. A kick from the illustrious general broke it down and brought to life this scene: a dead animal being skinned by the owner of the house, who in turn also fell down dead at the terrifying sight of the offended general!*

I do not dwell on these particulars by design. How many pages I omit! How many iniquities, proven and known by all, I silence! But I

---

*Official record of the province of San Juan:

> In consequence of the present law, the government of the province has stipulated with His Excellency General Don Juan Facundo Quiroga the following articles, in agreement with his note of 14 September 1833:
>
> 1. That he shall compensate the most excellent Government of Buenos Aires for the amount it has invested in said properties.
> 2. That he shall supply five thousand pesos to the province without encumbrance to the revenue, for its emergency need to supply the troops he has in the field, giving three thousand pesos in cash, and the rest from the sale of livestock, the payment of which exclusively affects the slaughtering trade.
> 3. That he alone shall be permitted to supply the markets, selling to the public at the rate of five reales per arroba of meat, which today is at six for bad quality, and at the rate of three to the State, without raising the current price of tallow.
> 4. That he shall have slaughtering provided without cost from the 18th of the present month until the 10th of January inclusive, and pasture at State expense at the price of two reales per month per head, which shall be charged from 1 October next.

> *San Juan, September 13, 1833*
> *Ruiz Viuente Atienzo*

(Author's note to the second edition.)

am giving the history of a barbaric government, and I have to make its mechanisms known. Mehemet Ali, master of Egypt by the same means as Facundo, gave himself over to a rapacity without precedent even in Turkey; he constituted a monopoly in all branches of trade and exploited them to his own benefit. But Mehemet Ali came from the bosom of a barbaric nation, and bettered himself to the point where he desired European civilization and grafted it onto the veins of the people he oppressed. Facundo, on the contrary, rejected all means of civilization that were already known, destroyed and demoralized them; Facundo, who didn't govern, because government was work benefiting others, abandoned himself to the instincts of an avarice without measure, without scruples.

Egotism is at the base of almost all great historical characters; egotism is the real mainspring that causes all great actions to be executed. Quiroga possessed this political gift to an eminent degree, and exercised it by concentrating about him everything he saw disseminated in his surrounding, uncultured society; wealth, power, authority, all this he had; everything he could not acquire, fine manners, an education, a basis for respectability, this he pursued, and destroyed in the people who possessed it. His rage against the decent people, against the city, was more visible every day; and the governor of La Rioja, put into place by him, finally resigned because of daily harassment. One day, Quiroga was in a good mood, and he played with a young man like a cat plays with a timid mouse. He played at killing or not killing him; the victim's terror had made him appear so ridiculous that it put the executioner in a good mood, he had laughed heartily, in contrast with his usual custom. His good mood had to be known: he needed to let it out, to spread it over a large area. The call to arms rang out in La Rioja, and the citizens took to the streets, armed at the sound of the alarm. Facundo, who had ordered the call rung to amuse himself, had the residents form ranks in the plaza at eleven at night, sent away the common people, and kept only the men who were affluent heads of households, and the young men who still preserved some appearance of culture. He made them march and countermarch all night long, halt, fall in, forward march, side march. He was a drill sergeant teaching recruits, and his sergeant's stick went for the heads of the clumsy, for the chests of those who didn't fall in right; what else do you expect? That's the way to teach! Daylight came, and the pale faces of the recruits, their fatigue and exhaustion, revealed all they had learned during the night. Finally he let the troops rest, and took his generosity to the point of buying empanadas and distributing one to each man, which they rushed to eat, because that was a part of his amusement.

Lessons of this type are not lost on cities, and the clever politician who has made these procedures systematic in Buenos Aires has refined them and made them produce marvelous effects.[7] For example, between 1835 and 1840, almost the entire city of Buenos Aires went to jail. At times, there were 150 citizens who stayed in prison for two, three months, ceding their places to 200 substitutes who stayed six months. Why? what had they done? . . . what had they said? Imbeciles! don't you see that the city is being disciplined? . . . Don't you recall how Rosas used to say to Quiroga that it wasn't possible to establish a republic, because of lack of custom? He was just getting the city accustomed to being governed! He concluded his work, and in 1844 he presented the world a people that has but one thought, one opinion, one voice, one limitless enthusiasm for the person and the will of Rosas! Yes, now a republic really can be established!

But let us return to La Rioja. In England, businesses had been stirred into feverish movement regarding the mines of the new American states: powerful companies proposed to exploit the mines of Mexico and Peru; and Rivadavia, then residing in London, urged businessmen to put their capital into the Argentine Republic. The Famatina mines were ready for large enterprises. At the same time, speculators in Buenos Aires obtained the exclusive rights to this exploitation, with the intention of selling to the English companies for enormous sums. These two exploitations, that of England and that of Buenos Aires, were at cross-purposes with each other and could not come to an agreement. Finally, there was a transaction with another English firm that was to supply the funds and that indeed sent English miners and managers. Later, speculation was made on the establishment of a mint in La Rioja, which, when the national government was organized, would be sold to it for a great sum. Facundo, who was solicited, joined in with a great number of shares that he paid for with the Jesuit College, which he had had allotted to himself as payment for his salary as general. A commission of shareholders went to La Rioja to carry out this enterprise, and of course made known their wish to be introduced to Quiroga, whose mysterious, terrifying name was starting to resound everywhere. Facundo received them at his lodgings, in fine silk stockings, badly made breeches, and a poncho of rough cloth. Despite the grotesqueness of this figure, none of the elegant citizens of Buenos Aires even thought to laugh, because they were too well informed not to decipher the riddle. He wanted to humiliate the cultured men, and to show them just how much their European dress mattered to him.

Finally, exorbitant rights charged for the exportation of livestock not belonging to him completed the administrative system established in his province. But, besides these direct means to wealth, there is one that I hasten to set out, to rid myself once and for all of a fact that embraced Facundo's entire public life. Gambling! Facundo had a rage for gambling, as some do for liquor, as others do for snuff. A powerful soul, but one incapable of embracing the great sphere of ideas, he needed this fictitious occupation in which passion is continuously exercised, opposed, and flattered at the same time, annoyed, aroused, tormented. I have always believed that a passion for gambling is, in most cases, a positive kind of spirit not put to use because of society's bad organization. These forces of will, abnegation, and constancy are the same ones that shape the fortunes of the enterprising merchant, the banker, and the conqueror who gambles empires in battle. Facundo had gambled since childhood; gambling had been his only pleasure, his release, his whole life. But do you know what it is for a player to have power, terror, and the life of his table companions as funds? This is something that can only be imagined by someone who has seen it for twenty years. Facundo played unfairly, his enemies say. . . . I won't swear to this charge, because bad faith was of no use to him, and because he pursued to the death those who practiced it. But Facundo played with unlimited funds; he never permitted anyone to take playing money away from the table; it wasn't possible to stop playing, unless he allowed it; he would play for forty consecutive hours or more; terror didn't upset him, and he could order his table companions, who often were men devoted to him, whipped or shot. Here you have the secret of Quiroga's luck. Few won considerable sums from him, although many may be those who, at certain moments in a game, had before them pyramids of gold ounces won from Quiroga. The game continued, because the winning player wasn't allowed to leave, and in the end, he was left only with the glory of telling how he had won so much and then lost it right away.

So then, gambling was for Quiroga a favorite form of amusement and a system of spoliation. No one in La Rioja received money from him, no one possessed it, without immediately being invited to play and to leave it in the caudillo's power. The majority of the merchants in La Rioja failed, disappeared, because their money ended up in the general's pocket; and it wasn't because he didn't give them lessons in prudence. A young man had won four thousand pesos from Facundo, and Facundo didn't want to play any longer. The young man thought a trap was being laid for him, that his life was in danger. Facundo repeated that he would not play any longer; the heedless young man insisted, and Facundo, condescending, won the four thousand pesos from him, and ordered that he be given two hundred lashes for his barbarism.

I tire of reading infamies, confirmed in all the manuscripts I consult. I sacrifice their telling to an author's vanity, to literary aspirations. By saying more, the scenes would end up overdone, mean, repulsive.

The life of the campaign commander stops here, after he had abolished the city and suppressed it. Facundo, up to this point, was like Rosas on his *estancia,* although before taking power Rosas was not so dishonored either by gambling or by the brutal satisfaction of all his passions. But Facundo was going to enter a new sphere, and so we will have to follow him through the whole Republic, to go looking for him on the battlefields.

What consequences did the destruction of civil order bring to La Rioja? About this one does not reason, or discuss. One goes to see the theater where these events unfolded and gazes over it: that is the answer. Today the Llanos of La Rioja are deserted; the population has immigrated to San Juan; the reservoirs that gave water to thousands of herds have dried up. In those Llanos, where twenty years ago so many thousands of herds were grazing, the tiger wanders in tranquillity, having reconquered his dominion; a few families of beggars gather carob beans for subsistence. This is how the Llanos have paid for the evils that they spread over the Republic. Woe to you, Bethsaida and Chorazin! Truly I say to you, that Sodom and Gomorrah were treated better than you should be.[8]

CHAPTER VII

Social Life (1825)

La société du moyen-âge était composée des débris de mille autres sociétés. Toutes les formes de liberté et de servitude se rencontraient; la liberté monarchique du roi, la liberté individuelle du prêtre, la liberté privilégiée des villes, la liberté représentative de la nation, l'esclavage romain, le servage barbare, la servitude de l'aubain.

Chateaubriand[1]

Facundo possessed La Rioja as absolute master and arbiter: there was no voice but his, no concerns but his. Since there was no literature, there were no opinions, and since there were no differing opinions, La Rioja was a war machine that would go where it was taken. Up to this point, however, Facundo hadn't done anything new. This was the same thing that Dr. Francia, Ibarra, López, Bustos had done, what Güemes and Aráoz had attempted in the north: to destroy all existing rights in order to impose their own. But a world of ideas, of contradictory interests, was stirring outside La Rioja, and the far-off rumor of debates in the press and the political parties reached Facundo's residence in the Llanos. Moreover, in his rise to power he hadn't been able to keep the racket made by the civilized structure he was destroying from being heard far away, or the neighboring towns from taking a closer look at him. His name had passed the borders of La Rioja. Rivadavia invited him to take part in the organization of the Republic; Bustos and López, to oppose it; the government of San Juan prided itself on counting him among its friends; and men he didn't know came to the Llanos to see him and ask for his support for this or that party. The Argentine Republic at that time presented a lively and interesting picture. All interests, all ideas, all passions met together to agitate and argue for their cause. Here, a caudillo who wanted nothing to do with the rest of the Republic; there, a people that asked only to emerge from isolation; farther away, a government that brought Europe to America; elsewhere, another one that hated even the name of civilization; in some places, the Inquisition was reinstated; in others, freedom of religion was declared the first right of man; some shouted "federation," others "central government"; each of these diverse positions had strong interests and passions, invincible in their support. I need to clear up this chaos a bit, to show the role that Quiroga was called upon to play and the great work he should have achieved. To portray the campaign commander who takes power over the city and finally annihilates it, I have had to describe the Argentine land, the customs it engenders, the characters it develops. Now, to show Quiroga coming out of his province and proclaiming a principle, an idea, and carrying it everywhere on the point of his lances, I also need to trace a geographical map of the ideas and interests that were agitating in the cities. To this end, I must examine two cities, in which opposite ideas predominated: Córdoba and Buenos Aires, as they were up to 1825.

Córdoba

Córdoba was—I shall not say the most coquettish of American cities, because that would offend its Spanish gravity, but certainly one of the prettiest cities of the continent. Situated in a hollow formed by an elevated terrain called Los Altos, it has been forced to fold back over itself, to crowd and push together its symmetrical buildings. The sky is very pure, the winter, dry and tonic, the summer, hot and stormy. On the eastern side, it has a beautiful promenade of capricious shapes, suddenly magical to the eye. It consists of a pool of water squared in by a broad walkway, shaded by colossal, ancient willows. Each side is a block long, enclosed by wrought-iron grating with enormous doors in the centers of the four sides, so that the promenade is an enchanted prison within which one circles, always around a gorgeous pavilion with Greek architecture. In the main plaza is the magnificent Gothic cathedral, with its enormous cupola carved into arabesques, the only example I know of in

South America of medieval architecture. A block away is the church and convent of the Jesuits, in whose presbytery there is a trapdoor leading into tunnels that extend underneath the city, ending up no one yet knows where; dungeons have also been found where the Jesuits buried their prisoners alive. So, if you wish to see monuments of the Middle Ages, and to examine the power and the ways of that celebrated order, go to Córdoba, where one of its great central establishments in America was located.

On each block of the compact city, there is a proud convent or monastery, a house for pious women or one for religious observance. Back then every family had a priest, monk, nun, or chorister; the poor contented themselves with being able to count among them a hermit, lay brother, sacristan, or acolyte.

Each convent or monastery had a contiguous shantytown, in which eight hundred slaves of the order were reproducing: blacks, zambos, mulattoes, and little mulatto women with blue eyes, blond, healthy, with legs gleaming like marble; true Circassians endowed with every grace, plus teeth of African origin that fed human passions; all for the greater honor and fortune of the convent to which these houris belonged.

Moving on a bit in this visit we are making, we find the celebrated University of Córdoba, founded no less than in 1613, and in whose gloomy cloisters eight generations of doctors in both types of law, famed debaters, commentators, and casuists have spent their youth. Let us listen to the celebrated Dean Funes describe the teaching and spirit of this famous university, which has provided a large part of America with theologians and doctors for two centuries: "The course of study in theology lasted five and a half years. Theology shared in the corruption of philosophical studies. When Aristotelian philosophy was applied to theology, a mixture of the profane and the spiritual was formed. Purely human reasoning, subtleties and tricky sophisms, frivolous and impertinent questions: this was what came to form the dominant taste in those schools." If you wish to penetrate a bit more into the spirit of freedom this instruction would give, listen further to Dean Funes: "This university was born and created exclusively in the hands of the Jesuits, who established it in the college they called Maximum, in the city of Córdoba." Very distinguished lawyers have come out of there; but as for men of letters, none that haven't had to reeducate themselves in Buenos Aires with modern books.

This learned city to this day has not had a public theater, has known no opera, still has no daily newspapers, and the printing industry has not been able to establish itself there. The spirit of Córdoba, up to 1829, was monastic and scholastic; drawing-room conversations always revolved around processions, saints' days celebrations, about university examinations, nuns' professions, the receiving of a doctor's tassel.

To what point this may influence the spirit of a people concerned with these ideas for two centuries, one cannot say; but it must have some influence, because you see how the inhabitant of Córdoba casts his eyes around him and does not see open space; the horizon is four blocks beyond the plaza. He goes out in the afternoon for a stroll, and instead of coming and going down a street of poplars that broadens the soul and enlivens it, long and spacious like the stream through Santiago, he circles around an artificial lake of motionless water, lifeless, in whose center is a pavilion of majestic, but immobile, stationary form. The city is a cloister locked in by cliffs; the promenade is a cloister with an iron fence; every block has a cloister of nuns or monks; the colleges are cloisters; the legislation that is taught, theology; the entire scholastic knowledge of the Middle Ages is a cloister, in which intelligence locks itself in and parapets itself against all that may come from the text and its commentary. Córdoba knows of nothing on the face of the earth but Córdoba; true, it has heard tell that Buenos Aires is out there somewhere; but if it believes this, which isn't always the case, it asks: "Do they have a university? But it must be brand new. Let's see: How many convents are there? Is there a promenade like this one? If not, it's nothing."

"What book do you use there to study legislation?" the grave Dr. Jigena asked a young man from Buenos Aires. "Bentham." "What did you say? Little Bentham?" showing with his fingers the size of the volume in duodecimo edition in which Bentham is published. "Little Bentham! In one paper of mine there is more doctrine than in those old tomes. What a university and what stupid little doctors!" "And what author do you teach?" "Hah! Cardinal Luca! What do you say, sir? Seventeen volumes in folio!"

It is true that the traveler nearing Córdoba looks for, but does not find, the holy city, the mystical city, the city with a doctor's hat and tassels. Finally, the driver tells him: "Look there . . . down below . . . between the grasses . . . " And, in fact, staring down at the ground, and at a short distance, one sees pop up one, two, three, ten crosses in a row on the cupolas and spires of the many churches that decorate this Pompeii of medieval Spain.

Apart from this, the people of the city, made up of artisans, shared in the spirit of the upper classes: the master shoemaker took on the airs of a doctor of shoemaking and addressed a Latin text to you while he gravely measured your size; the word *ergo* was in the kitchens and in the mouths of the beggars and fools of the city, and every argument among errand boys took on the tone and the form of a summation. Add to this that during the entire revolution Córdoba was a haven for Spaniards who were mistreated everywhere else. What effect could the revolution of 1810 have on a people educated by the Jesuits and cloistered by nature, education, and art? What support could revolutionary ideas, the children of Rousseau, Mably, Raynal, and Voltaire, find there, if by chance they crossed the Pampas to descend into the Spanish catacombs, into those heads disciplined by peripatetic philosophy to look beyond all new ideas, into those minds that, like their promenade, had an immobile idea in the center, surrounded by a lake of dead waters, making them difficult to penetrate?

Around 1816, the enlightened and liberal Dean Funes succeeded in introducing into that ancient university the courses of study so scorned up until then: mathematics, modern languages, public law, physics, drawing, and music. From then on, the youth of Córdoba began to set their minds on new paths, and it didn't take long for effects to be felt which we will take up elsewhere, because for now, I am only characterizing the mature, traditional spirit that predominated.

The revolution of 1810 found closed ears in Córdoba, at the same time that the provinces, all together, were responding to the call "To arms! Liberty!" In Córdoba, Liniers began to raise armies to go to Buenos Aires, to kill the revolution; it was to Córdoba that the Junta sent one of their own with his troops, to decapitate Spain. Córdoba, finally, insulted by this offense and awaiting vengeance and reparations, with the learned hand of the university, and in the language of the breviary and the commentators, wrote that famous anagram marking for the traveler the tomb of the first royalists sacrificed on the altars of the homeland:

C	L	A	M	O	R
o	i	l	o	r	o
n	n	l	r	e	d
c	i	e	e	l	r
h	e	n	n	l	í
a	r	d	o	a	g
	s²	e		n	u
				a	e
					z

In 1820, an army rebelled in Arequito, and its leader, a native of Córdoba, abandoned the flag of the homeland and peacefully established himself in Córdoba, which took pleasure in having grabbed away an army. Bustos created a colonial government without responsibilities; he introduced court etiquette, the secular quietism of Spain; and thus prepared, Córdoba reached the year 1825, when at issue was the organization of the Republic and constituting the revolution and its results.

Buenos Aires

Now let us examine Buenos Aires. For a long time, it struggled with the indigenous people that swept it off the face of the earth; it rose again, fell immediately, until around 1620 when it rose, now sufficiently on the map of Spanish dominions to be elevated to a captaincy-general, separating it from that of Paraguay, to which it had been subordinate until then. By 1777, Buenos Aires was now very visible, so much so that it was necessary to redo the administrative geography of the colonies in order to put it at the head of a viceroyalty created for it *ex profeso*.

In 1806 the speculating eye of England ran over the map of America and saw only Buenos Aires, its river, its future. In 1810, Buenos Aires pulsated with revolutionaries seasoned in all the anti-Spanish, French, European doctrines. What forward movement had been operating on the western bank of the Río de la Plata? Spain, as colonizer, was not a trader or a navigator; the Río de la Plata was nothing much to it: *official* Spain looked at it with scorn, a shore and a river. As time went by, the river had deposited its sediment of riches on that shore, but very little of the Spanish spirit, of the Spanish government. Trading activity had brought the spirit and general ideas of Europe; the ships that frequented its waters brought books from all over and news of all the world's political events. Note that Spain did not have any other trading city on the Atlantic coast. The war with the English speeded up the movement toward emancipation and awoke a feeling of self-importance. Buenos Aires was a little child that defeated a giant, became infatuated with itself, considered itself to be a hero, and risked greater things.

Carried by this feeling of self-sufficiency, it initiated the revolution with an audacity that had no model, took it everywhere, considered itself entrusted by on High with the realization of a great work. The *Social Contract* flew from hand to hand; Mably and Raynal were the oracles of the press, Robespierre and the Convention, the models. Buenos

Aires considered itself a continuation of Europe, and if it didn't frankly confess to being French and North American in spirit and tendencies, it did deny Spanish origins, because the Spanish government, it said, had claimed it after the age of adulthood. With the revolution came the armies and the glory, the triumphs and reversals, the revolts and the sedition.

But Buenos Aires, in the midst of all these swings, showed the revolutionary strength with which it was endowed. Bolívar was everything, Venezuela was the pedestal for that colossal figure; Buenos Aires was an entire city of revolutionaries. Belgrano, Rondeau, San Martín, Alvear, and the hundred generals who commanded their armies were its instruments, its arms, not its head or its body. In the Argentine Republic one cannot say, "General So-and-so liberated the country," but rather, "the Junta, the Board, the Congress, the Government of this or that era ordered General So-and-so to do this." Contact with Europeans from all nations was greater, even from the start, than in any other place on the Spanish American continent. De-Hispanicization and Europeanization took place over ten years in a radical way, but only in Buenos Aires, it should be understood.

Nothing more is needed than a list of the residents of Buenos Aires, to see how abundant English, French, German, Italian last names are among the country's children. In 1820 society began to be organized according to the new ideas impregnating it, and that movement continued until Rivadavia was put at the head of the government. Until that moment, Rodríguez and Las Heras had been laying the usual foundations for free governments. Political amnesty, personal security, respect for property, responsibility of civil authority, balance of powers, public education; everything, finally, was peacefully set down and constituted. Rivadavia came from Europe, bringing Europe with him, but what is more, he had contempt for Europe; Buenos Aires (and of course, they said, the Argentine Republic) would achieve what republican France hadn't been able to, what the English aristocracy didn't want, what tyrannized Europe lacked. This wasn't an illusion of Rivadavia, it was the general thinking of the city, it was its spirit, its tendency.

The parties were divided by greater or lesser pretensions, but not by basically antagonistic ideas. And how could it have been otherwise for a people who, in only fourteen years, had made an example out of England, overrun half the continent, outfitted ten armies, given a hundred major battles, triumphed everywhere, taken part in every event, broken every tradition, tried out every theory, risked everything, and succeeded in everything: that was alive, growing rich, becoming civilized? How could it have been otherwise, when the bases of government, the political faith given to it by Europe, were plagued with error, with absurd and deceptive theories, with bad principles? Because its politicians could not be expected to know more than the great men of Europe, who at that time knew nothing definitive about political organization. This is a grave fact that I want to emphasize. Today, studies of constitutions, races, beliefs—history, in a word—have made common a certain practical knowledge that instructs us against the glitter of theories conceived *a priori;* but before 1820, none of this had spread through the European world. With the paradoxes of the *Social Contract,* France rose up; Buenos Aires did the same; Montesquieu separated three distinct powers, and at once we had three powers; Benjamin Constant and Bentham annulled the executive, here it was constituted null at birth; Say and Smith preached free trade, and free trade, we repeated. Buenos Aires professed and believed everything that the learned European world believed and professed. Only after the revolution of 1830 in France, and its incomplete results, did the social sciences take a new direction and illusions begin to vanish. From then on, European books started to reach us showing that Voltaire was not really right, that Rousseau was a sophist, and Mably and Raynal, just anarchists; that there were not three powers, or a social contract, et cetera. From then on, we learned something about races, tendencies, national customs, historical causes. Tocqueville revealed to us, for the first time, the secret of North America; Sismondi showed us the futility of constitutions; Thierry, Michelet, and Guizot, the spirit of history; the revolution of 1830, all the deception of Benjamin Constant's constitutionalism; the Spanish Revolution, all that is incomplete and backward in our race. For what, then, do they blame Rivadavia and Buenos Aires? For not knowing more than the knowledgeable Europeans who led them astray? Moreover, how could a people who had contributed so much and with such good results to the spread of revolution not ardently embrace these general ideas? How to rein in the flight of fantasy of the inhabitants of a limitless plain, looking toward a river with no facing banks, a step away from Europe, unaware of its own traditions, in reality with none; a new, improvised people, that from the cradle has heard itself hailed as a great people?

Thus brought up, spoiled until then by good fortune, Buenos Aires set about constituting itself and the Republic just as it had set about liberating itself and America: decidedly, with no middle ground, with no accommodation of obstacles. Rivadavia was the living incarnation of the poetic, grandiose spirit that dominated the entire society. Rivadavia, then, continued the work of Las Heras on the large mold into which a great American state, a republic, would be poured. He brought in learned Europeans for the press and the universities, settlement colonies for the deserts, ships for the rivers, concern and freedom for all beliefs, credit and the Banco Nacional to stimulate industry, all the great social theories of the era for modeling his government; in short, he brought in Europe, so as to pour it all at once into America, and to realize in ten years the work that before would have required the passing of centuries. Was this a chimerical project? I protest that it was not. All his administrative creations subsist, except those that Rosas's barbarism found inconvenient for his assaults. Freedom of religion, which the highest-level clergy of Buenos Aires supported, has not been suppressed; the European population is disseminated over the *estancias,* and takes up arms *motu propio* to break with the only obstacle that deprives it of the blessings offered by the soil; the rivers are crying out to break through the official blindness that keeps them from being navigated; and the Banco Nacional is an institution so deeply rooted that it has saved society from the misery to which the tyrant would have led it. Above all, however fantastic and inopportune that great system—toward which all the peoples of America are now heading and hurrying—might have been, at least it was easy and tolerable for people; and however much men without conscience may scream about him every day, Rivadavia never spilled a drop of blood or destroyed anyone's property, descending voluntarily from the luxury of the presidency to the noble, humble poverty of the exile. Rosas, who so slanders him, would drown in the lake formed by all the blood he himself has spilled; and the forty million pesos from the national treasury and the fifty from private fortunes that Rosas has consumed in ten years to support the interminable war that his brutalities have ignited, in the hands of that fatuous dreamer, Rivadavia, would have been turned into canals for navigation, great, built-up cities, and many establishments of public utility. May there be left, then, to this man now dead to his country, the glory of having represented European civilization in its most noble aspirations, and may his adversaries claim what is theirs, the demonstration of American barbarism in its most odious, repugnant form; because Rosas and Rivadavia are the two extremes of the Argentine Republic, which is bound to savages by the Pampas and to Europe by the Río de la Plata.

I make not a eulogy, but rather an apotheosis of Rivadavia and his party, who have died as a political element within the Argentine Repub-

lic, although Rosas may insist, suspiciously, on calling his current enemies "Unitarists." The old Unitarist Party, like that of the Girondists,
succumbed many years ago.[3] But in the midst of its mistakes and fantastic illusions, it had so much that was great and noble that the succeeding generation owes it the most elaborate funeral rites. Many of
those men are still among us but no longer in an organized party: they
are the mummies of the Argentine Republic, as venerable and noble as
those of the Napoleonic empire. These Unitarists of 1825 make up a separate type that we know how to distinguish by their figure, their manners, their tone of voice, and their ideas. I think that from among a
group of a hundred Argentines, I could say that one is a Unitarist. The
Unitarist type marches straight forward, head high; does not turn back,
although he hears a building fall down; speaks arrogantly; completes
sentences with disdainful gestures and conclusive motions; has set, invariable ideas; and on the eve of battle will still be involved in arguing
about all the aspects of a regulation, or establishing a new legal formality, because legal formulas are the external worship he pays to his idols:
the Constitution, individual rights. His religion is the future of the Republic, whose image—colossal, indefinable, but grand and noble—appears to him at all times covered with the mantle of past glories and
doesn't allow him to think about the events he is witnessing. It is impossible to imagine a generation more given to reasoning, more deductive, with more initiative, and more lacking in common sense. News of
an enemy triumph arrives; everyone repeats it, the official report describes it in detail, the losers come in wounded. A Unitarist does not believe that triumph, and bases his opinion on reasons so conclusive he
makes you doubt what your eyes are seeing. He has such faith in the superiority of his cause, and such loyalty and abnegation in consecrating
his life to it, that neither exile, poverty, nor the passing of years will cool
his ardor one bit.

Regarding the nature of their energy and soul, they are infinitely superior to the generation that has succeeded them. Above all, what most
distinguishes them from us are their fine manners, their ceremonious
politics, and their pompously cultured gestures. In drawing rooms they
have no equal, and although by now cut down by age, they are more
gallant, more lively and gay with the ladies, than their sons.

Today good form is neglected among us, as the movement toward
democracy becomes more pronounced, and it isn't easy to get an idea
of the culture and refinement of Buenos Aires society before 1828. All
the Europeans that came into port thought they were in Europe, in the

salons of Paris; nothing was lacking, not even the French petulance, which was noticeable back then in elegant Buenos Aires.

I have dwelled on these details to characterize the era in which the Republic was being established, and the diverse elements that were in combat with one another. Córdoba, Spanish through its literary and religious education, stable, and hostile to revolutionary innovations, and Buenos Aires, all novelty, all revolution and movement, are the two prominent aspects of the parties that were dividing all the cities; in every city these two diverse elements, which exist in all cultured peoples, were in conflict. I do not know if another phenomenon like this has appeared in America; that is, the two parties, the retrograde and the revolutionary, the conservative and the progressive, each represented to a high degree by a city civilized in a different manner, each nourished by ideas extracted from different sources: Córdoba, from Spain, the Councils, the Commentators, the Pandects; Buenos Aires, from Bentham, Rousseau, Montesquieu, and all of French literature.

To these antagonistic elements another cause no less grave was added: this was the loosening of all national ties produced by the Revolution of Independence. When authority is taken away from one center in order to establish it somewhere else, much time goes by before it takes root. *El republicano* said the other day that "authority is nothing more than an agreement between governors and governed." It seems there are still many Unitarists here! *Authority is founded on the undeliberated consent that a nation gives to a permanent fact.* Where there is deliberation and will, there is no authority. That state of transition is called federalism, and after every revolution and consequent change of authority, all nations have their phase of efforts toward federation.

I will explain what I mean. Expelled from Spain, Ferdinand VII—the authority, that permanent fact—ceased to be, and Spain met in provincial juntas that denied authority to those who governed in the name of the king. This was the federation of Spain. The news came to America, and it broke off from Spain, separating into various sections: the federation of America.

From the viceroyalty of Buenos Aires, when the battle was over, four states emerged: Bolivia, Paraguay, the Banda Oriental, and the Argentine Republic: the federation of the viceroyalty.

The Argentine Republic divided into provinces, not by the old intendancies, but by cities: the federation of cities.

It is not that the word *federation* means separation, but rather that, given the previous separation, it expresses the union of different parts. The Argentine Republic found itself in a social crisis, and many notable, well-intentioned men from the cities thought it possible to make federations every time a man or a people felt itself without respect for a nominal authority, existing only by agreement.

In this way, then, there was another apple of discord in the Republic, and the parties, after having called themselves royalists and patriots, congressionalists and executivists, *pelucones* and liberals, ended up calling themselves federalists and unitarists.[4] I lie, the fun isn't over yet: for Don Juan Manuel Rosas has taken to calling his present and future enemies "savage, vile unitarists," and twenty years from now, just as today all those who wear the label he has put on them are federalists, one will be born a *savage,* according to this stereotype.

But the Argentine Republic is geographically constituted in such a way that it must always be unitarist, although the label on the bottle may say the opposite. Its continuous plains, its rivers confluent to a single port, make it fatally "one and indivisible." Rivadavia, knowing better the needs of the country, advised the people to unify under one common constitution, making the port of Buenos Aires a national one. Agüero, his echo in Congress, used to say to the *porteños* with his magisterial, unitarist tone: "Let us give voluntarily to the people what they will later demand from us with weapons in hand."[5]

The prediction missed by one word. The people did not demand the port from Buenos Aires with weapons, but with the barbarism they sent to it in Facundo and Rosas. But Buenos Aires kept the barbarism and the port, which has only served Rosas and not the provinces. So Buenos Aires and the provinces have mutually hurt each other, without producing any advantages.

I have had to establish all these causes in order to continue the life of Juan Facundo Quiroga, because, although it may seem ridiculous to say so, Facundo was Rivadavia's rival. Everything else was transitory, intermediate, and of little moment: the federal party of the cities was a link connected to the barbarous party of the countryside. The Republic was courted by two unitarist forces: one coming out of Buenos Aires, supported by the liberals of the interior; another coming out of the countryside, supported by the caudillos who had by then succeeded in dominating the cities. One, civilized, constitutional, European; the other, barbarous, arbitrary, American.

These two forces had reached their fullest stage of development, and just a word was needed to set off the fight; and since the revolutionary party was called Unitarist, the opposing party had no problem adopting the denomination of Federalist, without comprehending it.

But this barbarous force was disseminated throughout the Republic, divided into provinces, into personal strongholds; a powerful hand was needed to mold it and present it as a homogenous whole, and Quiroga offered his arm to realize this grand work.

The Argentine gaucho, although he has instincts common to all shepherds, is eminently provincial: there is a Buenos Aires type, a Santa Fe one, a Cordoban, a *llanista*, etc. He limits all his aspirations within his province; other people are enemies, or strangers; they are all different tribes, who wage war among themselves. López, in control of Santa Fe, took no notice of what went on outside unless they started to bother him, in which case he got on his horse and threw the intruders out. But just as it was not in their power to make the provinces stop bordering each other everywhere, so they could not avoid finally uniting in common interest, and that is how they ended up with the same unity they wanted so much to combat.

Remember that in the beginning I said that the travels and journeys of Quiroga's youth had been the basis of his future ambition. And in fact, Facundo, although a gaucho, had no ties to any one place; he was from La Rioja, but he had been educated in San Juan, had lived in Mendoza, had been in Buenos Aires. He knew the Republic; his gaze extended over a large horizon; master of La Rioja, he naturally wanted to show up invested with power in the town where he learned to read, in the city where he built mud walls, in the other one where he was jailed and did a glorious deed. If events pulled him outside his province, he wouldn't resist leaving because of fear or intimidation. Very different from Ibarra or López, who only liked to defend themselves within their own territory, he would attack someone else's and take power over it. Thus does Providence realize great things through insignificant and imperceptible means, and the barbarous unity of the Republic was to begin because a bad gaucho had wandered from province to province, building mud walls and stabbing with his knife.

CHAPTER VIII

Tests of Strength

¡Cuánto dilata el día! porque mañana quiero galopar diez cuadras sobre un campo sembrado de cadáveres.

Shakespeare[1]

Just as I have depicted it was the political physiognomy of the Republic in 1825, when the government of Buenos Aires invited the provinces to meet as a congress to form a general government. This idea was welcomed with approval everywhere, perhaps because each caudillo was counting on being named the legitimate caudillo of his province, perhaps because the glitter of Buenos Aires so dazzled everyone that it would not have been possible to refuse such a rational plan without scandal. Some have imputed the government of Buenos Aires with error for having promoted this issue, whose solution would be so dire for that government itself and for civilization, which, just like religion, tends to spread and propagandize, and if men didn't want everyone to think like them they wouldn't be real believers.

Facundo received the invitation in La Rioja and welcomed the idea with enthusiasm, perhaps because of the sympathy that highly gifted spirits have with essentially good things.

In 1825, the Republic was preparing for war with Brazil, and each province had been entrusted with the formation of an army regiment. Arriving in Tucumán with this order was Colonel Lamadrid, who, impatient to obtain recruits and the resources necessary to raise his regiment, didn't hesitate much before toppling those morose authorities and taking over the government himself, to expedite the required decrees. This subversive act put the government of Buenos Aires in a delicate position. There was mistrust between the governments, provincial jealousies, and Colonel Lamadrid, coming from Buenos Aires and upsetting a provincial government, made the former, in the eyes of the nation, look like the instigator. To dispel that suspicion, the government of Buenos Aires urged Facundo to invade Tucumán and reinstate the provincial authorities. Lamadrid explained to the government the motive that had driven him, real but quite frivolous to be sure, and protested his inalterable loyalty. But it was too late: Facundo was on the move, and preparations had to be made to repel him. Lamadrid had at his disposal armaments en route through Salta, but out of courtesy, so as not to aggravate further the charges weighing against him, he limited himself to taking fifty rifles and an equal number of sabers—sufficient, according to him, to finish off the invading forces.

General Lamadrid was one of those types native to Argentine soil. At the age of fourteen, he began waging war on the Spanish, and the wonders of his legendary valor passed the limits of the possible. He had been present in 140 encounters, in all of which Lamadrid's sword had emerged chipped and dripping blood; gunpowder smoke and horses' whinnies absolutely enraptured him; and as long as he could cut up everything in his path—cavalry, cannons, infantry—losing the battle mattered little to him. I said he was a type native to this country, not because of this fabulous courage, but because he was a cavalry officer and a poet besides. He was a Tyrtaeus who inspired soldiers with fighting songs, the *cantor* of whom I spoke earlier; he was the gaucho spirit, civilized and consecrated to liberty.[2] Unfortunately, he was not a complete general, such as Napoleon liked; valor predominated over the other qualities of this general, in a ratio of a hundred to one. If you doubt it, look at what he did in Tucumán: he didn't convene sufficient forces, although he could have, and with a fistful of men, he went into battle, despite being accompanied by Colonel Díaz Vélez, who was almost as brave as he. Facundo had two hundred infantrymen and his Colorados cavalry. Lamadrid had fifty infantrymen and some militia squadrons. The combat began, Facundo's cavalry was overrun, and so was Facundo, who only returned to the battlefield after everything was over. The infantrymen were left in closed ranks; Lamadrid ordered a charge, was not obeyed, and charged them alone. This is true: he alone trampled the masses of infantry; they threw his horse over, he got up, charged again; he killed, wounded, stabbed everything within his reach, until horse and horseman fell, run through by bullets and bayonets, and with this the victory was decided by the infantry. Still on the ground, they plunged the bayonet of a rifle into his back, they shot him, and bullet and bayonet passed through him—roasting him, moreover, with the flash. Facundo finally returned to recover his lost black flag, and found the battle won and Lamadrid dead, very dead. His clothing was there; his sword, his horse, nothing was missing except the cadaver, which could not be found among the many mutilated and naked ones lying in the field. Colonel Díaz Vélez, taken prisoner, said that his brother had a lance wound in one leg; there was no cadaver with such a wound.

Lamadrid, pierced by eleven wounds, had dragged himself into some bushes where his aide found him, ranting deliriously about the battle, and responding to the noise of footsteps coming near: "I will not surrender!" Until then, Colonel Lamadrid had never surrendered.

Here you have the famous Battle of Tala, Quiroga's first test outside the boundaries of his province. In it, he had vanquished the most valiant of valiant men, whose sword he kept as a victory trophy. Would he stop there? But let us look at the force that had risen up against the colonel of the Fifteenth Regiment, who had overthrown a government in order to outfit his corps. Facundo raised a flag in Tala that was not Argentine, one that he had invented. It was a black cloth with a skull and crossbones in the middle. This was his flag, which he lost at the beginning of the battle, and which he was "going to recover"—as he told his routed soldiers—"even it it's at the gates of hell." Death, fear, hell, appear on the banner and in the proclamation of the general of the Llanos. Haven't you seen this same burial sheet over the coffins of the dead, when the priest chants *a porta inferi*?

But there is still something more that revealed from then on the spirit of the pastoral, Arab, Tartar force that was going to destroy the cities. The Argentine colors are sky-blue and white, the transparent sky of a calm day and the clear light of the disk of the sun: peace and justice for all. Because of our hatred for tyranny and violence, our flag and our shield excommunicate the blazon and warlike bearings. Two hands, in a sign of unity, uphold the Phrygian cap of the freed slave; the united cities, this symbol says, will uphold the freedom they have acquired; the sun begins to illuminate the scene of this oath, and the night disappears little by little. The armies of the Republic, who took war everywhere to make that future of light a reality, and to turn into day the dawn that the shield announces, wore dark blue with varying details: they dressed like Europeans. Very well; in the bosom of the Republic, from the depths of its bowels, arose the color red, and it became the soldier's uniform, the flag of the army, and ultimately, the national cockade that every Argentine must wear, under pain of death.

Do you know what the color red means? I don't know either, but I will gather together some references.

I have before me a picture of the flags of all the world's nations. There is only one cultured, European one in which red predominates, despite the barbarous origins of their flags. But there are other red ones. I read them off: Algeria, red flag with skull and crossbones; Tunisia, red flag; Mongolia, *idem;* Turkey, red flag with crescent; Morocco, Japan, red with the exterminating blade; Siam, Surat, etc., the same thing.

I recall that travelers who attempt to penetrate the African interior equip themselves with red cloth to please the black princes. "The king of Eboe," say the Lardner brothers, "wore a Spanish coat of red cloth, and trousers of the same color."

I recall that the gifts sent by the government of Chile to the Araucanian caciques consist of red blankets and clothing, because this color greatly pleases the savages.

The cape of the Roman emperors who represented the dictator was purple; that is, red.

The royal robe of the barbarian kings of Europe was always red.

Spain has been the last European country to repudiate the color red, worn in the scarlet cape.

Don Carlos, in Spain, the absolutist pretender, raised a red flag.

The royal edict of Genoa,* ordering that the senators wear a purplish red toga, foresees that this should be the practice especially "in esecuzione de giudicato criminale ad effetto di incutere colla grave sua decorosa presenza il terrore e lo spavento nei cativi." [3]

The executioner, in all the European states, wore red until the last century.

Artigas added a red diagonal stripe to the Argentine flag.

Rosas's armies wear red.

His portrait is stamped on a red ribbon.

What mysterious link connects all these facts? Is it just a coincidence that Algeria, Tunisia, Japan, Morocco, Turkey, Siam, the Africans, the savages, the Roman Neros, the barbarian kings, *il terrore e lo spavento,*

---

*Señor Alberdi supplied me with this item, noted in his trip to Italy. (Author's note to the first edition.)

the executioner and Rosas, dress in a color banned today by Christian, cultured societies? Is not red the symbol expressing violence, blood, and barbarism? And if not, why this antagonism?

The Revolution of Argentine Independence is symbolized by two sky-blue stripes and one white one, as if to say: justice, peace, justice!

The reaction commanded by Facundo, and taken advantage of by Rosas, is symbolized in a red ribbon, which says: terror, blood, terror!

The human species, in all times, has given this meaning to the color scarlet, red, purple. Study the government of the peoples who brandish this color, and you will find Rosas and Facundo: terror, barbarism, blood flowing every day. In Morocco, the emperor himself has the singular prerogative of killing criminals.

I must stop and consider this point. Each civilization expresses itself in its costume, and each costume indicates an entire system of ideas. Why do we wear full beards today? Because of the studies done lately on the Middle Ages: the direction in romantic literature is reflected in fashion. Why does the latter vary each day? Because of the freedom in European thinking; make thinking fixed, enslave it, and you will have an invariable manner of dress. Thus in Asia, where men live under governments like that of Rosas, they have worn long robes since the time of Abraham.

There is still more: every civilization has had its costume, and every change in ideas, every institutional revolution, a change in dress. One costume for Roman civilization, another, the Middle Ages; the tailcoat does not come into use in Europe until after the renaissance in knowledge; fashion is imposed on the rest of the world only by the most civilized nation; all the Christian peoples wear tailcoats, and when the sultan of Turkey, Abdul Medhil, wants to introduce European civilization into his states, he removes his turban, his caftan, and his wide pants in order to wear a tailcoat, trousers, and cravat.

Argentines know about the obstinate war that Facundo and Rosas have made on the tailcoat and fashionable dress. In 1840, a group of *mazorqueros* surrounded, in the darkness of night, an individual who wore a frock coat on the streets of Buenos Aires. The knives were two fingers' width from his throat. "I am Simón Pereira," he exclaimed. "Señor, a man who goes dressed like this puts himself in danger." "That's just why I dress like this; who but I wears a frock coat? I do it so I will be recognized from far away." This man is a cousin and business partner of Don Juan Manuel Rosas. But to end this explication that I propose to give on the color red brought in by Facundo, and to illustrate through its symbols the character of the civil war, I must relate here the story of the red ribbon, which today is starting to be displayed abroad. In 1820, the Colorados de las Conchas appeared in Buenos Aires with Rosas; the countryside had sent this contingent. Twenty years later, Rosas finally covered the city in red: houses, doors, wallpaper, china, tapestries, wall hangings, etc., etc. Ultimately, he officially consecrated this color and imposed it as a state measure.

The history of the red ribbon is a very curious one. At first, it was an emblem adopted by supporters; later on it was ordered that everyone wear it, to "prove the uniformity" of public opinion. People meant to obey, but when they changed clothes, they forgot. The police came to the aid of their memory: *mazorqueros* spread out along the streets and, above all, at church doors, and when the ladies exited, lashes with bulls' pizzles were dispensed mercilessly. But there was still much more to be done. Did someone wear the ribbon carelessly tied? Lash him! he was a unitarist. Was it worn too small? Lash him! he was a unitarist. Was he not wearing it at all? Cut his throat for disobedience! Neither the government's attention nor public education stopped there. It wasn't enough to be a federalist or to wear the ribbon, which was also required to display the portrait of the illustrious Restorer over the heart, as a sign of "intense" love, and the motto "Death to the savage, filthy unitarists." Might you think that with this, the work of debasing a cultured people and of making them renounce all personal dignity was done? Ah! they were not yet well disciplined. At dawn one morning, on a Buenos Aires corner, appeared a huge, ridiculous figure painted on paper, with a streamer of ribbon half a yard long. The instant that someone saw it, he ran away terrified, sounding the alarm everywhere; he went into the first store, and came out with a streamer of ribbon half a yard long. Ten minutes later, the entire city appeared in the streets, each with his streamer of ribbon half a yard long. The next day, another figure appeared with a slight alteration in the ribbon: the same maneuvers. If some young lady forgot her red bow, the police stuck one on her head for free—with melted tar! This is how uniformity of opinion has been achieved! Ask anywhere in the Argentine Republic if there is someone who will not hold and believe himself a federalist! It has happened a thousand times that someone has stepped outside the door to his house and seen that the end of the street has been swept; in an instant he has ordered his own swept, in the belief that it was a police order. A shopkeeper raises a flag to attract attention; his neighbor sees it, and fearful of being tainted as lazy by the government, raises his own, the people across the street raise theirs, it spreads to other streets, and in a moment, Buenos Aires is dressed in flags. The police become alarmed, inquire what important news has been received unbeknownst to them. . . . And this is the people that made eleven thousand Englishmen surrender in the streets, and then sent five armies all over the American continent to hunt down Spaniards!

What happens is that terror is a disease of the mind that attacks a people like cholera, smallpox, or scarlet fever. No one, finally, escapes the contagion. And when work is done for ten straight years to inoculate it, even those already vaccinated cannot resist in the end. So do not laugh, peoples of Spanish America, on seeing such degradation! You too are Spanish, and this is how the Inquisition educated Spain! We carry this disease in our blood.

Let's again take up the thread of events. Facundo entered Tucumán triumphantly and returned to La Rioja after a few days, without committing notable acts of violence and without imposing taxes, since Rivadavia's constitutional norms had shaped a public consciousness that couldn't be confronted all in one blow.

Facundo returned to La Rioja. Although an enemy of the president, Quiroga didn't know exactly what to say about his motive for this opposition, which was quite natural. He himself couldn't have realized it. "I'm not a federalist," he would always say, "would I be that stupid?" "Do you know," he said once to Don Dalmacio Vélez, "why I've gone to war? For this!" And he took out an ounce of gold. Facundo was lying.

At other times he would say: "Carril, the governor of San Juan, slighted me by not paying attention to my recommendation of Carita, and that's why I threw in with the opposition to the Congress." He was lying.

His enemies would say: "He had a lot of shares in the mint and proposed to sell them to the national government for three hundred thousand pesos. Rivadavia rejected this proposal, because it was an outrageous robbery, and since then, Facundo counts himself among his enemies." These facts are true, but this wasn't his motive.

It is believed that he yielded to the suggestions of Bustos and Ibarra that he oppose the government, but there is a document that proves the contrary. In a letter written to General Lamadrid in 1832, he said: "When I was invited by the lowly and worthless Bustos and Ibarra, not considering them capable of opposing the despot President Don Bernardino Rivadavia with any success, I rejected them; but the late Bustos's aide-de-camp Colonel Manuel del Castillo having assured me that you were involved in this business, and were the one most interested in it, I did not hesitate for a moment in deciding to carry through with my commitment, counting only on your sword for a happy outcome. . . . Imagine my disappointment!, etc."

He wasn't a federalist, and how could he have been? Is it necessary to be as ignorant as a campaign caudillo to understand the form of government best suited to the Republic? Is a man's ability to judge the arduous questions of high-level politics greater, the less his education? Were thinkers like López, like Ibarra, like Facundo, with their historical, social, geographical, philosophical, and legal studies, the ones who were going to resolve the problem of a suitable organization of the state? Bah! . . . Let's put aside the useless words with which the unwary have been duped with such impudence. Facundo went against the government that had sent him to Tucumán for the same reason that he went against Aldao, who had sent him to La Rioja. He felt strong, and with a will to action; he was driven to this by a blind, undefined instinct, and he obeyed it; he was the campaign commander, the bad gaucho, enemy of civil justice, of civil order, of educated men, of learned men, of the tailcoat—of the city, in a word. He was entrusted with the destruction of all this from on High, and he could not abandon his mission.

Around this time, a singular issue came to complicate matters. In Buenos Aires, seaport residence of sixteen thousand foreigners, the government proposed to grant those foreigners freedom of religion, and the most enlightened sector of the clergy supported and sanctioned the law. The convents had already been regulated and the priests given pensions. In Buenos Aires this issue caused no controversy, because these were points on which all opinion was in agreement; they were of patent necessity. The question of freedom of religion is, in America, a political and economic question. Whoever says freedom of religion is saying European immigration and settlement. It caused so little stir in Buenos Aires that Rosas has not dared to touch anything agreed upon back then, and anything Rosas would not attempt must be an inconceivable absurdity.

However, in the provinces this was a question of religion, of salvation and eternal condemnation. Imagine how Córdoba received it! In Córdoba an inquisition was begun. San Juan experienced a "Catholic" insurrection, because that was what the party called itself, to distinguish it from the "libertines," its enemies. This revolution in San Juan then snuffed out, one day they find Facundo at the city gates, with a black flag divided by a bloody cross, surrounded by this motto: "Religion or death!"

Does the reader recall that I have copied from a manuscript that Facundo "never went to confession, never went to Mass or prayed, and that he himself said he did not believe in anything"? Very well: party spirit led a celebrated preacher to call him the "Envoy of God" and to incite the mob to follow his flag. When this same priest opened his eyes and distanced himself from the criminal crusade he had preached, Facundo said he was only sorry not to have him in his hands, so as to give him six hundred lashes.

When he arrived in San Juan, the principal men of the city—the magistrates who hadn't fled, the priests, pleased with this divine assistance—went out to meet him and formed two long rows in the street. Facundo passed by without looking at them; they followed him at a distance, upset, looking at each other in common humiliation, until they got to the middle of an alfalfa pasture, lodgings that the shepherd general, this modern Hykso, preferred to the decorated buildings of the city.[4] A black woman who had been his childhood servant appeared to see her Facundo; he sat her at his side, conversed affectionately with her, while the priests and notables of the city stood there with no one talking to them, without their chief deigning to dismiss them.

The "Catholics" must have been left a little doubtful of the importance and suitability of the assistance that had come to them so unexpectedly. A few days later, learning that the priest of the Conception was a "libertine," Facundo ordered him brought in by soldiers, given lashes on the way, and shackled, ordering him to prepare to die. Because my Chilean readers should know that at that time in San Juan there were libertine priests, clerics, friars, who belonged to the party of the president. Among others, the presbyter Centeno, well known in Santiago, along with six others, one of those who worked the most on ecclesiastical reform. But it was necessary to do something in favor of religion, to justify the flag's motto. With so laudable a goal, Facundo wrote a little note to a priest who was a supporter of his, asking for advice regarding the decision he had made, he said, to shoot all the authorities, by virtue of the fact that they hadn't yet decreed a restitution of benefits to the clergy.

The good priest, who hadn't foreseen what giving arms to criminals in the name of God would mean, at least had some scruples about the way in which reparations would be made and was able to get an official letter sent to the authorities, asking or ordering them to do this.

Was there a religious issue in the Argentine Republic? I would emphatically deny it, if I didn't know that the more barbarous and therefore the less religious a people is, the more susceptible it is to fanaticism and prejudice. But the masses didn't act spontaneously, and those who adopted that motto, Facundo, López, Bustos, etc., were completely indifferent. This is of capital importance. The religious wars of the fifteenth century in Europe were supported on both sides by sincere believers, exalted, fanatic, and committed to the death, without political concerns, without ambitions. The Puritans read the Bible the moment before combat, they prayed and prepared themselves with fasting and penitence. Above all, the sign by which the spirit of parties becomes clear is when they carry out their proposals after a triumph, even beyond what was already assured before the struggle. When this does not occur, their words are deceptive. After having triumphed in the Argentine Republic, what has the party calling itself "Catholic" done for religion or for the interests of the priesthood?

The only thing as far as I know is to have expelled the Jesuits and cut the throats of four respectable priests in Santos Lugares* after having flayed their scalps and hands; and to put a portrait of Rosas alongside the Eucharist and carry it in procession under a canopy! Did the "libertine" party ever commit such horrific profanations?

But I've dwelled too much on this point. Facundo occupied his time in San Juan with gambling, leaving the authorities to worry about raising the sums he needed to make up for expenses incurred by his defense of religion. The whole time he stayed there, he lived under a canopy of hides in the middle of an alfalfa field, and flaunted (because it was a premeditated flaunting) his *chiripá*.[5] A challenge and an insult to a city where the majority of citizens rode on English saddles, and where the dress and barbarous tastes of the countryside were detested, insofar as it is an exclusively agricultural province!

Still one more campaign in Tucumán, against General Lamadrid, completed the debut or first showing of this new emir of the shepherds. General Lamadrid had returned to the government of Tucumán, sup-

---

*These priests were: Villafañe, from the province of Tucumán, who was seventy-six years old; two persecuted priests named Frías, from Santiago del Estero, settled in the Tucumán countryside, one sixty-four, and the other sixty-six; the canon Cabrera, of the Córdoba cathedral, sixty years old. The four were taken to Buenos Aires and had their throats cut in Santos Lugares, after the profanations I have recounted. (Author's note to the first edition.)

ported by the province, and Facundo thought himself obligated to remove him. A new expedition, a new battle, a new victory. I omit the details, because we won't find in them anything but trifles. Nonetheless, there is one illustrative fact. Lamadrid had 110 infantrymen at the Battle of Rincón; when the action ended, 60 had died on the line of battle, and except for 1, the 50 others were wounded. The following day, Lamadrid again presented himself in combat, and Quiroga sent one of his aides, naked, to tell him simply that the action would begin with the 50 prisoners he left on their knees and a company of soldiers aiming at them. With this hint, Lamadrid abandoned any effort to keep resisting.

In each of these three expeditions in which Facundo tested his strength, one still notes little flow of blood, little violation of morality. It is true that in Tucumán he seized cattle, leather, and hides, and imposed heavy taxes in metal specie; but there were not yet any citizens flogged, there were no assaults on ladies; there were the evils of conquest, but still without horror; the pastoral system did not unfold unchecked and with all the ingenuity it would show later on.

What role did the legitimate government of La Rioja have in these expeditions? Oh! The appearance of form still existed, but the spirit was all in the campaign commander. Blanco left office, fed up with humiliations, and Agüero took over the government. One day, Quiroga brought his horse up to the door of Agüero's house, and told him: "Governor, I came to advise you that I am camped with my escort two leagues from here." Agüero resigned. An attempt was made to elect a new government, and by petition of the citizens he deigned to pick Galván for them. The latter was installed, and that night was assaulted by a posse; he fled, and Quiroga had a good laugh from this adventure. The Representative Assembly was made up of men who didn't even know how to read.

Facundo needed money for his first expedition into Tucumán, and asked for eight thousand pesos from the treasurer of the mint against his own shares, for which he had never paid; in Tucumán he asked for twenty-five thousand pesos to pay his soldiers, who received nothing, and later on, he sent a bill for eighteen thousand to Dorrego, to pay the costs of an expedition he had made by order of the government of Buenos Aires. Dorrego hurried to satisfy such a just demand. This sum was divided between him and Moral, governor of La Rioja, who suggested the idea; six years later, he gave the same Moral seven hundred lashes in Mendoza, as punishment for his ingratitude.

During Blanco's government, an argument started over a card game.

Facundo took his contender by the hair, shook him, and broke his neck. The body was buried and the certificate noted: "Dead of natural causes." On leaving for Tucumán, he sent out a posse to the home of Sárate, a peaceful landowner but one known for his valor and scorn for Quiroga; the former came to his door, and pushing aside his wife and children, they shot him, leaving his widow to take care of his burial. Having returned from the expedition, he met Gutiérrez, ex-governor of Catamarca and supporter of the Congress, and urged him to come live in La Rioja, where he would be safe. The two spent a period in the greatest intimacy; but one day, after he was seen at the races surrounded by gaucho friends, they arrested him, giving him an hour to prepare to die. Shock reigned in La Rioja; Gutiérrez was a respectable man who had won the affection of all. The presbyter Dr. Colina, the priest Herrera, the provincial Father Tarrima, the guardian of San Francisco, Father Cernadas, and the priory priest of Santo Domingo, appeared to ask that Facundo at least give the prisoner time to write his will and to confess. "So, I see," he answered, "that Gutiérrez has a lot of supporters here. Orderly, come here! Take these men to jail and kill them instead of Gutiérrez." They were indeed taken away; two started sobbing and ran away; another had something worse than fainting happen to him; the rest were put on death row. Hearing the story, Facundo burst out laughing and ordered them freed. These scenes with priests were frequent ones for the "Envoy of God." In San Juan, he had a black man dressed as a cleric paraded around; in Córdoba, he would only receive Dr. Castro Barros, with whom he had an account to settle; in Mendoza, he walked beside a cleric imprisoned and sentenced to death, who was then seated on the bench to be shot; in Antiles he did the same with the priest of Alguia, and in Tucumán with the prior of a convent. It is true that none of them were shot; that was something reserved for Rosas, also a chief of the "Catholic" party; but he degraded them, humiliated them, insulted them, none of which stopped all the old people and pious women from sending their prayers to heaven that Facundo's arms be granted victory.

But Gutiérrez's story doesn't end there. Two weeks later, he received an order to go into exile with an escort. Once he reached a place to stay for the night, a fire was lit for supper, and Gutiérrez offered to blow on it. The head officer struck him with a wooden stick; others followed, and his brains splattered all over. A messenger left immediately, to advise Governor Moral that, the prisoner having attempted to flee. . . . The officer didn't know how to write, and among his provisions for the trip he had brought along the sealed letter from La Rioja!!

These were the principal events that occurred during Facundo's initial testing of union with the Republic; because this was just a test; the moment had not yet come for an alliance of all the pastoral forces, when a new organization of the Republic would emerge from the struggle. Rosas was by now big in the countryside of Buenos Aires, but as yet he had no titles or name; he worked, however, at agitating, stirring up revolt. The Constitution the Congress made was rejected by all the areas where the caudillos had influence. In Santiago del Estero the envoy appeared in a tailcoat, and Ibarra received him in shirtsleeves and a *chiripá*. Rivadavia "resigns, since the will of the people is in opposition"; "but the barbarians will devour you," he added in his farewell. He did well to resign! Rivadavia took it as his mission to present us with Benjamin Constant's constitutionalism, with all its hollow words, deceptions, and nonsense. Rivadavia didn't know that in the matter of civilization and the liberty of a people, a government has, before God and before generations to come, heavy obligations to fulfill, and there is no charity or compassion in abandoning a nation, for thirty years, to the devastations and the knives of the first one who shows up to tear it to pieces and cut its throat. Nations, in their infancy, are children who foresee nothing, who know nothing, and men of much foresight and much knowledge must serve as their fathers. The barbarians have devoured us, indeed, and it is some sad glory to foretell it in a proclamation and not make the slightest effort to stop it.

CHAPTER IX

Society at War

Il y a un quatrième élément qui arrive; ce sont les barbares, ce sont des hordes nouvelles, qui viennent se jeter dans la société antique avec une complète fraîcheur de moeurs, d'âme et d'esprit, qui n'ont rien fait, qui sont prêts à tout recevoir avec toute l'aptitude de l'ignorance la plus docile et la plus naïve.

Lerminier[1]

La Tablada

The president had fallen, amid the whistles and boos of his adversaries. Dorrego, the able leader of the opposition in Buenos Aires, was a friend of the governments of the provincial interior, which had favored and supported his triumphant parliamentary campaign. Abroad, it seemed that victory and the Republic had parted ways; and although its armies suffered no disasters in Brazil, the need for peace was felt everywhere. The interior chiefs' opposition had weakened the army by destroying, or by refusing to send, contingents that would have reinforced it. In the interior an apparent tranquillity reigned; but the ground seemed to be shifting, and strange rumors disturbed the quiet surface. The Buenos Aires press shone with a sinister gleam; there were threats behind the articles that the opposition and the government hurled at each other daily.

The Dorrego administration felt a vacuum beginning to form around it, that the party of the city that had called itself "Federalist" and had put him into power had no resources to maintain its luster after the fall of the president. The Dorrego administration hadn't resolved any of the questions that kept the Republic divided, demonstrating on the contrary all the impotence of federalism.

Dorrego was a *porteño* before all else. What did the interior provinces matter to him? Taking care of their interests would have shown him to be unitarist, that is, national. Dorrego had promised the caudillos and the towns to do all he could to consolidate the perpetuity of the former and to favor the interests of the latter. Now elevated to power in the government, "What do we care," he would say there, among his own circles, "if petty tyrants rule like despots over those people? What are four thousand pesos a year for López to us, eighteen thousand for Quiroga to us, we who have the port and the customshouse making a million and a half which that fatuous Rivadavia wanted to turn into national income?" Because let's not forget that the isolationist system translates with one very short phrase: "Every man for himself." Could Dorrego and his party have foreseen that the provinces one day would come to punish Buenos Aires for denying them its civilizing influence, and that, having scorned their backwardness and their barbarism, that backwardness and that barbarism were going to penetrate into the streets of Buenos Aires, become established, and set up camp in the Fort?[2]

But Dorrego could have seen it, if he or his men had had a sharper eye. The provinces were there at the gates of the city, waiting for the moment to penetrate. Since the days of the president, the civil authorities' decrees met an impenetrable barrier in the outlying areas of the city. Dorrego had used this outside resistance as an instrument for the opposition, and when his party triumphed, he decorated his ally from outside the city walls with the title of campaign commander in chief.[3] What ironclad logic is this, which makes elevation to campaign commander an indispensable step for a caudillo? Where this scaffolding did not exist, as was the case then in Buenos Aires, it was raised *ex profeso*, as if before letting the wolf into the fold they wanted to lift him up on their shields for everyone to see.

Dorrego later found out that the campaign commander who had made the president wobble and had contributed so powerfully to his overthrow was a lever constantly applied to the government, and that, with Rivadavia fallen and Dorrego taking his place, the lever continued its unhinging work. Dorrego and Rosas were watching each other, observing and threatening one another. Everyone from Dorrego's circle remembers his favorite phrase: "That gaucho rogue!" "Let him keep scheming," he would say, "and when he least expects it, I'll have him shot." This is what the Ocampos said too, when they felt Quiroga's robust claw on their shoulder!

Indifferent to the towns of the interior, weak among the federalist element of the city, and already in a struggle with the power of the countryside that he had called to his aid, Dorrego, who had come into the government through parliamentary opposition and polemic, tried to attract the support of the unitarists he had defeated. But political parties have neither charity nor foresight. The unitarists laughed in their sleeves; they conspired and passed the word: "He's wavering," they said, "let's let him fall." The unitarists didn't understand that along with Dorrego, those who had wanted to be intermediaries between them and the countryside were withdrawing from the city, and that the monster they were running from didn't want Dorrego, but rather the city, the civil institutions, and they themselves, who were its highest expression.

With things in this state, peace was declared with Brazil, and the first division of the army, commanded by Lavalle, disembarked. Dorrego knew the feelings of the veterans of the Wars of Independence, who saw themselves covered with wounds, hair graying beneath the weight of their helmets, and nevertheless merely colonels, majors, captains; at most two or three had tied on a general's sash, while, in the bosom of the Republic, without ever having crossed its borders, there were dozens of caudillos who in four years had been elevated from bad gauchos to commanders, from commanders to generals, from generals to conquerors of towns, and finally to absolute sovereigns of the latter. Why look for another motive for the implacable hatred that boiled beneath the veterans' armor? What was left for them, after the new order of things had prevented them, as they had intended, from waving their plumes down the streets of the capital of the Brazilian empire?

The morning of December 1, the disembarked troops formed ranks in the Plaza de la Victoria. Governor Dorrego had taken to the countryside, and the unitarists filled the streets, splitting the air with their cheers and shouts of triumph. A few days later, seven hundred armored men commanded by general officers left along the Calle del Peru for the Pampas to meet a few thousand gauchos, their Indian allies, and some regular forces led by Dorrego and Rosas. A moment later the battlefield of Navarro was full of cadavers, and the next day a dashing officer, now in the service of Chile, delivered Dorrego into headquarters as a prisoner. One hour later Dorrego's cadaver lay shot through with bullets. The chief who had ordered his execution announced it to the city in these terms of abnegation and arrogance:

I hereby inform the Deputy Governor that Colonel Don Manuel Dorrego has been shot by my order, before the regiments making up this division.

History, Mr. Minister, will judge impartially if Señor Dorrego should have died or not, and if, in sacrificing him for the calm of a people he has put into mourning, I have been possessed by any other sentiment than that of the public good.

May the people of Buenos Aires be persuaded that the death of Colonel Dorrego is the greatest sacrifice that I can offer them.

I salute you, Mr. Minister, with all due consideration.
Juan Lavalle.

Was Lavalle wrong? . . . This has been said so many times that it would be tiresome to add another "yes" in support of those who, after the consequences could be felt, have carried out the easy task of incriminating the motives that caused them. "When evil exists, it is because it is in things, and only there should one search for it; if represented by a man, when the personification disappears, it is renewed. Caesar, assassinated, was reborn more terribly in Octavius." It would be an anachronism to oppose this opinion of L. Blanc,[4] expressed earlier by Lerminier and thousands of others, taught so many times by history before 1829 to our parties, who were educated with the exaggerated ideas of Mably, Raynal, Rousseau regarding despots, tyranny, and so many other words that we still see, fifteen years later, forming the basis of what is published in the press.

Lavalle didn't know, at that time, that by killing the body one does not kill the soul and that political personages draw their character and their existence from the fund of ideas, interests, and aims of the party they represent. If Lavalle had shot Rosas instead of Dorrego, he perhaps would have saved the world a frightful scandal, humanity an opprobrium, and the Republic much blood and many tears; but, even by shooting Rosas, the countryside would not have lacked its representatives, and no more would have been done than to change one historical frame for another. But what people pretend not to know today is that, despite the purely personal responsibility for the act of which Lavalle accuses himself, Dorrego's death was a necessary consequence of the dominant ideas of the time, and that by concluding this affair the soldier, intrepid to the point of defying the judgment of history, did no more than realize the admitted and proclaimed wish of the citizens. Surely no one will accuse me of designs to excuse the dead man, at the expense of those who survive, for doing what he did, except perhaps for the way it was done—surely the least important thing in this sort of case. What else had prevented the proclamation of the 1826 Constitution but the hostility against it of Ibarra, López, Bustos, Quiroga, the Aldaos, each one dominating a province and some of them influencing the others? So then, what could have seemed more logical at that time and for those men, logical *a priori* because of their literary education, than to clear away the only obstacle that, according to them, presented itself to the much desired organization of the Republic? These political errors, which belong more to an era than to a man, are nevertheless very worthy of consideration because upon them depends the explanation for many social phenomena. Lavalle, by shooting Dorrego as he intended to shoot Bustos, López, Facundo, and the rest of the caudillos, was responding to the demands of his era and his party.

In 1834, there were still men in France who thought that by getting rid of Louis Philippe the French Republic would again rise up great and glorious, as in times past. Maybe the death of Dorrego was also one of those fatal, predestined events that form the knot of historical drama and that, when left out, leave it incomplete, cold, absurd. Civil war had been incubating for some time in the Republic: Rivadavia had seen it coming, pale, frenetic, armed with torches and daggers. Facundo, the youngest and most enterprising of the caudillos, had brought his hordes over the slopes of the Andes and had holed up, to his regret, in his lair. Rosas, in Buenos Aires, by now had his work ripe and ready for show; it was the work of ten years, accomplished around the gauchos' campfire, in the *pulpería*, with the *cantor*. Dorrego wasn't needed by anyone: not by the unitarists, who scorned him; or by the caudillos, to whom he was indifferent; or by Rosas, finally, who by now was tired of waiting, of developing in the shadow of the parties of the city, and who wanted to govern right away, unrestrained. In a word, what was fighting to emerge was the element that was not federalist in the strict sense of the word, because it couldn't be; the one that had been stirring and agitating from Artigas to Facundo, a third social element, full of vigor and strength, impatient to appear in all its nakedness, to measure itself against the cities and European civilization. If you were to take Dorrego's death out of history, would Facundo have lost the force of expansion he felt boiling over in his soul, would Rosas have interrupted the work of personifying the countryside in which he had been engaged, without rest or break, since long before its manifestation in 1820, or the whole movement initiated by Artigas and now incorporated into the bloodstream of the Republic? No! What Lavalle did was to cut with his sword the Gordian knot in which the entire Argentine society had become entangled; by bleeding it, he wanted to avoid the slow cancer of stagnation; by lighting the fuse, he made the mine, prepared long before by the hands of unitarists and federalists, explode.

From that moment, the only thing timid men could do was to cover their ears and close their eyes. The rest flew to arms everywhere, and the tumult of their horses made the Pampas tremble and the cannon show its black mouth at the cities' gates.

I must leave Buenos Aires, to return to the backdrop of the other provinces to see what was being planned there. One thing I should note in passing is that López, beaten in various encounters, solicited in vain tolerable terms for peace, and that Rosas seriously considered leaving for Brazil.* Lavalle rejected any kind of deal, and succumbed. Do you not see the absolute unitarist in this scorn toward the gaucho, in this confidence in the triumph of the city? But I've already said it: the *montonera* was always weak on the battlefield but terrible in a long campaign. If Lavalle had adopted another line of action, and maintained the port under the control of men in the city, what would have happened? . . . Would the bloody government by the Pampas have taken place?

Facundo was in his element. A campaign was about to begin; messengers were passing each other everywhere; feudal isolation was going to be turned into a wartime confederacy; everything was put under requisition for the upcoming campaign. It wasn't necessary to go all the way to the banks of the Plata to find a good battlefield; no, General Paz, with eight hundred veterans, had come to Córdoba, had beaten and destroyed Bustos and taken over the city, which was just a step away from the Llanos and which the *montoneras* from the sierras of Córdoba now harassed and besieged with their huzzahs.

Facundo speeded up his preparations; he burned to go hand to hand with a one-armed general who couldn't hold a lance, or make his saber cut circles. He had defeated Lamadrid; what could Paz do to him! From Mendoza, Don Félix Aldao was going to join him with an auxiliary regiment, disciplined and perfectly turned out in red; and even before a force of seven hundred men from San Juan joined his ranks, Facundo

*I get these facts from Don Domingo del Oro, who then was with López's side, and who served as a sponsor for Rosas, at that moment greatly weakened by López. (Author's note to the second edition.)

set out for Córdoba with four thousand men, anxious to measure their power with the armored Second Regiment and its arrogant officers.

The Battle of La Tablada is so well known that the details no longer matter. It has been brilliantly described in the *Revista de Ambos Mundos*,[5] but there is something that should be noted. Facundo attacked the city with his entire army, and during a day and night of attempted assaults, was forced back by one hundred young clerks, thirty artisan artillerymen, eighteen retired soldiers, six sick men in armor, parapeted behind hastily made trenches defended only by four pieces of artillery. Only when he announced his intention to set fire to the beautiful city could he get them to surrender its center, which was the only place not under his control. Knowing that Paz was nearing, he left behind the useless infantry and marched off to meet him with the cavalry, which nevertheless had triple the numbers of the enemy army. Then came the hard battle, then the repeated cavalry charges; but to no avail!

Those enormous masses of horsemen who were going to roll over the eight hundred veterans had to retreat every time and charge again, to again be forced back. In vain Quiroga's terrible lance made as much havoc in the rear guard of his men as the cannon and sword of Ituzaingó made in the front lines.[6] To no avail! In vain the horses whirled before the bayonets and the cannons' mouths. To no avail! They were the waves of an angry sea that crashed, in vain, against a rough, unmoving rock: sometimes it was buried in the turmoil raised in the wake of the crash, but a moment later, its black crest, unmoving, calm, reappeared, outwitting the rage of the agitated element. Out of four hundred auxiliary troops, only sixty were left; out of six hundred Colorados, not even a third survived, and the rest of the nameless corps had come apart and become an unformed, undisciplined mass, dispersed over the fields. Facundo flew to the city, and at dawn the next day was like a tiger in wait, with his cannons and infantry; however, it was all over very quickly, and fifteen hundred cadavers made patent the rage of the vanquished and the resolve of the victors.

In those bloody days, two things happened that had repercussions later on. Facundo's troops in the city killed Major Tejedor, who was carrying a flag of truce in his hand; in the battle of the second day, one of Paz's colonels shot nine imprisoned officers. We will be seeing the consequences of this.

In Córdoba's La Tablada, the forces of the countryside and those of the city took measure of one another under their highest inspirations, Facundo and Paz, worthy personifications of the two tendencies that

were going to fight for dominance over the Republic. Facundo, ignorant, barbarous, who for long years had led a wandering life only illumi-
nated, now and then, by the sinister reflections of the dagger spinning
about him; brave to the point of rashness, endowed with Herculean
strength, a gaucho on horseback before all else, dominating everything
through violence and terror, he knew only the power of brute force, he
only had faith in his horse; he expected everything to come from valor,
from his lance, from the terrible push of his cavalry charges. Where in
the Argentine Republic could you find a more complete version of the
perfect bad gaucho? Do you think it was stupid to leave his infantry and
artillery in the city? No, it was instinct, it was gaucho pride. The infantry would dishonor the triumph, whose laurels should be gained on
horseback.

Paz, on the contrary, was the legitimate son of the city, the most total representative of the power of civilized peoples. Lavalle, Lamadrid,
and so many others were always Argentines, cavalry soldiers, as brilliant
as Murat, if you wish; but their gaucho instinct made its way through
the armor and the epaulets. Paz was a European-style military officer.
He didn't believe in valor alone, if it wasn't subordinate to tactics, to
strategy, and to discipline; he barely knew how to ride a horse; he was,
moreover, one-armed, and couldn't handle a lance. The ostentation of
large forces made him uncomfortable. Fewer soldiers, but well-trained
ones. Let him form an army, wait for him to tell you, "It is in ready
condition," and allow him to pick the terrain where the battle will be
fought, and then you could trust him with the future of the Republic.
He was the spirit of a European warrior, even down to the branch in
which he served: he was an artillery officer, and therefore a mathematician, a scientist, a calculator. A battle was a problem he would resolve
with equations, until he would give you the unknown factor, which was
victory. General Paz was not a genius, like the artillery officer of Tou-
lon, and I am glad he wasn't; liberty doesn't often have much to thank
geniuses for. He was an able officer and an honest administrator, who
had known how to preserve civil, European traditions, and who looked
to science for that which others expected from brute force; he was, in
a word, the legitimate representative of the cities, of European civilization, which we are threatened with losing in our homeland. Poor
General Paz! Take glory in your repeated setbacks! The Penates of the
Argentine Republic go with you! Destiny has not yet decided between
you and Rosas, between the city and the Pampas, between the sky-blue
stripe and the red ribbon. You have the only quality of spirit that, in the

end, vanquishes the resistance of brute matter, the one that made up the power of martyrs! You have faith. You have never doubted! Faith will be your salvation and civilization depends on you!

There must have been something of predestination in this man. Emerging from the middle of such an ill-advised revolution as that of December 1, he was the only one who was able to justify it with victory; snatched from the head of his army by the gaucho's eminent power, he went from prison to prison for ten years, and Rosas himself didn't dare kill him, as if a guardian angel were looking over the rest of his days. Escaping as if by miracle in the middle of a stormy night, the agitated waves of the Plata allowed him, at last, to touch the eastern shore; rejected here, disappointed there, the exhausted forces of a province that had already seen two armies succumb were finally delivered to him. From these crumbs, which Paz gathered with patience and care, he formed his means of resistance, and when Rosas's armies had triumphed everywhere and brought terror and slaughter to every end of the Republic, the one-armed general, the general caught by bolas, shouted from the marshes of Caaguazú: "The Republic still lives!"[7] Despoiled of his laurels by the hands of those he had saved, and yanked without dignity from the head of his army, he found safety among his enemies in Entre Ríos, because heaven unloosed its elements to protect him, and because the gaucho of the Montiel forest didn't dare kill the good one-armed man who killed no one. Arriving in Montevideo, Paz learned that Ribera had been overthrown, perhaps because he wasn't there to ensnare the enemy with his own maneuvers. The whole city, filled with dismay, crowded the humble dwelling of the fugitive to ask from him a word of consolation, a vision of hope. "If you give me twenty days, they will not take the town," was the only answer he gave, without enthusiasm but with a mathematician's assurance. Oribe gave Paz what he asked for, and three years now have gone by since that dismal day in Montevideo.

When he had the town well secured and had gotten the improvised garrison accustomed to daily fighting, as if this were an occupation just like any other in life, he left for Brazil, staying at court there longer than his allies would have liked. Rosas, expecting him to be under surveillance by the imperial police, then learned he was in Corrientes training six thousand men, that he had made an alliance with Paraguay; and later on, he heard that Brazil had invited France and England to take part in the struggle. So the issue between the pastoral countryside and the cities had become, in the end, an issue between the one-armed mathematician, the scientist Paz, and the barbarous gaucho Rosas; between the Pampas on one side, and Corrientes, Paraguay, Uruguay, Brazil, England, and France on the other.

What honors this general most is that the enemies whom he had fought neither feared nor hated him. Rosas's *Gaceta,* so prodigal with calumny and defamations, was unable to damage him successfully, discovering each time the respect he inspired in his detractors; it called him one-armed, castrated, caught by bolas, because there always must be brutality and stupidity mixed with the bloody cries of the Carib.[8] If one were to penetrate deep into the hearts of those who serve Rosas, one would discover the affection they all had for General Paz, and the old federalists hadn't forgotten that it was he who always protected them from the wrath of the old unitarists. Who knows if Providence, which holds the fate of states in its hands, had decided to watch over this man who so many times had escaped destruction, so as to rebuild the Republic under the rule of law that permits liberty without license and that makes futile the terror and violence stupid men need in order to govern! Paz was from the provinces, and thus was guaranteed not to sacrifice the provinces to Buenos Aires and to the port, as Rosas does today to have millions with which to impoverish and barbarize the people of the interior, and as the federalists of the cities accused the 1826 Congress of doing.

The triumph at La Tablada opened a new era for the city of Córdoba, which until then, according to the message sent to the provincial representatives by General Paz, "had held last place among Argentine towns." "Remember that it is here," the message continued, "where measures have been canceled and obstacles placed against everything tending toward constituting the nation and this very province, whether under the federalist system or the unitarist."

Córdoba, like all Argentine cities, had its liberal element, up until then strangled by the absolute, quietist government of Bustos. Upon Paz's entry, this oppressed element emerged, demonstrating how much more robust it had become during the nine years of that Spanish government.

Earlier, I depicted Córdoba as the antagonist of Buenos Aires in its ideas, but there is a circumstance that powerfully recommends it for the future. Knowledge is the greatest degree for a Cordoban: a university two centuries old has left a consciousness of this civilizing activity that is not as deeply rooted in other interior provinces. Thus, not long after revising the subjects and direction of university study, Córdoba could already count on a great number of supporters of civilization, whose cause and effect are the dominance and cultivation of intelligence.

This respect for learning, this traditional value conceded to university degrees, in Córdoba reaches down even to the lower classes of society. There is no other way to explain why the civic masses in Córdoba embraced the civil revolution brought in by Paz with an ardor that the past ten years have not belied, and that has readied thousands of victims from the artisan and proletarian classes of the city for the ordered, cold fury of the *mazorqueros*. Paz brought an interpreter along with him in order to be understood by the Cordoban masses: Barcala, the black colonel who had so gloriously distinguished himself in Brazil, and who walked arm in arm with the chief army officers. Barcala, the freed slave who devoted so many years to showing artisans the right road, and to making them love a revolution that considered neither color nor class when recognizing merit; Barcala was the one entrusted with popularizing the change in ideas and aims at work in the city, and he accomplished this beyond what anyone hoped. The citizens of Córdoba, since then, belong to the city, to civil order, to civilization.

Cordoban youth has distinguished itself in the present war by the abnegation and loyalty it has displayed, the number of youths who have succumbed on the battlefields and in the slaughters of the Mazorca being infinite, and greater still, the number suffering the woes of exile. In the St. John's Day battles,[9] the streets were left sown with those Cordoban scholars, who were swept aside by the cannons they were trying to snatch away from the enemy.

Moreover, the clergy, who had fomented such opposition to the Congress and the Constitution, had had more than enough time to measure the abyss toward which civilization was being led by defenders of the true faith of the likes of Facundo, López, and the rest, and they didn't hesitate to give wholehearted support to General Paz.

And so, scholars as well as youth, clergy as well as the masses, seemed united in one sole opinion, willing to uphold the principles proclaimed by the new order of things. Paz could now commit himself to reorganizing the province and to securing friendly relations with the others. A treaty was declared with López in Santa Fe, who was convinced by Don Domingo del Oro to ally himself with General Paz; Salta and Tucumán already were allies even before La Tablada, with only the western provinces remaining hostile.

CHAPTER X

Society at War

_____

Que cherchez-vous? Si vous êtes jaloux de voir un assemblage
effrayant de maux et d'horreurs vous l'avez trouvé.
                                                    Shakespeare[1]

Oncativo

In the meantime, what had become of Facundo? He had left everything
behind in La Tablada: weapons, officers, soldiers, reputation, everything,
except his rage and valor. Governor Moral of La Rioja, surprised by the
news of such a huge defeat, used a flimsy excuse to leave the city, heading for Los Pueblos, and from Sañogasta he sent an official letter to
Quiroga upon his arrival, offering him the province's resources. Before
the expedition to Córdoba, relations between the two provincial leaders, the nominal governor and the caudillo, the caretaker and the lord
of the manor, had seemed to cool. Facundo hadn't found as many weapons as calculations would have indicated, adding up what existed in the
province at that time with what had come from Tucumán, San Juan,
Catamarca, etc. Another singular circumstance aggravated the suspicions
weighing against the governor in Quiroga's mind. Sañagosta was the
manorial home of the Doria-Dávilas, Facundo's enemies, and the governor, foreseeing the conclusions that Facundo's suspicious nature would
draw from the date and place of the letter, dated it from Uanchín, a
place four leagues distant. Quiroga knew, however, that it was from
Sañagosta that Moral had written him, and all his doubts were confirmed. Bárcena, a hateful instrument of slaughter that he had acquired

in Córdoba, and Fontanel went out with posses to cover Los Pueblos and arrest all the wealthy men they found. The search, however, did not end happily: the quarry smelled the hounds and fled terrified in all directions. The posses returned with only eleven men, who were shot at once. Don Inocencio Moral, uncle of the governor, with his two sons, one fourteen and the other twenty; Ascueta, Gordillo, Cantos (a Chilean), Sotomayor, Barrios, another Gordillo, Corro, a nonresident from San Juan, and Pasos were the victims of that day's work. This last one, Don Mariano Pasos, on another occasion had already experienced Quiroga's resentment. As he was leaving on one of his first excursions, upon seeing the slovenliness and disorder of the troops, Pasos had said to a certain Rincón, a merchant like him: "Some group of fighters!" Quiroga, learning of this, had these two demanding critics brought in, tied one of them to a pillar of the town hall, and had him given two hundred lashes, while the other one stood there with his pants down waiting for his turn, from which he was pardoned by Quiroga. Later on, this lucky man was governor of La Rioja and a great follower of the general.

Governor Moral, then, knowing what awaited him, fled the province, although later on he got seven hundred lashes for his ingratitude; for this was the same Moral who shared the eighteen thousand pesos taken away from Dorrego.

That Bárcena whom I mentioned before was the one ordered to assassinate the commissioner of the British mine company. I have heard from him myself the horrible details of this murder, committed in the man's own home, pushing aside his wife and children to make way for the bullets and sabers. This same Bárcena was the leader of the Mazorca that accompanied Oribe to Córdoba, which, at a dance held to celebrate the triumph over Lavalle, made the bloodied heads of three young men whose families were present roll through the ballroom. Because it must be kept in mind that the army that went to Córdoba in pursuit of Lavalle had a company of *mazorqueros* who carried at their left sides the convex knife, like a small scimitar, that Rosas ordered made *ex profeso* by the cutlers of Buenos Aires for cutting men's throats.

What was Quiroga's motive for these atrocious executions? It is said that in Mendoza, he told Oro that his only objective was to terrorize. The story is told that as the slaughter of unlucky peasants—of whoever happened to pass through Atiles, his general headquarters—went on in the countryside, one of the Villafañes asked him, with a tone of compassion, fear, and pleading: "How much longer, general?" "Don't be an idiot," Quiroga answered, "how else can I rebuild everything?" Here we have his complete system: terror over the citizen, so that he will give up his fortune; terror over the gaucho, so that he will fight to support a cause no longer his; terror supplants a lack of activity and administrative work, supplants enthusiasm, supplants strategy, supplants everything. And one should not be deluded: terror is a means of governing that produces greater results than patriotism and spontaneity. Russia has exercised it since the time of Ivan and has conquered all the barbarian peoples; the bandits in the forest obey the leader who has in his hand this rope that yokes the most arrogant of necks. It is true that it degrades men, impoverishes them, takes away all the elasticity of their minds; that in one day, indeed, it wrenches from states what they would have given in ten years; but what does all this matter to the czar of Russia, to the bandit chief, or to the Argentine caudillo?

One of Facundo's edicts ordered all the inhabitants of the city of La Rioja to immigrate to the Llanos, under pain of death, and this order was carried out to the letter. The implacable enemy of the city was afraid he wouldn't have sufficient time to kill it bit by bit, and he gave it the coup de grâce. What was the motive behind this useless immigration? Was Quiroga afraid? Yes indeed, at that moment he was afraid! In Mendoza, an army was being raised by the unitarists, who had taken over the government; Tucumán and Salta were to the north, and to the east, Córdoba, La Tablada, and Paz; he was, therefore, surrounded, and a general hunt could finally bring the Tiger of the Llanos to bay.

Facundo had had the cattle taken away toward the mountains, while Villafañe went to Mendoza with troops to aid the Aldaos, and he amassed his new recruits in Atiles. Terrorists too have their moments of terror; Rosas too cried like a little child and pounded the walls when he learned of the rebellion in Chascomús, and eleven enormous trunks were brought into his house to pack his effects and embark, an hour before the news of Alvarez's triumph reached him. But, for God's sake! Never scare terrorists! Woe to the people once the conflict is over! Then come the September slaughters and a display of pyramids of human heads in the marketplace!

Despite Facundo's order, a girl and a priest, Severa and Father Colina, stayed on in La Rioja. The story of Severa Villafañe is a pitiful romance, a fairy tale in which the most beautiful princess of her time wanders as a fugitive, sometimes disguised as a shepherdess, at others begging for shelter and a piece of bread, to escape the pursuit of some frightful giant, some bloody Bluebeard. Severa had the misfortune to excite the concupiscence of the tyrant, and no one could help her get away from his ferocious attention. It was not only virtue that made her resist his seduction: it was an invincible repugnance, the fine instincts of a delicate woman who detested men of brute force because she feared they would wilt her beauty. A beautiful woman will often trade a bit of her own dishonor for a bit of the glory surrounding a celebrated man; but only for that kind of noble, high glory that need not debase or stoop a man to make him stand out, so that a spiny, faded bush can be seen in the midst of so much creeping scrubland. This was the only cause of the pious Madame de Maintenon's frailty, and that attributed to Madame Roland and to so many others who sacrificed their reputations to be associated with illustrious men. Severa resisted for long years. One time she escaped being poisoned with a fig by her Tiger; another, Quiroga himself, forlorn, took opium to end his life. One day she slipped from the hands of the general's aides, who were going to stretch her out spread-eagled against a wall to affront her modesty; on another, Quiroga surprised her in the patio of her house, grabbed her by the arm, bathed her in blood with his blows, threw her on the ground, and split her head with his boot heel. My God! Was there no one to help this poor girl? Didn't she have family? Didn't she have friends? Yes, she did! She belonged to one of the first families of La Rioja. General Villafañe was her uncle; she had brothers who witnessed these insults; there was a priest who closed the door to her when she sought to hide her virtue in the sanctuary. Severa finally fled to Catamarca and shut herself up in a house for pious women. Two years later, Facundo passed through there and ordered that the shelter be opened and that the mother superior bring the inmates before him. One cried out upon seeing him and fell lifeless to the floor. Wasn't this a fine romance? It was Severa!

But let us return to Atiles, where an army was being readied to recover the reputation lost at La Tablada; because what this was all about was the reputation of the gaucho leading the charge. Two unitarists from San Juan fell into his hands: the young Castro y Calvo, a Chilean, and one Alejandro Carril. Quiroga asked the first: "How much will you give for your life?" "Twenty-five thousand pesos," he answered trembling. "And you, how much will you give?" he said to the second. "I can only give four thousand; I am a merchant and have no more." They ordered the money brought from San Juan, and now there were thirty thousand pesos for the war, raised at such little cost. While waiting for the money to arrive, Facundo lodged them beneath a carob tree, busying them with making cartridges, paying them two reales a day for their work.

The San Juan government was aware of the efforts that Carril's family was making to send the ransom, and took advantage of this knowledge. A government of citizens, although federalist, it didn't dare shoot citizens and felt powerless to extort money from the unitarists. The government hinted at an order to send the prisoners held in the jail to Atiles; the mothers and wives knew what Atiles meant, and first some, then others, managed to get together the amounts requested, to have their relatives returned from the road leading to the Tiger's lair. In this way, Quiroga governed San Juan solely with his terrifying name.

When the Aldaos had taken power in Mendoza, and he hadn't left behind a single man, young or old, married or single, able to bear arms in La Rioja, Facundo moved to San Juan to establish his general headquarters in that town, rich at the time in wealthy unitarists. He came in and had a citizen notable for his influence, talent, and fortune given six hundred lashes. Facundo himself walked beside the cannon carrying the moribund victim all around the plaza, because Facundo was very attentive to this aspect of administration. He was not like Rosas, who, from deep within his office where he drinks his *mate,* sends the Mazorca the orders they must carry out, afterward blaming the federalist enthusiasm of the poor people for the atrocities with which he has made humanity shudder. Not thinking even this preliminary step to be enough, Facundo had a little old lame man brought in, accused, or not accused, of having served as *baqueano* for some fugitives, and had him shot immediately, without confession, without allowing him even a word, because the "Envoy of God" didn't always take care that his victims confessed.

With public opinion thus prepared, there was no sacrifice that the city of San Juan wasn't ready to make in defense of the federation; taxes were imposed without complaint; weapons were dug up from underground; Facundo bought rifles, sabers from anyone who offered them to him. The Aldaos triumphed over the incompetence of the unitarists by violating the treaties of Pilar, and then Quiroga went on to Mendoza. There, terror was useless: the daily slaughters ordered by the Friar, which I detailed in his biography, had the city as cold as a corpse, but Facundo needed to confirm the fear that his name instilled everywhere.[2] Some young men from San Juan had fallen prisoner; these, at least, belonged to him. He ordered that one of them be asked this question: "How many rifles can you bring in within four days?" The young man answered that if he were given time to send to Chile to procure them, and to his home to raise the money, he would see what he could do. Quiroga repeated the question, asking him to answer categorically.

"None!" A minute later they took the body away to be buried, and six more San Juan natives followed at short intervals. The question was put to the prisoners from Mendoza, orally or in writing, and the answers were more or less satisfactory. A higher-category prisoner showed up: General Alvarado had been apprehended. Facundo had him brought before him. "Sit down, General," he told him. "How many days will it take for you to deliver six thousand pesos to me for your life?" "None, sir; I have no money." "What! but you have friends, they won't let you be shot." "I have none, sir; I was just passing through this province, when, by public demand, I took over the government." "Where do you want to retreat now?" Facundo continued, after a moment of silence. "To wherever Your Excellency orders me." "Tell me, where do you want to go?" "I repeat, wherever you order me." "How about San Juan?" "Fine, sir." "How much money do you need?" "None, sir, thank you." Facundo went over to a desk, opened two drawers stuffed with gold, and stepping back, said: "General, take what you need." "Thank you, sir, nothing." An hour later, General Alvarado's carriage was at the door of his house with his luggage and with General Villafañe, who accompanied him to San Juan, and who upon arrival gave him one hundred ounces of gold from General Quiroga, pleading with him not to refuse it.

As one can see, Facundo's soul wasn't completely closed to noble inspiration. Alvarado was an old soldier, a grave, circumspect general, and had caused him little harm. Later on he would say of him: "That General Alvarado's a good officer, but he doesn't understand anything about this war of ours."

In San Juan, they brought him a Frenchman, Barreau, who had written things about him that the French were able to write. Facundo asked him if he was the author of the articles that had done so much harm, and receiving an affirmative answer, "What do you expect now?" responded Quiroga. "Death, sir." "Take this gold and get out of here."

In Tucumán, Quiroga was leaning over a bar. "Where's the general?" he was asked by an Andalusian who had gotten a little tipsy to get through a bad spot with his pride intact. "Inside; what do you want with him?" "I came to pay the four hundred pesos he's hit me with for a tax . . . that animal gets everything for free!" "Mister, do you know the general?" "I don't want to know him, that outlaw!" "Come on, let's have a drink." This unique dialogue had gone even further, when an aide appeared and directing himself to one of the interlocutors, said, "General . . . " "General!" repeated the Andalusian, his mouth dropping wide open. "But . . . you're the general? Damn! General," he continued, getting down on his knees, "I'm just a poor devil, a shopkeeper . . . what can I tell you! . . . it's going to ruin me, but the money is ready . . . come on . . . don't get mad!" Facundo burst out laughing, picked him up, calmed him down, and gave him back his money, taking just two hundred pesos as a loan, which he repaid religiously later on. Two years later, a paralyzed beggar shouted to him in Buenos Aires: "Hello, General; I'm the Andalusian from Tucumán; I'm crippled now." Facundo gave him six ounces of gold.

These gestures prove the theory that modern drama has exploited with such brilliance, namely, that even in the blackest historical characters there is always a spark of virtue that lights up for a moment, then is hidden. On the other hand, why shouldn't a man without brakes to control his passions do good? This is a prerogative of power, like any other.

But let's return to the thread of public events. After terror was begun so solemnly in Mendoza, Facundo retired to Retamo, where the Aldaos took the 100,000 pesos in taxes they had snatched from the terrified unitarists. There was the card table that always accompanied Quiroga; there the enthusiasts of the game arrived; there, finally, was where they stayed up all night by the opaque light of the torches. In the midst of so many horrors and so many disasters, gold circulated there in torrents, and Facundo won, after two weeks, the 100,000 pesos of the taxes, the many thousands that his federalist friends had, and as much as can be bet on a card. War, however, needs outlays, and the shorn sheep return to be shorn again. This story of the famous dirty tricks of Retamo, where there was a night when 130,000 pesos were on the table, is the story of Quiroga's whole life. "The stakes are so high, General," said someone to him during his last expedition to Tucumán. "Bah! this is nothing! In Mendoza and San Juan you could enjoy yourself! There the money flowed, all right! One night I won fifty thousand pesos from the Friar, another night twenty-five thousand from the priest Lima; but this? This is small change!"

A year was spent in these preparations for war, and finally, in 1830, a new and formidable army, composed of divisions recruited in La Rioja, San Juan, Mendoza, and San Luis, headed for Córdoba. General Paz, wanting to avoid bloodshed, although he was certain he would add another laurel to those that already wreathed his temples, sent Major Paunero, an officer full of prudence, energy, and wisdom, to meet Quiroga, proposing not only peace but an alliance. It is thought that Quiroga was disposed to embrace any possibilities for a deal; but the advice of the mediating commission from Buenos Aires, whose only object was to avoid any deals, and the pride and presumption of Quiroga, who saw himself leading a new army, more powerful and better disciplined than the first one, made him reject the peaceful proposals of the modest General Paz.

This time, Facundo had put together something resembling a planned campaign. Communications established in the sierras of Córdoba had stirred up the pastoral populace; General Villafañe was approaching from the north, with a division from Catamarca, while Facundo fell in from the south. It took little penetrating insight for General Paz to penetrate Quiroga's designs, and to frustrate them. One night the army disappeared from the area around Córdoba. No one could discover its whereabouts; everyone had found it, but in different places, at the same time. If anything like the complicated strategic moves of Bonaparte's campaigns in Italy has ever been carried out in America, it was then, when Paz had forty divisions cross the sierras of Córdoba in such a way that the fugitives from one battle would fall into the hands of another corps, stationed for that reason in a precise and inevitable place. The *montonera,* stupefied, surrounded everywhere, with the army at its front, its flanks, its rear guard, had to let itself be caught in the net laid out for it, whose strings were being moved like clockwork from the general's tent.

On the eve of the Battle of Oncativo, all the divisions hadn't yet formed from this marvelous two-week campaign in which they had acted in combination along a hundred-league front. I will omit the details of that memorable battle, in which General Paz, to add valor to his triumph, published in the *Bulletin* news of the death of seventy from his side, despite having only lost twelve men, in a battle where eight thousand soldiers and twenty pieces of artillery were engaged. A simple maneuver had defeated the valiant Quiroga, and all the horrors, all the tears spilled to form his army, had ended up giving Quiroga a season of dirty card tricks and Paz several thousand useless prisoners.

CHAPTER XI

Society at War

Un cheval! Vite un cheval! . . . Mon royaume pour un cheval!
Shakespeare[1]

Chacón

Facundo, the bad gaucho of the Llanos, didn't return to his home territory this time but headed toward Buenos Aires, and because of this unforeseen direction in his flight was saved from falling into the hands of his pursuers. Facundo understood that there was nothing left for him to do in the interior provinces; this time, there was no chance to torment and wring the towns of their resources without the victors coming to their aid from everywhere.

This battle at Oncativo, or Laguna Larga, had a very fruitful outcome; because of it, Córdoba, Mendoza, San Juan, San Luis, La Rioja, Catamarca, Tucumán, Salta, and Jujuy were freed from the rule of the caudillos. The unity of the Republic, proposed by Rivadavia through parliamentary channels, was put into effect from Córdoba by means of arms. General Paz, to this end, convened a congress of deputies of those provinces, so that they might agree on the best way to organize their institutions. Lavalle had been less fortunate in Buenos Aires, and Rosas, who was destined to play such a frightful, somber role in Argentine history, was by now beginning to influence public affairs and was governing the city. The Republic, then, was left divided into two factions: one in the interior, which wanted to make Buenos Aires the capital of the

Union; the other in Buenos Aires, which pretended it didn't want to be capital of the Republic, unless the latter abjured European civilization and civil order.

That battle had revealed another great fact, namely, that the *montonera* had lost its original strength and the armies of the cities could stand up to it and destroy it. This event was fruitful for Argentine history. As time passed, the pastoral bands lost their original spontaneity. Facundo now needed terror to move them, and on the battlefield they appeared dazed in the presence of troops disciplined and directed by the strategic maxims that European art had taught the officers of the cities. In Buenos Aires, however, the outcome was different. Lavalle, despite his valor, which he displayed at Puente de Márquez and everywhere else, and despite his numerous trained troops, succumbed at the end of the campaign, trapped inside the city limits by the thousands of gauchos that Rosas and López had amassed; and by a treaty that, in the end, was in effect a capitulation, he stripped himself of authority, and Rosas penetrated Buenos Aires. Why was Lavalle vanquished? For no other reason, in my opinion, than that he was the most valiant cavalry officer the Argentine Republic had. He was an Argentine general, and not a European general; his cavalry charges had given him a novelistic fame.

At the defeat of Torata—or Moquegá, I don't recall which—Lavalle, covering his army's retreat, gave forty charges in a day and a half, until he didn't have even twenty soldiers left for another. I don't recall if Murat's cavalry ever performed an equal feat. But look at the dire consequences that these deeds brought to the Republic. Lavalle, recalling in 1839 that the *montonera* had vanquished him in 1830, renounced his entire European-style military education and adopted the system of the *montonera*. He outfitted four thousand horses and arrived at the outskirts of Buenos Aires with his brilliant bands, at the same time that Rosas, the gaucho of the Pampas who had vanquished him in 1830, for his part renounced his own *montonera* instincts, dismissed the cavalry in his armies, and entrusted the success of his campaign solely to a regimented infantry and to the cannons.

The roles had switched: the gaucho put on a uniform, the officer of the Wars of Independence, a poncho; the first triumphed, the second would die pierced by a bullet fired at him in passing by the *montonera*. Harsh lessons, indeed! If Lavalle had made the 1840 campaign on an English saddle, wearing a French jacket, today we would be on the banks of the Río de la Plata, planning steam navigation for the rivers and distributing land to European immigrants. Paz was the first general of the city to triumph over the pastoral element, because he put all the resources of European military art into play against it, directed by a mathematical mind. Intelligence vanquishes matter; art, numbers.

So fruitful in results was the work of Paz in Córdoba, and so high did it raise the influence of the cities in two years, that Facundo felt it impossible to regain his power as a caudillo, despite having extended it over all the Andean borderlands, and only cultured, European Buenos Aires could offer a haven for his barbarism.

Córdoba's newspapers of that era transcribed European news items, the sessions of the French Assembly; portraits of Casimir Périer, Lamartine, and Chateaubriand were used as models in drawing classes; such was the interest that Córdoba showed for European movements. Read the *Gaceta Mercantil,* and you may judge the semibarbarous route the Buenos Aires press took from that time on.

Facundo fled to Buenos Aires, not without first shooting two of his officers to maintain order among those who accompanied him. His theory of terror was never refuted: it was his talisman, his palladium, his Penates. He would give up everything except this favorite weapon.

He arrived in Buenos Aires and presented himself to Rosas's government, in the reception rooms coming by chance upon General Guido, the most courteous and ceremonious of the generals who had made their careers by paying compliments in palace antechambers. He directed a most sincere one to Quiroga. "Why are you laughing in my face," says the latter, "as if I were a dog? You people sent me a committee of doctors to tangle me up with General Paz (Cavia and Cernadas). Paz beat me by the rules." Quiroga regretted many times afterward not having listened to Major Paunero's propositions.

Facundo disappeared in the whirlwind of the big city; one heard no more than talk about some gambling incidents. General Mansilla threatened to hit him with a candlestick at one point, saying, "Where do you think you are, in the provinces?" His provincial gaucho dress got attention; the wrap of his poncho, his full beard, which he had vowed to wear until he washed off the stain of La Tablada, drew for a moment the attention of the elegant and European city; but after that, no one cared about him.

At that time, a great expedition against Córdoba was being planned. Six thousand men from Buenos Aires and Santa Fe were enlisting for the enterprise; López was the chief general; Balcarce, Enrique Martínez, and other officers would go under his orders. By now the pastoral element dominated, but in alliance with the Federalist party of the city: there were still generals. Facundo took charge of a desperate attempt against La Rioja or Mendoza; for this, he received two hundred convicts pulled from all the jails, hitched up sixty more men from the Retiro barracks, gathered some of his officers, and readied his march.

In Pavón, Rosas was gathering his red cavalry; López, from Santa Fe, was there too. Facundo stopped in Pavón to come to an agreement with the other leaders. The three most famous caudillos were gathered in the Pampas: López, the disciple and immediate successor of Artigas; Facundo, the barbarian of the interior; and Rosas, the wolf cub still in training, who now was on the verge of starting to hunt on his own. The classics would have compared them to the triumvirate of Lepidus, Marc Antony, and Octavius, who divided the empire between them; and the comparison would be exact, down to the vileness and cruelty of the Argentine Octavius.

The three caudillos tested and displayed their personal importance. Can you guess how? All three got on their horses and went out every morning to be gauchos on the Pampas. Throwing the bolas at their horses, heading them into animal holes, they rolled on the ground, collided, ran races. Who was the biggest man? The best horseman, Rosas, the one who triumphed in the end. One morning he went to invite López to race: "No, *compañero*," the latter answered, "you're just too rough." Rosas, in fact, punished them every day, left them full of bruises and welts. These jousts in Arroyo de Pavón have had fabulous fame throughout the Republic, which has helped clear the way to power for the champion of the games, the empire for the "best on a horse."

With three hundred followers, most of them yanked from the arms of justice, Quiroga crossed the Pampas on the same road by which, twenty years before when he was just a bad gaucho, he had fled Buenos Aires, deserting the ranks of the Arribeños brigade.

At Villa del Río Cuarto, Facundo met with tenacious resistance, and was held back for three days by some ditches that acted as barricades for the garrison. He was ready to leave, when a rube appeared and told him that the men under siege didn't have a single cartridge left. Who was this traitor? In 1818, on the afternoon of March 18, Colonel Zapiola, leader of the cavalry of the Chilean-Argentine army, attempted to make a show of power of the patriots' cavalry against the Spanish, on a beautiful plain this side of Talca.[2] Six thousand men made up that brilliant parade. They charged, and since the enemy forces were much fewer, the line became concentrated, pressed together, became obstructed, and finally broke. At that moment the Spanish moved in, and the defeat was even more pronounced in that enormous mass of cavalry. Zapiola was the last one to turn back his horse, which got hit by a bullet at close range; and he would have fallen into enemy hands had not a soldier from the Granaderos cavalry dismounted and put him, like a feather, onto his own horse, slapping it with his sword to make it take off faster. A straggler then passed by, and the dismounted Granadero grabbed onto the horse's tail, stopped it in mid-race, jumped onto its rump, and both colonel and soldier were saved.

They called him Boyero, or Oxcart Boy, and this deed began the rise of his career. In 1820, they pulled a man skewered through both arms off the blade of his sword, and out of so many brave and illustrious men, Lavalle put him by his side. He served with Facundo a long time, immigrated to Chile in search of warrior adventures, and from there to Montevideo, where he died gloriously fighting to defend the city, cleansing himself of the mistake of Río Cuarto. If the reader recalls what I have said about the wagon-train foreman, he will guess the character, valor, and strength of Boyero; resentment toward his leaders and personal vengeance pushed him to take that ugly step, and Facundo took Villa del Río Cuarto thanks to his opportune disclosure.

In Villa del Río Quinto he met the valiant Pringles, that soldier of the Wars of Independence who, surrounded by the Spanish on a narrow pass, threw himself into the sea on his horse, and, amid the noise of the waves crashing against the shore, made resound his formidable cry of "Long live the homeland!"

The immortal Pringles—to whom Viceroy Pezuela, showering him with gifts, turned over his army, and for whom San Martín, as a prize for so much heroism, had a unique medal cast, which read "Honor and glory to the vanquished of Chancay!"—died in the hands of Facundo's convicts, and Facundo had the body wrapped up in his own blanket.

Heartened by this unexpected triumph, he advanced to San Luis, which barely offered him resistance. Past the *travesía,* the road divided into three. Which one would Quiroga take? The one on the right led to the Llanos, his own territory, the theater of his action, the cradle of his power, where there were no forces superior to his own, but neither were there resources. The one in the middle went to San Juan, where there were a thousand men-at-arms nevertheless incapable of withstanding a cavalry charge headed by Quiroga, shaking his terrible lance. The one on the left, lastly, led to Mendoza, where the real forces of the Cuyo region were, under the orders of General Videla Castillo. A battalion of eight hundred men was there, determined, disciplined, commanded by Colonel Barcala; a squadron of disciplined armored soldiers, commanded by Lieutenant Colonel Chenaut; lastly, the militia, and some detachments from the Second Light Brigade and the Armored Soldiers of the Guard. Which of these three roads would Quiroga take? He had at his command only three hundred undisciplined men, and besides that, he himself was sick and weakened. . . . Facundo took the road to Mendoza; he came, he saw, he conquered, because that was the swiftness with which events occurred. What happened? Treachery, cowardice? Nothing like that. An impertinent plagiarism of European strategy, a classic error on the one hand, and an Argentine prejudice, a romantic error on the other, caused the battle to be lost in the most shameful way. Let us see how.

Videla Castillo opportunely learned that Quiroga was approaching, and not believing, as no general would have believed, that he would invade Mendoza, he detailed to Las Lagunas his detachments of veteran troops, which, along with other details from San Juan under the command of Major Castro, formed a good observational force, able to resist an attack and to force Quiroga to take the road to the Llanos. Up to this point there was no error. But Facundo headed for Mendoza, and the entire army went out to meet him.

In the place called Chacón there was an open field that the advancing army left to its rear guard; but at a short distance, hearing the firing of troops in retreat, General Castillo ordered a rapid countermarch, in order to occupy the open field of Chacón. A double error: first, because a retreat in proximity to a terrible enemy makes a raw recruit go cold, since he doesn't understand the reason for the movement; second, and still more important, because the more broken, more impracticable field was better for beating Quiroga, who only had a detachment of infantry.

Can you imagine what Facundo would have done in an impassable terrain, against six hundred infantrymen, a formidable battery of artillery, and a thousand horses in the lead? Is this not the fox inviting the hen to dinner? Well, all the officers were Argentines, men on horseback. There was no true glory if they didn't conquer with their sabers; above all, an open field was needed for the cavalry charges. This was the error of Argentine strategy.

The line formed in a suitable place. Facundo came into view on a white horse; Boyero made known his presence, threatening his old comrades-at-arms from afar.

The combat began, and some militia squadrons were ordered to charge. An Argentine error, to begin the battle with a cavalry charge; an error that has caused the Republic to lose a hundred battles, because the spirit of the Pampas is there in every heart, since if you lift up a bit the lapels of the tailcoat in which the Argentine disguises himself, you will always find a gaucho, more or less civilized, but always a gaucho. On top of this national error came the European plagiarism. In Europe, where the great masses of troops are in columns and the field of battle surrounds various hamlets and towns, the elite troops remain in reserve, to go wherever they are needed. In America, the battle usually takes place on a bare field, the troops are few, the hard combat is of short duration; therefore it is always good to begin with the advantage. In the present case, the least suitable thing was to give a cavalry charge, and if it were to be given, the best troops should have been used, in order to run over the three hundred men who made up the battle force and the enemy reserves all at the same time. Far from doing that, the usual routine was followed, sending numerous militia units that advanced to the front. They started watching Facundo; every soldier feared meeting up with Facundo's lance, and when he heard the cry "Charge!" he stayed stuck to the ground, retreated, was himself charged, retreated, and surrounded the better troops. Facundo kept on going toward Mendoza, not bothering with the generals, infantry, and cannons that he left to his rear guard. This was the Battle of Chacón, which left the army of Córdoba that was about to attack Buenos Aires flanked. The inconceivable audacity of Quiroga's move was crowned by the most complete success. Removing him from Mendoza was now useless: the prestige of victory and terror would give him means of resistance, while his enemies were left demoralized by defeat; he would run over San Juan, where he would find resources and arms, and an interminable, unwinnable war would be waged. The leaders left for Córdoba, and the infantry, along with the officers from Mendoza, capitulated the next day. The unitarists of San Juan, two hundred in number, immigrated to Coquimbo, and Quiroga was left in peaceful possession of Cuyo and La Rioja. Those two towns had never suffered a catastrophe equal to this one, not so much because of the evils Quiroga caused directly as for the upset in business brought on by the mass emigration of the wealthy sector of society.

But the evil was greater in terms of the reverses experienced by the spirit of the city, which is what I am interested in noting. I have said it before, and here I must repeat it: considering the mediterranean position of Mendoza,[3] it was, until that time, an eminently civilized town, rich in illustrious men and endowed with a spirit of enterprise and progress not had by any other town in the Argentine Republic; it was the Barcelona of the interior. This spirit had reached its peak during the

Videla Castillo administration. In the south, forts were constructed that, besides extending the borders of the province, have left it forever secured against invasions of savages, and the desiccation of swamps in the immediate area was begun. Societies for agriculture, industry, mining, and public education were formed, all of them directed and supported by intelligent, enthusiastic, and enterprising men; a factory was promoted that made canvas and woolen fabrics, which provided clothing and tents for the troops; an armory was established, where swords, sabers, armor, lances, bayonets, and rifles were made, with only the barrels of the latter being of foreign manufacture; hollow cannonballs and printing type were forged. A French chemist, Charon, directed this latter work, along with the assay of provincial metals. It is impossible to imagine a more rapid or more extensive development of all the civilized faculties of a people. In Chile or Buenos Aires, all this manufacture would not attract much attention; but in an interior province, and only with the aid of local artisans, it was a prodigious effort. The printing press squealed under the load of the daily newspaper and periodical publications, in which poetry soon appeared. With the inclination I know that town to have, after ten years of a system like this it would have become a colossus; but then the trampling of Facundo's horses came and stomped these vigorous buds of civilization, and the friar Aldao had it plowed over and sowed the earth with blood for ten years. What could remain!

The movement toward ideas didn't stop, even after Quiroga's occupation. The members of the Mining Society who had immigrated to Chile devoted themselves, as soon as they arrived, to studying chemistry, minerology, and metallurgy. Godoy Cruz, Correa, Villanueva, Doncel, and many others gathered all the books dealing with these subjects, collected different metals from all over America, searched the Chilean archives for information about the history of the Uspallata mines, and through their diligence, succeeded in starting work there that, with the help of the knowledge they had gained, put to good use the scarce quantity of useful metal those mines contain. The new exploitation of mines in Mendoza, which is being done so profitably today, dates from that time. The Argentine miners, not satisfied with these results, spread out all over the Chilean territory, which offered them a rich arena in which to test their science, and what they have done in Copiapó and other spots, in exploitation and profit and the introduction of new machinery and apparatus, is not slight. Godoy Cruz, disappointed with the mines, took his research in another direction, and with the cultivation of the white mulberry thought he would solve the problem of the future of the San Juan and Mendoza provinces, which was to find a product that would hold great worth within a small volume.

Silk fulfills these conditions, which are imposed on those central areas because of their immense distance from the seaports and the high price of shipping. Godoy Cruz was not content with publishing in Santiago a voluminous, complete pamphlet about cultivation of the white mulberry, raising silkworms and cochineal. He also distributed it for free in those provinces, and has spent ten years agitating without a break, propagating the white mulberry, urging everyone to devote themselves to its cultivation, exaggerating its optimum advantages, while he maintains correspondence with Europe to learn about current prices, sending samples of the silk he has harvested, getting practical knowledge about its defects and improvements, learning and teaching others how to spin it. The fruits of this great, patriotic work have equaled the hopes of the noble craftsman. As of last year, there were several million white mulberry bushes in Mendoza, and silk, gathered by the hundredweight, had been spun, twisted, dyed, and sold to Europe in Buenos Aires and Santiago, at five, six, and seven pesos per pound, because the silk of Mendoza, in luster and fineness, does not take second place to the best of Spain or Italy. The poor old man has finally returned to his country to delight in the spectacle of an entire people devoted to accomplishing this most productive change in industry, promising himself that death will not shut his eyes before he sees a caravan of carts leaving for Buenos Aires, loaded up in deepest America with the precious product that for so many centuries has made China rich, and that the factories of Lyon, Paris, Barcelona, and all of Italy compete for today. Eternal glory of the unitarist spirit, of the city, and of civilization! Mendoza, with its initiative, has anticipated all of Spanish America in the large-scale exploitation of this rich industry!* Ask the spirit of Facundo and Rosas for a single drop of interest in the public good, of devotion to any useful objective; twist it and squeeze it, and it will only ooze blood and crimes!

I dwell on these details because, in the midst of so many horrors such as these about which I am condemned to write, it is pleasing to stop and consider the beautiful plants trampled over by the uncultured savage of the Pampas. I dwell on them with pleasure because they will prove to those who still doubt it that resistance to Rosas and his system—although up to now perhaps weak in its method, just the defense of

---

*The final results have not justified such hopeful promise; today the silk industry in Mendoza is languishing, and will disappear for want of promotion. (Author's note from the second edition.)

European civilization, of its forms and results—is what has given for fifteen years so much abnegation, so much constancy to those who, up to now, have spilled their blood or tasted the sadness of exile. There is a new world about to unfold that only awaits, before it appears in all its brilliance, some fortunate general who will succeed in removing the iron foot oppressing the intelligence of the Argentine people today. Besides, History mustn't be woven only of crimes and soaked in blood; nor is it extreme to make the nearly erased pages of past eras visible for a people that has strayed. May they at least wish for their children better times than their own; because it does not matter that today, the cannibal of Buenos Aires may tire of spilling blood and allow those subjugated and destroyed by misfortune and exile to return to their homes. None of this matters for the progress of a people. The evil that must be removed is the one born of a government that trembles in the presence of thinking, illustrious men, and that in order to subsist, needs to send them away or kill them; born of a system that, concentrating all its will and action in *one single man,* the good that he doesn't do, because he doesn't conceive of it, cannot do it, or doesn't want it, no one feels willing to do, for fear of attracting the suspicious gaze of the tyrant; or perhaps because where there is no freedom of thought and action, public spirit dies out, and the egoism that is concentrated on ourselves drowns any feeling of interest in others. "*Every one for himself,* the executioner's whip for all": this is a summary of the life and government of enslaved peoples.

If the reader is bored by these thoughts, I will tell him about some frightful crimes. Facundo, master of Mendoza, used the methods that by now we know so well in order to supply himself with money and soldiers. One afternoon, posses crossed the city in every direction, taking to an olive grove all the officers they could find who had surrendered in Chacón. No one knew the reason, nor did they fear anything at first, trusting in the good faith of the stipulated terms. Several priests, meanwhile, also received orders to appear; when there was a sufficient number of officers gathered, the priests were ordered to hear their confessions. That done, they were lined up and, one by one, began to be shot under the direction of Facundo, who indicated which one still seemed to be alive and pointed with his finger to the place where they should give him the bullet that would finish him off. The slaughter concluded, after lasting for an hour because it was done calmly and slowly, Quiroga explained to some people the motive for that terrible violation of the treaty's good faith: the unitarists, he said, had killed General Villafañe, and he was taking reprisals. The charge was well founded, but the satisfaction was a bit crude. "Paz," he said on another occasion, "shot nine of my officers; I've shot ninety-six of his." Paz was not responsible for an act that he deeply lamented and that was motivated by the killing of one of his representatives at a parley. But the system of giving no quarter, which Rosas followed with such tenacity, and of violating all accepted forms, pacts, treaties, capitulations, is the effect of causes that don't depend on the personal character of the caudillos. Individual rights, which have lessened the horrors of war, are the result of centuries of civilization; the savage kills his prisoner, doesn't respect any accord whenever there is an advantage in breaking it. What brakes could control the Argentine savage, who doesn't know about the individual rights of cultured cities? Where could he have become aware of these rights? In the Pampas?

Villafañe's murder occurred on Chilean territory. His killer has already suffered the talion law: an eye for an eye, a tooth for a tooth. Human justice has been satisfied; but the character of that bloody drama's protagonist fits my subject too well for me to deprive myself of the pleasure of introducing him. Among the emigrants from San Juan who headed for Coquimbo was a major from General Paz's army, endowed with those original characteristics that Argentine life develops. Major Navarro, from a distinguished San Juan family, with a small form and a flexible, thin body, was well known in the army for his bold daring. At the age of eighteen, he stood guard as a second lieutenant in the militia on the night in 1820 when the First Battalion of the Andes revolted in San Juan. Four companies formed across from the headquarters and called on the city militia to surrender. Navarro was the sole guard on duty; he half-opened the door and defended the entryway with his foil. The second lieutenant received fourteen saber and bayonet wounds, and pressing with one hand on three blows of the bayonet he had received to the thigh, with the other arm covering five that had pierced his chest, and choking on the blood that ran down in torrents from his head, he walked from there to his house, where he recovered his health and life after seven months of desperate, almost impossible treatment. On sick leave because of the militia's dissolution, he went into business, but a business accompanied by danger and adventure. At first he brought contraband shipments into Córdoba; after that he traded with Indians, from Córdoba; and finally, he married the daughter of a cacique, lived faithfully with her, took part in the wars of savage tribes, got used to eating raw meat and drinking blood during horse slaughters, until after four years he became a savage through and through. There, he learned that war with Brazil was going to start, and leaving his beloved savages behind, he returned to the army at his rank of second lieutenant, and was so skillful and dealt out so many blows with his saber that at the campaign's end he was a captain and brevet major, and one of the favorites of Lavalle, an admirer of brave men. In Puente Márquez his deeds left the army astonished, and after all those forays he stayed in Buenos Aires with the rest of Lavalle's officers. Arbolito, Pancho el Ñato, Molina, and other leaders of the campaign were the high-ranked personages who showed off their valor in cafes and inns. Animosity against the army officers became more poisoned every day. In the Cafe Comedia, some of these heroes of that era were drinking a toast to the death of Lavalle. Navarro, who heard them, approached and took the glass away from one, poured for both himself and the man, and said, "Here, have a drink to Lavalle's health!" They unsheathed their swords and Navarro left him lying on the ground. He had to escape, gain the countryside, and get to Córdoba through enemy lines. Before reentering the service, he penetrated inland to see his family, his father-in-law, and learned to his sorrow that his better half had died. He bid them farewell, and two of his relatives, two young fellows, one his cousin and the other his nephew, accompanied him back to the army.

In the Battle of Chacón a flash burn to his temple had rustled away all his hair and imbued his face with gunpowder. With this appearance and entourage, and an English aide who could handle the lasso and the bolas with the same gaucho aim as the boss and his relatives, young Navarro immigrated to Coquimbo, for young he was, and as cultured in his speech, as elegant in his manners, as any dandy; all of which didn't stop him from going to drink cattle blood whenever he saw an animal go down. Every day he wanted to go back, and the insistence of his friends almost could not contain him. "I'm the son of gunpowder," he would say with his grave, sonorous voice, "war is my element." "The first drop of blood spilled in the civil war," he would say at other times, "came from these veins, and from them will come the last." "I can't go on any farther," he would repeat, stopping his horse, "I miss having a general's epaulets on my shoulders." "But what will my comrades say," he exclaimed at other times, "when they hear that Major Navarro has stepped on foreign soil without a squadron with lances at the ready?"

The day they crossed the border through the mountains there was a pathetic scene. They had to lay down their arms, and there was no way to make the Indians understand that there were countries where it was not permitted to go about holding a lance. Navarro went over to them, spoke to them in their language; he became more and more emotional; two big tears rolled down from his eyes; and the Indians, with a show of anguish, stuck their lances into the ground. Even so, after the march began again, they turned their horses back and circled the weapons, as if to say an eternal good-bye.

With this inclination of spirit, Major Navarro entered Chile and lodged in Guanda, which is located at the mouth of the stream leading to the mountain range. There he learned that Villafañe was going back to join Facundo and announced publicly his intention to kill him. The other emigres, who knew what those words meant coming from Major Navarro, left the scene after attempting in vain to dissuade him. When Villafañe was warned, he asked for help from the authorities, who gave him some militia men, who left as soon as they learned what was going on. But Villafañe was perfectly well armed and, in addition, had six men from La Rioja with him. When he passed through Guanda, Navarro went out to meet him, and with a stream between them announced in solemn, clear sentences his plan to kill him, after which he calmly returned to the house where he was just then having his midday meal. Villafañe indiscreetly lodged in Tilo, a place only four leagues distant from the one where the challenge had taken place. That night, Navarro asked for his weapons and a group of nine men to accompany him, whom he left in a suitable place near the house in Tilo, advancing alone under the moonlight. When he had penetrated the open patio of the house, he shouted to Villafañe, sleeping with his men on the balcony: "Villafañe, get up! A man with enemies cannot sleep." Villafañe took up his lance, Navarro dismounted from his horse, unsheathed his sword, approached, and ran him through. Then Navarro fired off a gunshot, which was the signal to advance that he had given his party, who attacked the dead man's group, killed them, or ran them off. They then had Villafañe's animals brought out, loaded up his equipment, and left with all of it for the Argentine Republic to join the army. Taking the wrong road, they arrived at Río Cuarto, when they found Colonel Echevarría, pursued by the enemy. Navarro flew to his aid, and when his friend's horse fell down dead, urged him to get onto the rump of his own. Echevarría would not consent, Navarro insisted he wouldn't flee without saving him, and finally he dismounted from his own horse, killed it, and died at his friend's side. His family didn't learn of such a sad end until three years later, when the same men who killed them told the tragic story and dug up, for proof, the skeletons of the two unfortunate friends. In the entire life of this ill-fated young man there is such originality that without a doubt it is worthwhile to digress in favor of his memory.

During Major Navarro's short immigration, events had occurred that completely changed the face of public affairs. The celebrated capture of General Paz, yanked away from the head of his army by a throw of the bolas, decided the fate of the Republic. It could be said that the Constitution wasn't adopted at the time, and the cities and laws didn't consolidate their power, because of this singular occurrence; because Paz, with an army of forty-five hundred perfectly disciplined men, and with a wisely put-together plan of operations, was sure of defeating the army of Buenos Aires. Those who have seen him triumph everywhere since then will judge that there was not much presumption on his part in having such high expectations. We could join voices with the moralists, who give the most fortuitous events the power to upset the fate of empires; but if hitting an enemy general with a throw of the bolas is fortuitous, that it should have come from those who attack the cities—from the gaucho of the Pampas converted into a political element—is not. And so, it can be said that back then civilization was "all balled up."[4]

Facundo, after so cruelly avenging his General Villafañe, left for San Juan to ready the expedition against Tucumán, where the army of Córdoba had retreated after its loss of the general, which made any idea of invasion impossible. When he arrived, all the federalist citizens, as in 1827, came out to meet him; but Facundo didn't like receptions. He sent one company to advance past the street where the citizens had gathered, left another behind, had guards posted on all the avenues, and going by another road he entered the city. He thus made his officious hosts prisoners, who had to spend the rest of the day and the whole night crowded together in the street, making room for themselves amid the horses' hooves to doze off a bit.

When Facundo reached the central plaza, he had his carriage stopped in the middle of it, ordered that the pealing of the bells cease and that all the furnishings of the house the authorities had prepared to receive him be thrown into the street: rugs, drapes, mirrors, chairs, tables, everything piled up in confusion in the plaza, and he would only step out when it was certain that nothing was left but the bare walls, a small table, a single chair, and a bed. While this operation was being carried out, he called over a boy who happened to pass near his carriage, asked him his name, and upon hearing the surname Roza, told him: "Your father, Don Ignacio de la Roza, was a great man; tell your mother I am at her service."

The next day a bench six yards long for execution by firing squad appeared in the plaza. Who would the victims be? The unitarists had fled en masse, even the timid ones who weren't unitarists! Facundo began to impose a tax on the women, instead of their absent husbands, fathers, and brothers, and the results were no less satisfying. I omit an account of all the events of this period, which would have to include the sobs and cries of women threatened with being sent to the bench or with flogging; two or three men shot, four or five flogged, one or another lady condemned to making food for the soldiers, and other unspeakable violence. But there was one day of glacial terror I mustn't let pass in silence. It was the moment when the expedition against Tucumán was leaving. The divisions began filing out, one after another; in the plaza, the muleteers were loading the baggage; a mule got scared and went into the church of Santa Ana. Facundo ordered it to be roped inside the church; the muleteer went to take it with his hands, and at that moment, an officer entering on horseback, by Quiroga's order, roped the mule and the muleteer and tugged them out together, the unhappy man suffering from the beast's kicks and blows. Something wasn't ready at that moment: Facundo had the negligent authorities appear. His Excellency the governor and captain general of the province received a punch in the face; the chief of police escaped a bullet by running away, and both rushed through the streets to their offices to issue the orders they had omitted.

Later, Facundo saw one of his officers striking with the flat of his sword two soldiers who were fighting. He called the officer over, attacked him with his lance; the officer grabbed the shaft to defend his life. They struggled, and finally the officer took it from him and returned it respectfully; another attempt at running him through with it; another fight; another victory for the officer, who again returned it. Then Facundo, repressing his rage, called for assistance; six men took hold of the athletic officer; they stretched him over a window frame; and with hands and feet well tied down, Facundo ran him through repeatedly with that same lance that twice was returned to him, until he had finished off the last death throes, until the officer's head hung and the body lay still and motionless. The furies had been unleashed; General Huidobro was threatened with the lance, although he had the courage to unsheath his sword and prepare to defend his life.

And despite all this, Facundo wasn't cruel, wasn't bloodthirsty; he was just a barbarian who didn't know how to contain his passions, which, once irritated, knew neither measure nor limit; he was the terrorist who, upon entering a city, shot one person and whipped another, but with economy, many times with discernment. The one shot was blind, paralytic, or a sacristan; usually, the unhappy one whipped was an illustrious citizen, a young man from the best families. His brutality with the ladies came from being unaware of the delicate attention that weakness deserves; the insulting humiliations imposed on citizens came from being a crude peasant, and because of it he liked to mistreat and wound the pride and decorum of those he knew disdained him. This was his only motive for making terror into a system of government. What would Rosas have done without it, in a society such as that of Buenos Aires was back then? What other means could demand from an intelligent people the respect their conscience denies to that which, in itself, is abject and contemptible?

It is incredible how many atrocities must be piled up, one on top of the other, to pervert a people. And no one knows the ruses, the studying, the observations, and the sagacity that Don Juan Manuel Rosas has used to subject the city to that magical influence, which in six years completely changed consciousness of what is just and right, which finally broke the hearts of the bravest and bowed them to the yoke. The Terror in France in 1793 was not a means, but an effect. Robespierre didn't guillotine nobles and priests to create a reputation for himself, or to elevate himself on top of the bodies he piled up. He was an austere, severe soul who thought that all of France's aristocratic limbs had to be amputated in order to cement the revolution. "Our names," said Danton, "will go down in posterity as execrable; but we will have saved the Republic." Terror among us is an invention of government to choke all conscience, all spirit of the city, and finally to force men to recognize as a thinking brain the foot squeezing their throat. It is the satisfaction taken by an inept man armed with a dagger to avenge the scorn he knows his nullity inspires in a public infinitely superior to him. This is why we have seen repeated in our times the extravagances of Caligula, who had himself adored as God and made his horse an associate in the empire. Caligula knew that he was the lowest of the Romans, whom he had, nevertheless, under his foot. Facundo gave himself an air of inspiration, of clairvoyance, to supplant his natural incapacity to influence minds. Rosas had himself worshiped in churches and his image pulled through the streets on a cart, to which generals and ladies were yoked, to create the prestige he lacked. But Facundo was cruel only when the blood had risen to his head and his eyes, and all he saw was red. His cold calculations were limited to shooting a man, to whipping a citizen. Rosas never goes into a fury; he calculates in the quiet and seclusion of his study, and from there, the orders go out to his hired assassins.

CHAPTER XII

Society at War

Les habitants de Tucumán finissent leurs journées par des réunions champêtres, où à l'ombre de beaux arbres ils improvisent, au son d'une guitarre rustique, des chants alternatifs dans le genre de ceux que Virgile el Théocrite ont embellis. Tout, jusqu'aux prénoms grecs, rapelle au voyageur étonné l'antique Arcadie.

Malte-Brun[1]

Ciudadela

The expedition departed, and the federalist residents of San Juan and the wives and mothers of the unitarists breathed at last, as if they were waking up from a horrible nightmare. In this campaign, Facundo displayed a spirit of order and a swiftness in his march that showed how much past disasters had taught him. In twenty-four days, he crossed nearly three hundred leagues of territory with his army; and so he almost took by surprise some enemy army squadrons, which, with the unexpected news of his approach, watched him move into Ciudadela, the old encampment of the patriot armies under Belgrano. It would be inconceivable how an army like the one Lamadrid commanded in Tucumán, with such brave leaders and such experienced soldiers, could be defeated, if moral causes and antistrategic prejudices weren't the solution to such a strange enigma.

General Lamadrid, the army chief, had among his subordinates General López, a sort of caudillo from Tucumán who was personally against him, and beyond the fact that a retreat demoralizes the troops, General Lamadrid was not the most skilled at dominating the spirit of his subordinate leaders. The army presented itself in battle having become half federal, half *montonero,* while Facundo's army had the unity brought by terror and obedience to a caudillo who is not a cause but a person, and who, therefore, eliminates free will and smothers all individuality. Rosas has triumphed over his enemies because of this ironclad unity, which makes all of his satellites into passive instruments, blind executors of his supreme will. On the eve of battle, Lieutenant Colonel Balmaceda requested the general-in-chief to allow him to make the first charge. If this had been carried out, since it was the rule to begin battles with a cavalry charge and since a subordinate had taken the liberty to request it, the battle would have been won, because the armored Second Regiment never met anyone, either in Brazil or in the Argentine Republic, who could withstand its charge. The general acceded to the demand of the Second's commander, but one of the colonels felt that his best corps was being taken away; General López, that the elite troops, which according to all the rules should form the reserve, were being engaged at the start; and the general-in-chief, not having sufficient authority to quiet this clamor, sent the invincible squadron and the famous charger who commanded it back to the reserve.

Facundo deployed his forces at such a distance as to shelter them from the infantry commanded by Barcala, and to weaken the effect of the eight pieces of artillery directed by the intelligent Arengreen. Had Facundo foreseen what his enemies were going to do? A guerrilla battle had taken place earlier, in which Facundo's men overwhelmed the Tucumán division. Facundo called in the victorious leader. "Why have you returned?" "Because I pushed the enemy back to the edge of the forest." "Why didn't you penetrate the forest fighting with swords?" "Because they had superior forces." "Give me a firing squad!" And the leader was executed. From one end of Quiroga's line to the other, one could hear the rattling of the spurs and rifles of the soldiers, who trembled not with fear of the enemy, but of the terrible chief who went along their rear guard, up and down the line brandishing his ebony-tipped lance. As a relief, as a release of the terror oppressing them, they waited for the order to throw themselves on the enemy. They would tear it to pieces, break through the line of bayonets, in exchange for putting something between themselves and the image of Facundo, which pursued them like an angry ghost. As can be seen, then, on one side terror prevailed, on the other, anarchy. At the first attempted charge, Lamadrid's cavalry disbanded; the reserve followed, and five cavalry chiefs were left only with the artillery, which increased its fire, and the infantry, which threw itself on the enemy with bayonets. Why describe more? The victors give the details of a battle.

Dismay reigned in Tucumán; emigration happened en masse, because the federalists in that city were few. This was Facundo's third visit! The next day, a tax was imposed. Quiroga learned that there were precious objects hidden in a church; he went to the sacristan, whom he interrogated about this. The man was some sort of imbecile, who answered with a smile. "You laugh? Give me a firing squad!" . . . which shot him on the spot, and the roll call of taxes filled up in an hour. The general's coffers swelled with gold. If anyone hadn't fully understood, he would have no doubt left when he saw the Franciscan prelate and the presbyter Colombres taken prisoner, on their way to being flogged. Facundo immediately appeared where the prisoners were being held, separated out the officers, and retired to rest from so much hard work, leaving orders that all of them be shot.

Tucumán is a tropical land, where nature has shown off her most splendid finery; it is America's Eden, without rival anywhere around the world. Imagine the Andes covered with a blackish-green blanket of colossal vegetation, letting escape from beneath the border of this gown twelve rivers that run at equal distances in parallel directions, until they all begin to slant toward one course, and together form a navigable canal that ventures into the heart of America. The land between the tributaries and the canal comprises, at most, fifty leagues. The forests that cover the land's surface are primitive, but in them the splendors of India are clad with the graces of Greece.

The walnut tree laces its broad branches with the mahogany and the ebony; the cedar allows to grow by its side the classic laurel, which in turn protects beneath its foliage the myrtle, consecrated to Venus, still leaving space so that the balsamic spikenard and the white lily may raise their staffs.

The odoriferous cedar has taken control of a belt of land there that interrupts the forest, and in other places rose bushes block the way with their thick, thorny wickerwork.

The ancient trunks serve as a ground for diverse species of flowering mosses, and the lianas and mulberries festoon, entangle, and confound all these diverse generations of plants.

Above all this vegetation, which would exhaust a fantastic palette with its combinations and richness of colors, flutter swarms of golden butterflies, enameled hummingbirds, millions of parrots the color of emeralds, blue magpies, and orange toucans. The din of these noisy birds deafens you all day long, as if it were the sound of a melodious waterfall. Major Andrews, an English traveler who has devoted many pages to the description of all these marvels, tells how he would leave in the mornings and go into ecstasy contemplating that arrogant, brilliant vegetation; how he penetrated the aromatic forests, and in delirium, captivated by the rapture that overcame him, he would go deep into where he saw thick darkness, until finally he returned home, where they showed him how he had torn his clothing, scratched and wounded his face, which sometimes when he arrived would be running with blood without his having felt it.[2] The city is surrounded for many leagues by a forest, formed exclusively of orange trees rounded on top to a certain height, in such a way as to form a limitless vault supported by a million smooth, shapely columns. The rays of that torrid sun have never been able to watch the scenes taking place on the carpet of greenery covering the earth beneath that immense canopy. And what scenes! On Sundays the beauties of Tucumán go to spend the day in those limitless galleries. Each family chooses a suitable place; they push aside the oranges blocking the path, if it is autumn; or perhaps dancing couples poise on the thick carpet of orange blossoms that covers the ground, and with the perfume of its flowers they linger long, the melodic sounds of sad songs accompanied by guitars growing faint in the distance. Do you by chance think this description is copied from *A Thousand and One Nights* or other Oriental fairy tales? Imagine, instead, what I cannot describe about the voluptuousness and beauty of the women born under a sky of fire, who, as in a faint, at siesta time lie down comfortably under the shade of myrtles and laurels, falling asleep drunk with the essences that choke anyone unaccustomed to that atmosphere.

Facundo had taken over one of these dark canopies, perhaps to meditate on what he should do with the poor city that had fallen like a squirrel under the lion's claws. The poor city, meanwhile, was trying to accomplish a project full of innocent coquetry. A delegation of young girls brimming with youth, innocence, and beauty approached the place where Facundo was lying on his poncho. The most resolute or enthusiastic one walked ahead of the rest; she hesitated, stopped, the ones behind pushed her on, they all stopped overtaken by fear, turned away their chaste faces, encouraged each other, and stopping, timidly advancing, and pushing each other on, at last arrived in his presence. Facundo received them affably, had them sit around him, allowed them to compose themselves, and finally inquired about the reason for such a pleasant visit. They had come to plead for the lives of the army officers who were going to be shot. Sobs escaped from amid the shy, carefully chosen group; a smile of hope flashed on some faces; and all the delicate seductions of women were called into play to attain the merciful goal they had set for themselves. Facundo was keenly interested, and from amid the thickness of his black beard, contentment and complacency could be discerned on his features. But he had to question them one by one, know about their families, the houses where they lived, a thousand little details that seemed to amuse and delight him, and that took up an hour, maintaining hope and expectations. At last, he said to them with the greatest affability: "Do you hear those shots being fired?"

It was too late! They had been shot! A cry of horror went out from amid that chorus of angels, escaping like a flock of doves pursued by a falcon. They had shot them, indeed! And how they had! Thirty-three officers, from colonels on down, lined up in the plaza totally naked, received, standing, the mortal fire. Two young brothers, sons of a distinguished Buenos Aires family, embraced each other to die, and the dead body of one held back the bullets from the other. "I'm free now," he shouted, "I've been saved according to the law." Poor dreamer! How much he would have given for his life! At his confession he had taken a ring out of his mouth, where he had hidden it so they wouldn't take it from him, asking the priest to return it to his lovely fiancée, who upon receiving it gave in exchange her sanity, which she has not regained to this day, poor crazy woman!

The cavalry soldiers each tied up a body and dragged them off to the cemetery, although some bits of skull, an arm, and some other limbs remained in the plaza of Tucumán, serving as fodder for the dogs. Oh! How many glories have been dragged like this through the mud! In San Nicolás de los Arroyos, Don Juan Manuel Rosas had twenty-eight officers killed in the same way and almost at the same time, not counting the hundred or more who had perished in obscurity! Chacabuco, Maipú, Junín, Ayacucho, Ituzaingó! Why have your laurels been a curse for all those who wear them?

If anything could be added to the horror of these scenes, it is the fate of the respected Colonel Arraya, father of eight children: a prisoner, with three lance wounds in the back, he was made to enter Tucumán on foot, naked, bleeding profusely, and loaded down with eight rifles. Exhausted by the effort, he had to be given a bed in a private home. At the hour of the executions in the plaza, some riflemen penetrated all the way into his room and shot him through in his bed, making him die amid the flames of the burning sheets.

Colonel Barcala, the illustrious black man, was the only leader excepted from this slaughter, because Barcala was master of Córdoba and Mendoza, where he was idolized by the civil guards. He was a tool that could be saved for the future. Who knew what might happen later on?

The next day, all over the city there began an operation called sequestration. It consisted of putting sentinels at the doors of all the stores and warehouses, at the leather shops, the tanneries, the tobacco storehouses. All of them, because in Tucumán there were no federalists; that was a plant that couldn't grow until it had the three good waterings of blood Quiroga gave the ground, and another greater than those three together contributed by Oribe. Now, they say, there are federalists who wear a ribbon that certifies them, on which is written: Death to the savage, filthy unitarists!

How could it be doubted for a moment! All that property and the herds of the countryside belonged, by right, to Facundo. Two hundred fifty carts, each with sixteen oxen, began the journey to Buenos Aires, carrying the produce of the region. European goods were put into a warehouse as stock for auctions, where the commanders acted as auctioneers. Everything was sold, and at the lowest price. And there was yet more. Facundo himself sold shirts, women's petticoats, children's clothes; he unfolded them, showed them, and urged the crowd: a medio, a real, any price was good. The merchandise was dispatched, business was brilliantly successful, more workers were needed, the multitude shoved at each other, suffocating in the crush. But it did begin to be noticed that after a few days buyers were scarce, and in vain they were offered frothy, embroidered handkerchiefs for four reales; no one was buying. What had happened? Feelings of remorse from the common people? Nothing of the sort. All the money in circulation had been used up: imposed taxes on the one hand, the sequestration on the other, the cheap sale, had taken in the very last coins circulating in the province. If any were left in the hands of Facundo's officers or followers, the card table was there to leave every pocket empty in the end. At the front door of the general's house, rows of leather pouches filled with silver were drying in the sun. They remained there through the night, without out guards, and those who passed dared not even look.

But don't think the city had been abandoned to pillage, or that soldiers had shared in that immense booty! No; Quiroga would repeatedly say afterward in Buenos Aires, in the circle of his "comrades": "I've never allowed soldiers to steal, because I think it's immoral." During the first days, a farmer complained to Facundo that his soldiers had taken some fruit. He had them line up and the guilty ones were found. Six hundred lashes was the sentence each one got. The farmer, shocked, pled for the victims, and they threatened to give him the same. Because that's how the Argentine gaucho is: he kills because his caudillos order him to kill, and he doesn't steal, because they don't order him to. If you want to find out why it is that these men don't rise up and free themselves from the one who gives them nothing in return for their blood and their valor, ask Don Juan Manuel Rosas about all the wonders that terror can do. He knows all about it! Not only the miserable gaucho, but also the renowned general, the magnificent, vain citizen, is made to work miracles! Did I not tell you that terror produces greater results than patriotism? Don Manuel Gregorio Quiroga, colonel of the army of Chile, ex-governor of San Juan and one of the chiefs of staff of Facundo's army, convinced that the half-million in booty was solely for the general, who had just beaten up a commander who kept for himself a few reales from the sale of a handkerchief, conceived of a plan to remove a few pieces of jewelry from those piled up in the warehouse, and thus to make up for his salary. His robbery was discovered, and the general ordered him tied to a post and exposed to public shame; and when the army returned from San Juan, the colonel of the army of Chile, ex-governor of San Juan, one of the chiefs of staff, marched on foot along barely passable roads, collared to a young bull. The bull's companion succumbed in Catamarca, and no one knows if the bull made it to San Juan! To go on: Facundo learned that a young man named Rodríguez, among the most enlightened of Tucumán, had received a letter from the fugitives. He had him arrested, took him to the plaza himself, hung him to a post, and had him given six hundred lashes. But the soldiers didn't know how to give lashes such as that crime demanded, and Quiroga took the thick reins used to execute the sentence, swinging them in the air with his Herculean arm, and fired off fifty lashes to serve as a model. The act concluded, he personally stirred up the tub of brine, scrubbed Rodríguez's buttocks, yanked the loose pieces off of him, and stuck his fist into the hollows they had left. Facundo went back to his house, read the intercepted letters, and found in them messages from husbands to their wives, bills to pay from merchants, advice that they not worry about them, etc. Not one word was there of political interest; so Facundo asked about young Rodríguez and they told him he was about to expire. He immediately began gambling and won thousands. Don

Francisco Reto and Don N. Lugones had been murmuring to each other something about the horrors they had witnessed. Each one received three hundred lashes and the order to go home across the city completely naked, hands on their heads with their behinds dripping blood. Armed soldiers followed at a distance, so the order would be executed exactly. And do you wish to know what happens to human nature, when infamy is enthroned and there is no one on earth to whom an appeal can be made against the executioners? Don N. Lugones, who had a mischievous character, turned around to his companion in torture, and said to him with the greatest composure: "*Compañero,* pass me the tobacco, let's have a smoke!" To go on: Dysentery broke out in Tucumán, and the doctors said with certainty that there was no cure, that it came from lack of morale, from terror, a disease against which no cure has been found in the Argentine Republic to this day. Facundo showed up one day at a house and asked a group of little children playing marbles where the *señora* was; the most observant one answered that she wasn't there. "Tell her I've been here." "And who are you?" "I am Facundo Quiroga . . . " The boy keeled over, and only in the last year has he begun to show signs of recovering a bit of his reason. The others ran away crying and screaming; one climbed a tree, another jumped over a wall and took a terrible fall. . . . What did Facundo want with that lady? . . . She was a beautiful widow who had attracted his glance and he came to court her! Because in Tucumán, Cupid or the satyr was not lazy. A young woman attracted him, he spoke to her and proposed to take her to San Juan. Imagine what the poor girl could say to this dishonorable proposition made by a tiger. She blushed, and stammering, answered that she could not decide . . . that her father . . . Facundo went to her father, and the anguished father, hiding his horror, objected, asking who would be responsible for his daughter, that she would be abandoned. Facundo satisfied all his objections, and the unhappy father, not realizing what he was saying and thinking he would put an end to that abominable business, proposed that he be given a document. . . . Facundo took up his pen and handed him the required guarantee, passing paper and pen to the father so that he might sign the agreement. The father was a father in the end, and nature spoke, saying: "I won't sign; kill me!" "You filthy old cheat!" Quiroga answered, and he went out the door choking with rage.

Quiroga, the champion of "the cause the people have sworn," as they say in Buenos Aires, was barbarous, avaricious, and lewd, and he gave in to his passions without disguise. His successor does not sack towns, it is true; he does not insult the decency of women; he has but one passion, one need: the thirst for human blood and for despotism. Instead, he knows how to use words and formulas that give indifferent people what they need. The savage, the bloody, the perfidious, filthy unitarists, the bloody duke of Abrantes, the perfidious Brazilian minister, the federation! the American spirit! the filthy gold of France, the iniquitous claims of England, the European conquest! Words like these are enough to cover up the longest and the most frightful series of crimes seen in the nineteenth century. Rosas! Rosas! Rosas! I prostrate and humble myself before your powerful intelligence! You are as great as the Río de la Plata, as the Andes! Only you have understood how despicable is the human species, its freedom, its knowledge, and its pride! Trample on it! for all the governments of the civilized world will revere you, the more insolent you are! Trample on it! for you will not lack loyal dogs that, fetching the stale bread you throw to them, will spill their blood on the battlefields or display on their chests your red marker in every American capital! Trample on it! oh yes, trample on it!

In Tucumán, Salta, and Jujuy, a great progressive industrial movement, in no way inferior to the one we described in Mendoza, was left interrupted or weakened because of Quiroga's invasion. Dr. Colombres, whom Facundo loaded down with manacles, had introduced and promoted the cultivation of sugarcane, which is so appropriate to that climate, remaining unsatisfied with his work until ten great sugar mills were in operation. Buying plants from Havana, sending representatives to sugar mills in Brazil to study procedures and machinery, refining the molasses, everything had been accomplished with zeal and success when Facundo sent his herds of horses into the cane fields and dismantled most of the new mills. An Agricultural Society had already published its papers and was preparing to test the cultivation of indigo and cochineal. Artisans and workshops for wool fabric, fulled cloth, carpets, and morocco leather had been brought to Salta from Europe and North America, and all had already obtained satisfactory results. But what most concerned those towns, because it was in their most vital interest, was the navigation of the Bermejo River, a great commercial artery that, passing through the vicinity or the borders of those provinces, flows into the Paraná and opens an outlet for the immense riches that the tropical sky spills everywhere. The future of those beautiful provinces depends on the fitting out of water routes for commerce. From mediterranean cities, poor and underpopulated, they could turn into centers of civilization and wealth in ten years, if, favored by an able government, they could devote themselves to removing the slight obstacles that block their development. No, these aren't the chimerical dreams of a possible but distant future, they are not.

In North America, in less than ten years, the areas bordering the Mississippi and its tributaries have been covered not only with large and populous cities, but also with new states that have entered the Union. The Mississippi is not better situated than the Paraná; neither the Ohio, the Illinois, nor the Mississippi go through more fertile territory or more extensive regions than the Pilcomayo, the Bermejo, the Paraguay, and all the many great rivers Providence has placed among us to mark the path that will be followed, later on, by the new cities that will form the Argentine Union. Rivadavia put internal navigation of the rivers under consideration as a vital issue. In Salta and Buenos Aires, a great association with half a million pesos was formed, and the illustrious Soria finished his voyage and published a map of the river. How much time lost from 1825 to 1845! How much time, and even more, until God deigns to choke the monster of the Pampas! Because Rosas, opposing so tenaciously the free navigation of the rivers, protesting fears of European intrusion, harassing the cities of the interior and abandoning them to their own resources, does not simply obey the prejudices of a Goth against foreigners. He does not only give in to the persuasions of an ignorant Buenos Aires native who possesses the port and the main customshouse of the Republic, without caring to develop the civilization and wealth of this whole nation so that its port will be full of ships loaded with products from the interior and its customshouse with merchandise. Rather, he principally follows his instincts as a gaucho from the Pampas, who looks at water with horror, at ships with contempt, and who knows no happiness or joy equal to that of mounting a good racehorse to take him from one place to another. What does he care about white mulberry trees, sugarcane, indigo, river navigation, European immigration, and anything outside the narrow range of ideas with which he grew up? What does promoting the interior matter to him, he who lives amid riches and has a customshouse that, without any of this, gives him two million pesos annually? Salta, Jujuy, Tucumán, Santa Fe, Corrientes, and Entre Ríos today would be like Buenos Aires, if the movement toward industry and civilization so powerfully initiated by the early Unitarists, of which fertile seeds have remained, had continued. Today, Tucumán has large-scale exploitation of sugar and alcohol, which would make it wealthy if it could ship products to the coast at low cost, to trade them for merchandise in that ungrateful, stupid Buenos

Aires, from which it now gets the barbarizing movement begun by the gaucho with the red marker. But no evil is eternal, and one day those poor people will open their eyes, they who are denied all freedom of movement and deprived of all the capable and intelligent men who could carry out the work of realizing, in a few years, the grand future to which nature has destined those regions that today remain stationary, impoverished, and devastated. Why are they persecuted everywhere, or rather, why were they "savage" unitarists and not wise "federalists," that multitude of anonymous, enterprising men who devoted time to various social improvements: one to fomenting public education, another to introducing the cultivation of the mulberry tree, another of sugarcane, another to following the course of the great rivers, with no other personal interest, with no other reward than the glory of deserving the praise of their fellow citizens? Why have this movement and this concern ceased? Why do we not see the genius of European civilization that shone before, although only faintly, rise up again in the Argentine Republic? Why has its government, unitarist today in a way that Rivadavia himself never attempted, not dedicated a single glance to examining the inexhaustible and untouched resources of a privileged land? Why has it not devoted a twentieth of the millions that a fratricidal, exterminating war devours toward fomenting the people's education and promoting their happiness? What has it given them in exchange for their sacrifice and their suffering? A red rag! The government's care over fifteen years comes down to this; this is the only measure of national administration, the only point of contact between master and servant: a brand for the cattle!

CHAPTER XIII

Barranca-Yaco!!!

The fire that burned Albania for so long is put out now. All the red blood has been cleaned away, and our children's tears have been dried. Now we are bound by the ties of federation and of friendship.

Colden's History of Six Nations[1]

The victor at Ciudadela had pushed the last supporters of the unitarist system outside the Republic's borders. The cannon fuses were snuffed out, and horses' hooves no longer disturbed the silence of the Pampas. Facundo went back to San Juan and disbanded his army, but not before returning the sums violently wrenched from its citizens with money taken from Tucumán. What was still left to be done? Peace was now a normal condition in the Republic, just as a perpetual state of fluctuation and war had been before.

Quiroga's conquests had ended up destroying all sense of independence in the provinces, all administrative regularity. Facundo's name filled the vacuum of law, freedom and the spirit of the city had ceased to exist, and for this part of the Republic, all the provincial caudillos had been subsumed into one. Jujuy, Salta, Tucumán, Catamarca, La Rioja, San Juan, Mendoza, and San Luis lay dormant, rather than moving, under Quiroga's influence. I'll say it once and for all: federalism had disappeared along with the Unitarists, and the most complete unitarist fusion had just taken place in the Republic's interior provinces, in the person of the victor. In this way, then, the unitarist organization Rivadavia had wanted to give the Republic, and which had caused the struggle, was being realized in the interior; unless, to put this fact in doubt, we imagine that a federation may exist among cities that have lost all free movement and are at the mercy of a caudillo. But, despite the deceptiveness of the usual terms, the facts are so clear that they leave no doubt. In Tucumán, Facundo spoke with contempt of the dreamed-of federation; proposed to his friends that they focus on a man from the provinces to be president of the Republic; indicated as a candidate Dr. Don José Santos Ortiz, ex-governor of San Luis, his friend and secretary. "He's not a rough gaucho like me; he's educated and a good man," he said. "Above all, a man who knows how to do justice to his enemies deserves total confidence."

As we see, after defeating the Unitarists and dispersing the educated men, Facundo's original idea from before he entered the struggle reappeared—his support of the presidency and his conviction of the need to put order into the affairs of the Republic. However, he was seized by some doubts. "Now, General," someone said to him, "the nation will be constituted under a federal system. Not even a shadow of the Unitarists is left." "Hah!" he answered, shaking his head. "There are still a few rags to beat."* And with a meaningful air he added: "Our friends from down below don't want a Constitution."† He was already voicing these words in Tucumán. When communications from Buenos Aires reached him, and gazettes recording promotions given to commanding officers who had made the useless Córdoba campaign, Quiroga would say to General Huidobro: "They've never even sent me two titles to reward my officers, after we did everything. That's the *porteños* for you!" He learned that López was holding his Arabian horse and hadn't sent it back, and Quiroga became furious with the news. "You gaucho, you cow rustler!" he exclaimed. "The pleasure of that fine mount is going to cost you plenty!" And as the threats and the insults continued, Huidobro and other leaders became alarmed at the indiscretion with which he voiced them in such a public manner.

What were Quiroga's secret thoughts? What ideas concerned him at this point? He wasn't the governor of any province and didn't keep

---

*A vulgar phrase taken from the manner in which common people wash clothing, by beating it; it means that there are still many difficulties to be overcome. (Author's note from the first edition.)

†Cities below, Buenos Aires, etc., above, Tucumán, etc. (Author's note from the first edition.)

an army at the ready; all he had left was a name known and feared in eight provinces, and some armaments. While passing through La Rioja, he had left hidden in the forests all the rifles, sabers, lances, and short carbines he'd collected in the eight areas where he had been; there were more than twelve thousand weapons. A fleet of twenty-six pieces of artillery was left in the city, with abundant deposits of ammunition and leather holders; sixteen thousand select horses went to graze in the Huaco Ravine, which is an immense valley closed off by a narrow pass. La Rioja was, besides the cradle of his power, the center point of the provinces that were under his influence. At the slightest signal, that arsenal would provide the elements for war to twelve thousand men. And don't think that this hiding of rifles in the forests is some kind of poetic fiction. Up to 1841, deposits of rifles were being dug up, and it is still thought, though without any basis, that not all the arms hidden in the ground back then have been exhumed. In 1830, General Lamadrid took control of a treasure of thirty thousand pesos belonging to Quiroga, and very soon afterward, another of fifteen was reported.

Quiroga wrote to him afterward, holding him responsible for ninety-three thousand pesos that, according to Quiroga, were contained in those two buried treasures, which without a doubt he had left in La Rioja along with others back before the Battle of Oncativo, at the same time that he was killing and tormenting so many citizens in order to grab their money for war. As for the true amounts that were hidden, General Lamadrid suspected afterward that Quiroga's assertion was correct, because having fallen prisoner, the discoverer offered ten thousand pesos for his freedom, and not having obtained it, killed himself by cutting his own throat. These events are too illustrative for me to refrain from telling them.

The interior provinces, then, had a leader; and the loser at Oncativo, who had been entrusted in Buenos Aires with no more troops than a few hundred convicts, could now see himself as the second, if not the first, in command. To make the splitting of the Republic into two factions even clearer, the provinces bordering the Río de la Plata had signed an agreement, or a confederation, in which they mutually guaranteed each other independence and freedom. It is true that feudal federalism existed there, strongly represented by López in Santa Fe, Ferré, Rosas, native leaders of the peoples they dominated; because Rosas was now beginning to be influential as an arbiter of public affairs. With Lavalle's defeat he had been named governor of Buenos Aires, serving in that position until 1832 according to law, just as anyone else could have. I should not, however, omit a fact that is an essential antecedent. From the be-

ginning, Rosas sought to be invested with "extraordinary powers," and
the resistance with which his partisans in the city opposed him is impossible to describe in detail. Nevertheless, he obtained those powers
through pleas and seduction, for as long as the war in Córdoba lasted;
when it ended, the demands to strip him of that unlimited power began
anew. At that time the city of Buenos Aires, whatever the partisan ideas
that divided its politicians might have been, could not imagine the
existence of an absolute government. Rosas, meanwhile, resisted mildly,
craftily. "It's not that I want to make use of those powers," he would
say, "but because as my secretary García Zúñiga says, a schoolteacher
needs to have a whip in his hand so his authority will be respected." This
comparison seemed irreproachable to him, and he repeated it ceaselessly. The citizens, children; the governor, the man, the master. The ex-
governor, however, did not step down to become just another citizen.
The work of so many years of patience and action was at the point of
completion; the legal period in which he had been in power had taught
him all the secrets of the fortress; he knew its avenues, its weak spots,
and if he left the government, it was only so he could take it by assault
from the outside, without constitutional restrictions, without fetters or
responsibility. He laid down the staff of command but armed himself
with a sword so as to return with it later on and then to lay down both
of them in exchange for the ax and the rods, ancient insignia of the Roman kings. A powerful expedition, of which he appointed himself the
leader, had been organized during the last period of his government to
secure and extend the southern borders of the province, the scene of
frequent incursions by savages. A general raid was to be made, as part of
a grand plan; an army composed of three divisions would operate along
a four-hundred-league front, from Buenos Aires to Mendoza. Quiroga
would command the interior forces, while Rosas would come down the
Atlantic coast with his division. The colossal size and usefulness of the
enterprise concealed from the eyes of the common people the purely
political idea that was hidden under such an attractive veil. Indeed: what
could be more beautiful than to secure the southern frontier of the Republic, choosing a great river as the Indian border and reinforcing it
with a chain of forts, not at all an impracticable goal, and one that had
been brilliantly developed in the voyage of Cruz from Concepción to
Buenos Aires?[2] But Rosas was very far from involving himself in enterprises that only tended toward the welfare of the Republic. His army
made an unceremonious trip to the Río Colorado, marching slowly and
making observations about the terrain, climate, and other conditions of
the land they covered. A few Indian huts were destroyed, some rabble

taken prisoner; this was the extent of the results of that pompous expedition, which left the frontier as undefended as it was before and as it remains to this very day. The divisions from Mendoza and San Luis had even less happy results, returning after a useless incursion into the deserts of the south. Rosas then raised for the first time his red flag, similar in every way to that of Algeria or Japan, and had himself be given the title of Hero of the Desert, corroborating the one he already had obtained of Illustrious Restorer of the Law, of that same law whose basis he proposed to abrogate.*

Facundo, too sharp to let himself be fooled about the objective of the great expedition, stayed in San Juan until the interior army divisions returned. The one led by Huidobro, which had entered the desert through San Luis, left heading straight for Córdoba, and its approach snuffed out a revolt led by the Castillos, whose objective was to remove from government the Reinafé brothers, who obeyed López. This revolt was made on behalf of Facundo's interests and with his inducement; its first ringleaders were from San Juan, where Quiroga resided, and all its supporters—Arredondo, Camargo, etc.—were decidedly partisan to him. The newspapers of the time said nothing, however, about Facundo's connections with that movement, and when Huidobro withdrew to his quarters, and Arredondo and the other caudillos were shot, nothing was left to be said or done about it, because the war to be

---

*Ranchers from southern Buenos Aires since have assured me that the expedition secured the border, driving off the untamed barbarians and subjugating many tribes who have formed a barrier protecting the *estancias* from incursions by the former, and that thanks to these benefits the population has been able to expand toward the south. Geography also made important conquests, discovering territories unknown until then and clearing up many questions. General Pacheco made a reconnaissance of the Río Negro, where Rosas had allotted Choelechel Island to himself, and the Mendoza division discovered the entire course of the Río Salado out to where it channels into the Yauquenes Lagoon. But an intelligent government would have secured once and for all the southern frontiers of Buenos Aires. The Río Colorado, navigable from slightly below Cobu-Sebu, forty leagues' distance from Concepción, where it was crossed by General Cruz, offers along its entire course, from the Andes to the Atlantic, a border that at little cost would be impassable for the Indians. As for the province of Buenos Aires, a fort established where the Guamaní stream channels into the Monte Lagoon, supported by another in the area of the Salinas Lagoon toward the south, another in the Ventana sierra, finally relying on Fort Argentina in Bahía Blanca, would have permitted settlement of the immense space of territory lying between this last point and Fort Independence in the Tandil sierra, the southern border of the populated area of Buenos Aires. To complete this system of occupation, it would also be necessary to establish agricultural settlements in Bahía Blanca and at the mouth of the Río Colorado, in such a way for them to serve as a market for the exporting of products of the surrounding regions; because, since the entire coast from there to Buenos Aires lacks ports, the products of the most advanced *estancias* of the south are lost, as wool, tal-

waged between the two factions of the Republic, the two caudillos who silently fought for command, would have to be one of ambushes, snares, and betrayals. It was a bitter combat, in which strength did not square off against strength, but rather audacity on one side and astuteness and cunning on the other. This struggle between Quiroga and Rosas is little known, although it spans a period of five years. They detested each other, scorned each other; neither lost sight of the other for a moment, because each felt that his life and his future depended on the results of this terrible game.

I think it opportune to make clear with a chart the Republic's political geography from 1832 on, so the reader will better understand the movements that began to come about:

ARGENTINE REPUBLIC

ANDEAN REGION	RIO DE LA PLATA BASIN
Unit under the influence of Quiroga	*Federation under the pact of the League of the Plata*
Jujuy	Corrientes—Ferré
Salta	
Tucumán	Entre Ríos
Catamarca	Santa Fe ⎫
La Rioja	Córdoba ⎬ López
San Juan	Buenos Aires—Rosas
Mendoza	
San Luis	

FEUDAL FACTION

Santiago del Estero, under the domination of Ibarra

---

low, hides, horns, etc. cannot be transported without losing their value in the costs of shipping.

The navigation and settlement of the upper Río Colorado would bring, besides the products that it could create, the benefit of evicting the savages, few in number, who would be cut off from the north, causing them to look for territory south of the Colorado.

Far from having secured the frontier in a permanent manner, since the time of the southern expedition the barbarians have invaded and depopulated the entire countryside in Córdoba and San Luis, in the first up to the very edge of the Río Tercero, and in the second up to San José del Morro, which is at the same latitude as the city. Since then, both provinces live in continual alarm, with troops constantly at the ready; this, along

López extended his influence from Santa Fe into Entre Ríos through Echagüe, a Santa Fe native and one of his creations, and into Córdoba through the Reinafés. Ferré, a man of independent, provincial spirit, kept Corrientes out of the struggle until 1839; under the government of Berón de Astrada, he turned that province's arms against Rosas, who, with the growth of his power, had made the pact of the League of the Plata illusory. In 1840 that same Ferré, because of that spirit of narrow provincialism, declared Lavalle a deserter for having crossed the Paraná with the army of Corrientes; and after the battle of Caaguazú, he took the victorious army from General Paz, thus wasting the decisive advantages that triumph could have produced.

Ferré, in these operations as in the League of the Plata, which he had promoted years earlier, was inspired by a provincial spirit of independence and isolation that the Revolution of Independence had awakened in everyone's soul. So then, the same sentiment that had thrown Corrientes into opposition to the Unitarist Constitution of 1826, after 1838 threw it into opposition to Rosas, who was centralizing power. Here is born the error of that caudillo, and the disasters that followed the battle of Caaguazú, useless not only for the Republic in general, but also for the province of Corrientes itself; for, with the rest of the nation centralized by Rosas, it could hardly maintain its feudal, federal independence.

With the southern expedition over—or better put, broken up, since it didn't have a true plan or a real end—Facundo left for Buenos Aires accompanied by his escort and by Barcala, and entered the city without having bothered to announce his arrival to anyone. These operations, subversive to all accepted form, could be the subject of a very long commentary had they not been systematic and characteristic. What objective took Quiroga to Buenos Aires this time? Was it another invasion, like that of Mendoza, which he was making into the center of his rival's

---

with the system of depredation by government officials, makes a more ruinous plague than the incursions of the savages. Cattle raising has almost died out, and the ranchers hurry along its extinction to free themselves at last from the levying of the government on the one hand and the depredations of the Indians on the other.

Because of an inexplicable political system, Rosas forbids the frontier governments from undertaking any expeditions against the Indians, letting them invade the region periodically and devastate more than two hundred leagues of the frontier. This is what Rosas did not do, as he should have done, in the much-exaggerated southern expedition, whose results were ephemeral, leaving to survive the ills that later became more aggravated than before. (Author's note to the second edition.)

power? Had the spectacle of civilization, finally, dominated his wild roughness, and did he want to live in the bosom of luxury and comfort? I think all these causes together advised Facundo to take his ill-advised trip to Buenos Aires. Power educates, and Quiroga had the highly gifted spirit that allows a man always to fit his new position, however lofty it may be. Facundo established himself in Buenos Aires, and very soon he was surrounded by the most notable men: he bought six hundred thousand pesos' worth of public funds, played for high and low stakes, spoke scornfully of Rosas, declared himself a unitarist among unitarists, and the word "Constitution" never left his lips. His past life, his acts of barbarism, little known in Buenos Aires, were explained and justified by the need to triumph, by that of self-preservation. His conduct was measured; his air, noble and imposing, despite the fact that he wore a jacket, a poncho slung over him, and his beard and hair enormously full.

Quiroga, during his residence in Buenos Aires, made some tests of his personal power. A man, knife in hand, did not want to surrender to the night watchman. Quiroga happened to pass by the scene, wrapped in his poncho as always; he stopped to watch, and suddenly threw the poncho, seized and immobilized the man. After disarming him, he himself took him to the police station, without having given his name to the watchman, nor did he give it at the station either, where nevertheless he was recognized by an officer. The next day the newspapers published that bold act. Quiroga found out one day that a certain apothecary had spoken scornfully of his acts of barbarism in the provincial interior. He went to his shop and interrogated him. The apothecary asserted himself and told him he wasn't in the provinces anymore and couldn't knock people around with impunity. This event filled the whole city of Buenos Aires with pleasure. Poor Buenos Aires, so naive, so proud of its institutions! One year later, you would be treated with more brutality than that of Quiroga in the interior! The police had their agents enter Quiroga's very room, in pursuit of the man in residence, and Quiroga, seeing himself treated with such lack of consideration, extended his arm, grabbed his knife, sat up straight in the bed where he was lying down, and then immediately reclined again and slowly let go of the homicidal weapon. He knew there was another power besides his own, and that they could put him in jail if he defended himself.

His sons were in the best schools; he never permitted them to wear anything but a tailcoat or a frock coat, and when one of them tried to leave his studies and embrace a career at arms, Quiroga made him a drummer in a battalion until he regretted his foolishness. When some colonel talked to him about enlisting one of his sons in his corps as an officer, he answered mockingly: "If it were a regiment commanded by Lavalle, sure, but in this corps . . . !" Regarding writers, there was none that, in his conception, could rival the Varelas, who had said so many bad things about him. The Republic's only honorable men were Rivadavia and Paz: "They both had the best intentions." To the unitarists, he said he needed only a secretary like Dr. Ocampo, a politician who could write a constitution; and then with a printing press, he would march to San Luis and from there show it to the whole Republic on the point of a lance. Quiroga, then, presented himself as the center of a new attempt to reorganize the Republic, and one could say that he openly conspired, if all these proposals, all that talk, had had deeds behind them that gave them substance. The lack of work habits, the laziness of the shepherd, the custom of expecting terror to do everything, perhaps the novelty of the theater of events, paralyzed his thoughts, kept him in a deadly expectancy that ultimately compromised him and delivered him, in shackles, to his astute rival. We have no facts to prove that Quiroga meant to act immediately, besides his communications with the provincial governors and his indiscreet words, repeated by unitarists and federalists, without convincing the former to place their future in hands such as his, or the federalists to reject him as a deserter from their ranks.

And while he abandoned himself like this to a dangerous indolence, every day he saw the boa that would suffocate him in its redoubled coils coming nearer. In 1833, Rosas was busy with his fantastic expedition and had his army operating to the south of Buenos Aires, from where he observed the Balcarce government. The province of Buenos Aires shortly thereafter presented a most singular spectacle. I imagine what would happen on the earth if a powerful comet were to come near it: at first, a general disturbance, then vague, muffled noises; next, oscillations of the globe pulled out of its orbit; until finally, the convulsive shaking, the collapse of mountains, the cataclysm, would bring the chaos that precedes every one of the successive creations to which our globe has been witness.

Such was the influence Rosas exercised in 1834. The government of Buenos Aires felt itself ever more circumscribed in its action, more restricted in its movement, more dependent on the Hero of the Desert. Every communication from the latter was a reproach directed to the governor, an exorbitant amount needed for his army, some unusual demand. Then the countryside stopped obeying the city and a complaint had to be made to Rosas about this defiance of his followers. Later on, the disobedience entered the city itself; ultimately, armed men went through the streets on horseback, firing shots that killed passersby. This disorganization of society grew larger, day by day, like a cancer, advancing right to the heart, although one could discern a path that went from Rosas's camp to the countryside, from the countryside to the suburbs of the city, and from there to a certain class of men, the slaughterers, who were the principal instigators. The Balcarce government succumbed in 1833 to the drive of the countryside spilling into the city. Rosas's party worked ardently to clear a wide-open path for the Hero of the Desert, who was close to getting the ovation he deserved, the government; but the Federalist party in the city still resisted his efforts and wanted to oppose him. The Chamber of Representatives met in the midst of the conflict caused by the acephalism of the government, and General Viamonte, at its call, appeared quickly, in civilian clothes, and even dared to take over the government. For a moment, it seemed that order had been restored and the poor city could breathe; but then began the same agitation, the same maneuvers, the bands of men going through the streets, dealing out lashes to passersby. The state of alarm in which the entire city lived for two years, with this strange, systematic unhinging, is indescribable. Suddenly people were seen scattering through the streets, and the sound of doors slamming shut repeated from block to block, from street to street. What were they running from? Why did they lock themselves inside, in the middle of the day? Who knows! Someone had said that they were coming . . . that a band had been seen in the distance . . . that the faraway tumult of horses had been heard.

One of those times, Facundo Quiroga was marching down a street, followed by an aide, and upon seeing these men in tailcoats running down the sidewalks, the ladies fleeing without knowing from what, Quiroga stopped, let a gaze of contempt wander over those crowds, and said to his aide-de-camp: "These people have gone crazy!" Quiroga had arrived in Buenos Aires soon after the fall of Balcarce. "It would have happened differently if I'd been here," he would say. "And what would you have done, General?" replied one of those who was listening to him, "Your Excellency has no influence over these common people of Buenos Aires." Then Quiroga, raising his head, shaking his black mane and with flashing eyes, said to him in a terse, short voice: "Look here! I would have gone into the street and said to the first man I met: 'Follow me!' and that man would have followed me!" Such was the overwhelming energy of Quiroga's words, so imposing his physiognomy, that the incredulous man lowered his eyes, terrified, and for a long time no one dared unseal his lips.

General Viamonte finally resigned because he saw that governing wasn't possible, that there was a powerful hand stopping the wheels of administration. A search was made for someone wanting to replace him. The most enthusiastic men were asked to please take over the office, and no one wanted to; they all shrugged their shoulders and went home, frightened. Finally Dr. Maza, the teacher, mentor, and friend of Rosas, was placed at the head of government, and they thought they had cured the ill that afflicted them. A vain hope! Far from diminishing, the illness grew. Anchorena petitioned the government, asking that the disorder be put down, knowing that it had no means at all at its disposal, that the police force did not obey, that orders were coming from outside. General Guido and Dr. Alcorta, in the Chamber of Representatives, still made some energetic protests against the convulsive agitation in which the city was held, but the ills continued, and to make them worse, Rosas reproached the government from his camp for the disorder that he himself had fomented. What was it that this man wanted? To govern? A committee from the Chamber went to offer him the government: they told him that only he could put an end to that anguish, that two years of agony. But Rosas didn't want to govern, so new committees, new pleas. Finally he found a way to reconcile everything. He would do them the favor of governing, if the legal three-year term was lengthened to five, and if he was given the sum of public power, a new word whose scope only he understood.[3]

The city of Buenos Aires and Rosas were engaged in these transactions when news arrived of a disagreement between the governments of Salta, Tucumán, and Santiago del Estero that could cause an outbreak of war. Five straight years had gone by since the Unitarists disappeared from the political scene, and two since the Federalists of the city, the *lomos negros,* had lost all their influence in the government; at most, they had the strength to demand a few conditions that made capitulation tolerable.[4] While the city surrendered at discretion, along with its institutions, its individual rights, its restrictions on government, outside of Buenos Aires Rosas put into motion another, no less complicated machinery. His relationship with López, in Santa Fe, was ongoing, and besides that he had a meeting where both caudillos conferred. The government of Córdoba was under the influence of López, who had put the Reinafés at its head. Facundo was asked to go and use his influence to put out the sparks that had flared up in the north of the Republic; he was the only one summoned to carry out this peace mission. Facundo resisted, hesitated, but finally accepted. On December 18, 1835, he left Buenos Aires, and climbing up into the carriage, with several friends present, said his good-byes to the city.[5] "If I succeed," he said, waving his hand, "I'll see you again; if not, good-bye forever!" What sinister premonitions raised their ghastly heads at that moment in the soul of this undaunted man? Does the reader not recall something similar to what Napoleon expressed as he left the Tuilleries for the campaign that would end at Waterloo?

Scarcely having gone half a day's journey, he came to a muddy stream that stopped the carriage. The master of the local post solicitously came to aid in its crossing. New horses were hitched, all efforts were stepped up, and the carriage did not advance. Quiroga became furious and had the master himself yoked to the carriage shaft. Brutality and terror appeared once again as soon as he found himself in the country, in the midst of that nature and that semibarbarous society. That first obstacle overcome, the carriage kept crossing the Pampas like a shot; it went every day until two in the morning and started out anew at four. Quiroga was accompanied by his secretary, Dr. Ortiz, and by a young acquaintance he had come upon while leaving the city, unable to continue the journey because his own vehicle's wheels were broken. Upon arriving at each post, he immediately asked: "When did a courier from Buenos Aires pass through?" "An hour ago." "New horses and don't waste a second!" Quiroga cried. And the march continued. To make the situation even sorrier, it seemed like waterfalls had opened up from the sky; for three days, the rain didn't cease for a moment and the road had become a torrent.

Entering the jurisdiction of Santa Fe, Quiroga's uneasiness increased and turned into visible anguish when, at the Pavón post, he learned that there were no horses and that the postmaster was absent. The time that went by before a new team was obtained was mortal agony for Facundo, who kept on shouting: "Horses! Horses!" His traveling companions understood nothing of this strange fright, amazed to see this man, the terror of all the towns, now so scared and full of seemingly chimerical fears. When the carriage was able to get under way, he murmured in a low voice, as if talking to himself: "If I can get through Santa Fe, I won't have to worry about the rest." At the Río Tercero crossing, the gauchos from the area came to see the famous Quiroga, and they almost carried the carriage across on their shoulders.

Finally, he arrived in the city of Córdoba at nine-thirty at night, one hour after the arrival of the Buenos Aires courier, whose heels he had been on from the start. One of the Reinafés came to the post, where Facundo still sat inside the carriage asking for horses, of which there were none at that moment. He greeted Facundo with respect and effusion, pleading with him to spend the night in the city, where the government was preparing to host him in a worthy manner. "I need horses!" was the brief answer Quiroga gave. "Horses!" he replied to each new expression of attention or courtesy on the part of Reinafé, who finally left in humiliation, and Facundo departed for his destination at twelve midnight.

Meanwhile, the city of Córdoba was stirring with the strangest rumors: the friends of the young man who had come along with Quiroga by chance and who stayed on in Córdoba, his hometown, mobbed to visit him. They were amazed to see him alive, and told him of the imminent danger from which he had escaped. Quiroga was to have been assassinated at a certain place, the assassins were A and B, the pistols were bought at a certain store, C and D were asked to carry out the execution and they had refused. Quiroga had surprised them with the astonishing speed of his march, since the courier had scarcely come to announce his arrival when he himself showed up, making them abort all their plans. Never had an assault been more blatantly premeditated; all Córdoba knew the smallest details of the government's intended crime, and Quiroga's death was the subject of everyone's conversation.

Quiroga, meanwhile, arrived at his destination, settled the differences between the hostile leaders, and returned through Córdoba, despite the reiterated pleas of the governors of Santiago and Tucumán, who offered him a heavy escort for his safety, advising him to return by the road through Cuyo. What vengeful temper closed his heart and his ears and made him obstinately challenge his enemies again, without escort, without adequate means of defense? Why didn't he take the road to Cuyo, dig up his immense stockpile of arms on the way through La Rioja, and arm the eight provinces under his influence? Quiroga knew everything. He had received warning after warning in Santiago del Estero; he knew the danger from which his diligence had saved him; he knew the new, more imminent one that awaited him, because his enemies had not desisted from their already conceived design. "To Córdoba!" he cried to the postilions as they set out, as if Córdoba would be the end of his journey.*

Before arriving at the Ojo de Agua post, a young man came out of

---

*In the criminal case made against the accomplices in the death of Quiroga, the prisoner Cabanillas declared in an effusive moment, kneeling in the presence of Doctor Maza—whose throat was cut by Rosas's agents—that his only plan was to save Quiroga; that on

the woods and headed toward the carriage, forcing the postilion to halt. Quiroga put his head out the door and asked what he could do for him. "I want to speak with Dr. Ortiz." The latter climbed down from the carriage and learned the following: "In the area near the place called Barranca-Yaco, Santos Pérez is stationed with a posse. When the carriage arrives they are to open fire on it from both sides and immediately kill everyone from the postilions on up. No one is to escape. Those are the orders." The young man, who at another time had been helped by Dr. Ortiz, had come to save him; he had a horse right there so that he might mount and escape with him; his hacienda was nearby. The secretary, frightened, informed Facundo of what he had just learned, and urged him to get to safety. Facundo again interrogated the young Sandivaras, thanked him for his kind act, but calmed him of the fears he harbored. "The man isn't born yet," he told him in an energetic voice, "who's going to kill Facundo Quiroga. With one shout from me, tomorrow that posse will follow my orders and serve as my escort to Córdoba. You may go, my friend, don't worry."

These words of Quiroga's, of which I hadn't learned until this moment, explain the cause of his strange obstinacy in going out to defy death. Pride and terrorism, the two great impulses behind his rise, led him in shackles to the bloody catastrophe that would end his life. He thought avoiding danger was beneath him, and counted on making the knives held over his head drop with the terror of his name. This was the explanation I was giving myself before I learned that his own words made it superfluous.

The night the travelers spent at the post of Ojo de Agua was one of such anguish for the poor secretary, who was going to a certain and inevitable death and lacked the valor and rashness that drove Quiroga, that I believe I should omit none of its detail, all the more so since, luckily, its particulars are so authentic that it would be criminal neglect not

---

December 24 he had written to a friend of the latter, a Frenchman, to get word to Quiroga not to pass through the San Pedro forest, where he was waiting with twenty-five men to assassinate him by order of his government; that Toribio Junco—a gaucho of whom Santos Pérez would say: "There is someone braver than me: Toribio Junco"—had told this same Cabanillas that, observing a certain confusion in Santos Pérez's behavior, he began to follow him, until one day he found him kneeling in the chapel of the Virgin of Tulumba with his eyes burning with tears; that when he inquired what caused his suffering, he said: "I'm asking the Virgin to tell me if I should kill Quiroga like they've ordered me to; because they presented this to me as an action agreed on by Governors López of Santa Fe and Rosas of Buenos Aires, as the only means to save the Republic." (Author's note from the second edition.)

to record them. Because if ever there is a time when a man drinks down all the dregs of agony, if ever a time when death must seem horrible, it is when a sad duty, that of accompanying a rash friend, forces it on us, when there is no disgrace or dishonor in avoiding it.*

Dr. Ortiz took the postmaster aside and questioned him pleadingly about what he knew of the strange warnings they had received, assuring him that he would not betray his confidence. What details he heard! Santos Pérez had been there with his party of thirty men an hour before. They were all armed with sabers and carbines; they were by now stationed in the designated place; all those accompanying Quiroga had to die; Santos Pérez had said so to the postmaster himself. This confirmation of the news received earlier did not alter Quiroga's determination at all. After drinking a cup of chocolate, as was his custom, he slept profoundly. Dr. Ortiz also went to bed—not to sleep, but to think about his wife, his children, whom he would never see again. And all for what? To not face the anger of a fearsome friend, to not incur the stain of disloyalty. At midnight, his agony made the bed unbearable. He got up and went to look for his confidant: "Are you asleep, friend?" he asked in a low voice. "Who could sleep, *señor*, with such a terrible thing as this!" "So there is no question at all? What torment I must bear!" "Imagine, *señor*, how I feel, when I have to send out two postilions who will be killed too! This kills me. There's a boy here who's the nephew of the sergeant of Santos's party, and I'm planning to send him; but the other one . . . whom will I send? to have him die innocently!"

Dr. Ortiz made one last effort to save his life and that of his companion. He awakened Quiroga and informed him of the horrific details he had just learned, stating that he would not accompany him if he insisted on getting himself killed needlessly. Facundo, with angry gestures and crudely forceful words, gave him to understand that there was greater danger in opposing him there than in what awaited him at Barranca-Yaco, and he was forced to submit with no further discussion. Quiroga ordered his assistant, a brave black man, to clean a few firearms that were in the carriage and to load them. That was the extent of all his precautions.

Daylight arrived, finally, and the carriage set out. Besides the postil-

---

*I got these details from the unfortunate Doctor Piñero, killed in Chile in 1846 and a relative of Señor Ortiz, traveling companion of Quiroga from Buenos Aires to Córdoba. It is without doubt a sad necessity to cite none but the dead in support of the truth. (Author's note to the second edition.)

ion riding with the team, it was accompanied by that boy, two messengers who had joined it by chance, and the black man, who was on horseback. It reached the fatal spot, and two discharges pierced through the carriage on both sides, but without wounding anyone. The soldiers fell on it with their sabers bared, and in a moment had disabled the horses and cut the postilion, messengers, and assistant into pieces. Then Quiroga put his head out the door and, for a moment, made that mob hesitate. He asked who commanded the party, ordered him to approach, and to Quiroga's question of "What is all this?" received only the answer of a bullet in the eye, which left him dead. Then Santos Pérez repeatedly ran his sword through the ill-fated envoy, and, the execution completed, ordered the carriage full of bodies dragged into the woods, along with its shattered horses, and the postilion, still sitting on his horse with his head cut open. "Who is this boy?" he asked, seeing the child from the post, the only one left alive. "He's my nephew," answered the sergeant of the party, "I'll answer for him with my life." Santos Pérez came up to the sergeant, put a bullet through his heart, and then, dismounting, took the boy by the arm, laid him on the ground, and cut his throat despite his whining moans, which were those of a child who knew he was in danger. This last moan of the child was, nevertheless, the only torment that caused agony to Santos Pérez. Later on, fleeing from the posses pursuing him, hidden in the rocky crags or the tangled woods, the wind brought to his ears the pitiful moan of the boy. If, in the flickering starlight, he ventured out of his lair, his uneasy gaze bore into the darkness of the gloomy trees to assure himself that the whitish little shape of the boy was nowhere to be seen; and when he reached the place where two roads crossed, he dreaded seeing the boy riding on his horse, coming down the road he had just left.

Facundo also used to say that he suffered remorse for only one thing: the death of the twenty-six officers shot in Mendoza!

Meanwhile, who was this Santos Pérez? He was the bad gaucho of the Cordoban countryside, celebrated in the sierra and the city for his numerous murders, for his extraordinary daring, for his unprecedented adventures. While General Paz remained in Córdoba, he led the most stubborn, untouchable *montoneras* of the sierra, and for a long time, the area of Santa Catalina was its own little republic, into which the veteran soldiers of the army could not penetrate. With more lofty goals, he would have been a worthy rival of Quiroga; with his vices, he only managed to be his assassin. He was tall and had a handsome face, pale in color, with a curly, black beard. For a long time afterward he was pursued by the law, and no less than four hundred men were out on the search. At first the Reinafés had summoned him, and he was received warmly at the government palace. Leaving the meeting, he began to feel a strange stomach upset, and thought to consult a doctor friend of his, who, upon hearing that he had drunk a glass of liquor they offered, gave him an elixir that made him throw up—just in time—the arsenic the liquor had disguised. Later on, during the heaviest persecution, his old friend Commander Casanova got word to him that he had something important to tell him. One afternoon, while the squadron led by Commander Casanova went through exercises across from his house, Santos Pérez dismounted at the door and said to him: "Here I am; what did you want to tell me?" "Well! Santos Pérez, come in, sit down." "No! Why have you had me called here?" The commander, thus surprised, hesitated and didn't know what to say right away. His astute and bold interlocutor understood, and throwing him a look of contempt and turning away, said, "I was certain you wanted to betray me and arrest me! I only came to make sure." When the squadron was ordered to pursue him, Santos had disappeared. Finally, one night they caught him in the city of Córdoba, because of a woman's revenge. He had beaten up the mistress he was sleeping with. She, knowing he was profoundly asleep, got up cautiously, took his pistols and saber, went into the street, and denounced him to the police. When he woke up, surrounded by rifles pointed at his chest, he reached for his pistols, and not finding them, he said serenely: "I surrender. You've taken my pistols!" The day they brought him into Buenos Aires, an immense mob had gathered outside the government palace. On seeing him the masses cried: Death to Santos Pérez! and he, shaking his head contemptuously and running his gaze over that multitude, murmured only these words: "If only I had my knife with me!" Getting out of the wagon that took him to prison, he shouted repeatedly, "Death to the tyrant!" and on the way to the scaffold, his gigantic frame, like that of Danton, rose above the crowd, and his gaze sometimes fixed on the gallows as if it were an architect's scaffolding.

The government of Buenos Aires gave solemn pomp to the execution of the assassins of Juan Facundo Quiroga. The carriage, blood-stained and bullet-marked, was exhibited for examination by the public for a long time, and a portrait of Quiroga as well as a view of the gallows with the executed criminals were lithographed and distributed by the thousands; so were excerpts from the trial, published in a volume of folios. An impartial history still awaits facts and revelations, in order to point its finger at the instigator of the assassins.

CHAPTER XIV

Unitarist Government

No one knows just why it is that *he wants to govern*. Only one thing has been determined, which is that he is possessed of a fury that torments him: *he wants to govern!* He is a bear who has broken the bars of his cage, and as soon as he has *his government* in his hands, he will make everyone flee. Woe to the one who falls into his hands! He will not let him go until he expires under *his government*. He is a leech that will not come off until it fills with blood.

Lamartine[1]

In the introduction to these hasty notes, I have said that in my opinion Facundo Quiroga was the nucleus of civil war in the Argentine Republic, and the clearest, simplest expression of one of the forces that have been fighting under different names for thirty years. The death of Quiroga was not an isolated event, or without consequences. Social causes, which I have explained earlier, made it almost inevitable; it was a political denouement of the kind that could have caused a war.

The government of Córdoba, which was in charge of committing the assault, was too subordinate among existing governments to have dared undertake the project with such boldness, had it not believed itself supported by those who would reap the results. The murder of Quiroga was, then, an official act, extensively discussed among various governments, planned in advance, and carried out with tenacity, like a state policy. Given that his death doesn't end the series of events I have proposed to connect, in order not to leave it incomplete and cut short I must continue a bit further along this road, to examine the outcome produced in the internal politics of the Republic, until the number of bodies covering the path becomes so great that I am forced to halt and wait for time and bad weather to destroy them so they will not obstruct my march. Through the door left open by the murder at Barranca-Yaco, the reader will enter with me into a theater where the bloody drama is not yet finished.

Facundo died on February 18.[2] News of his death reached Buenos Aires on February 24, and by the beginning of March everything was in place for the necessary and inevitable government of the campaign commander in chief, who since 1833 had been torturing the city, causing it exhaustion, anguish, desperation, until finally, amid sobs and moans, he had wrested from it the "Sum of Public Power." Because this time Rosas hadn't been content to demand a dictatorship, extraordinary powers, etc. No, what he requested was what the phrase expressed: traditions, customs, accepted forms, rights, laws, religion, ideas, conscience, lives, possessions, concerns—sum up everything that has power over society and the result will be the Sum of Public Power he requested. On April 5, the Chamber of Representatives, complying with the stipulated terms, elected as governor of Buenos Aires, for five years, General Don Juan Manuel Rosas, Hero of the Desert, Illustrious Restorer of the Laws, holder of the Sum of Public Power.

But he wasn't satisfied with the election held by the Chamber of Representatives. What he was pondering was so big, so new, so unheard of, that first all imaginable precautions had to be taken; it should not be said later that the people of Buenos Aires hadn't delegated to him the Sum of Public Power. Rosas, as governor, put this question to the electorate: did they agree that Don J. M. Rosas should be governor for five years, with the Sum of Public Power? And I have to say, in tribute to historical truth, never was there a more popular government, more desired or better supported by public opinion. The Unitarists, who hadn't participated at all, received it at most with indifference; the Federalists, the *lomos negros,* with disdain, but without opposition; the peaceful citizens, as a blessing and an end to the cruel fluctuations of two long years; and lastly, the countryside, as a symbol of its power and the humiliation of the *cajetillas* from the city.[3] With such a positive disposition, elections or ratifications were begun in all parishes, and the vote was unanimous, except for three votes opposed to the delegation of the Sum of Public Power. How can we imagine it to have happened that in a province of four hundred thousand inhabitants, according to what the *Gaceta* reported, there were only three votes against the government? Could it perhaps be that the dissidents didn't vote? Not at all! There is still no evidence of a single citizen who did not vote; the sick got up from their beds to go give their assent, afraid that their names would be written on some blacklist, because such had been the insinuation.

Terror was already in the atmosphere, and although thunder hadn't yet exploded, everyone saw the grim, black cloud that had been covering the sky for two years. That vote is unique in the annals of civilized peoples, and the names of the three crazy men—rather than spirited opposers—have become part of the lore of the city of Buenos Aires.

There is a fatal moment in the history of every people, and it is when political parties, tired of struggling, before all else ask for the respite they have lacked for long years, even at the expense of liberty or of the goals to which they had aspired. This is the moment when the tyrants who found dynasties and empires rise up. Rome, tired of the struggles of Marius and Sulla, of patricians and plebeians, surrendered with delight to the sweet tyranny of Augustus, the first one heading the execrable list of Roman emperors. France, after the Terror, after the impotence and demoralization of the Directory, surrendered to Napoleon, who, down a road sown with laurels, subjected it to the allies who returned it to the Bourbons. Rosas had the cleverness to speed up that tiredness, to create it by making rest impossible. Once the master of absolute power, who would ask him for it back later? Who would dare dispute his title to dominance? The Romans granted dictatorships in rare cases, and for short, fixed terms, and even so, the use of a temporary dictatorship authorized a perpetual one, which destroyed the republic and brought all the unbridledness of the empire. When Rosas's term expired, he announced his definite decision to retire to private life. The death of his dear wife, that of his father, had eaten into his heart; he needed to go far away from the tumult of public affairs, to cry in the comfort of his own home over such bitter losses. The reader should recall, on hearing such language from Rosas's mouth—he who hadn't seen his father since his youth and who had given his wife such bitter times—something similar to the hypocritical protests of Tiberius before the Roman senate. The Buenos Aires Assembly begged him, beseeched him to continue making sacrifices for the homeland. Rosas allowed himself to be persuaded, he would stay only for six more months; the six months passed, and the farce of an election was abandoned. And, in fact, why did a chief who had rooted power in his own person need to be elected? Who would call him to account, trembling with the terror he had inspired in all?

When the Venetian aristocracy snuffed out the Tiepolo conspiracy in 1300, it named from its own bosom ten individuals who, invested with discretionary powers, were to pursue and punish the conspirators, but the duration of their authority was limited to only ten days. Let us hear the count of Daru, in his celebrated *History of Venice,* relating the event:

The danger was thought to be so imminent that a dictatorial authority was created after the victory. A council of ten members was named to safeguard the preservation of the state. It was armed with every means, it was freed of every form, every responsibility; every head was bowed to it.

It is true that its duration was not to go for more than ten days. Nevertheless, it was necessary to extend that for ten more days, then for twenty, then two months; but finally, it was extended six times in a row for this last term. After a year in existence, it had itself continued for five more. Then it became strong enough to extend itself for ten more years, until that terrible tribunal was declared in perpetuity.

What it had done to prolong its duration, it did to extend its powers. Instituted solely to deal with crimes of the state, this tribunal had taken control of the administration. Under pretext of safeguarding the security of the republic, it meddled in war and peace, used public funds and ended up assuming sovereign power.*

In the Argentine Republic, it is not a council that has taken control of supreme authority in this way; it is a man, and a very unworthy man. Temporarily in charge of foreign relations, he deposed, executed, murdered the governors of the provinces that had put him in charge. Clad with the Sum of Public Power in 1835 for five years only, in 1845 he is still clad with that power. And no one today would be so naive as to expect him to give it up, or that the people would dare ask him to. His government is for life, and if Providence allows him to die peacefully like Dr. Francia, long years of pain and misery await those unfortunate peoples, today the victims of a moment's exhaustion.

On April 13, 1835, Rosas was invested into government office. His easy manner and his self-assurance at the ceremony didn't fail to surprise those dreamers who had imagined themselves having a good time, watching the clumsiness and gaucherie of a gaucho. He appeared in a general's coat, unbuttoned to reveal a yellow cotton vest. I ask those who may not understand the spirit behind this singular toilette to forgive me for recalling that particular circumstance.

So now he had the government in his hands. Facundo had died a

Histoire de Venise, vol. II, bk. VII, p. 84. (Author's note to the first edition.)

month earlier; the city had surrendered of its own will; the people had confirmed, in the most authentic way, this surrender of all rights and every institution. The state was a *tabula rasa* upon which he would write something new, original; he was a poet, a Plato who would realize his ideal republic, according to how he had conceived it. This was a work he had pondered for twenty years and could finally give birth to, without old traditions, the concerns of this era, European-style copies, individual rights, institutions in force, standing in the way of its realization. He was a genius, finally, who had been lamenting the errors of his century and preparing himself to destroy them in one blow. Everything was going to be new, the work of his intelligence: let us look at this wonder.

From the Representative Assembly, where he had gone to receive the staff of office, he left in a red carriage, painted to order *ex profeso* for the ceremony, to which were tied red silk ribbons, and to these were yoked those men who since 1833 had held the city in a continual state of alarm with their assaults and impunity. They were called the Sociedad Popular, and they wore a dagger at the waist, a red vest, and a red ribbon, on which was written: "Death to the unitarists."[4] At the door to his home, these same men formed his honor guard; afterward came the citizens, then the generals, because it was necessary to make that show of limitless adherence to the person of the Restorer.

The next day, a proclamation and a list of banned persons appeared, on which was included one of his in-laws, Dr. Alsina. That proclamation, which is one of Rosas's few writings, is a precious document that I regret not having at hand. It was a program of his government, without disguise, without evasion:

HE WHO IS NOT WITH ME IS MY ENEMY.[5]

Such was the axiom of the policy it established. It announced that blood would flow, and merely promised that no attempts against property would be made. Woe to those who provoked his rage!

Four days later, the parish of San Francisco announced its intention to celebrate a Mass and Te Deum to give thanks to the Almighty, etc., inviting the neighborhood to solemnify, with its presence, the ceremony. The surrounding streets were paved, carpeted, decorated. It was like an Oriental bazaar, displaying woven damasks, purple, gold, and precious stones in fanciful designs. People filled the streets, young people came for the novelty, ladies made their afternoon stroll through the parish. The Te Deum was postponed from one day to the next, and the stir in the city, the coming and going, the excitement, the interruption of all work lasted for four, five consecutive days. The *Gaceta* recorded the most minimal details of the splendid affair. Eight days later, another parish announced its Te Deum; the neighbors proposed to rival in enthusiasm and surpass the first celebration. What luxurious decorations, what a display of riches and adornments! The portrait of the Restorer was in the street on a canopy which combined red velvet with gold tassels and cording. The same activity for even more days; everyone lived in the streets of the favored parish. A few days afterward, another parish, another fiesta in another neighborhood. But how long would these fiestas go on? Did these people never tire of spectacle? What kind of enthusiasm was this that didn't cool after a month? Why didn't all the parishes hold their affair at the same time? No, this was systematic, orderly enthusiasm, administered little by little. A year later, the parishes still had not finished giving their fiestas; the official vertigo went from the city into the countryside, and was unending. The *Gaceta* of the time was there, busy for a year and a half describing the federalist fiestas. The portrait was part of all of them, pulled along, in a cart made especially for it, by the generals, the ladies, the "pure" federalists. "Et le peuple, enchanté d'un tel spectacle, enthousiasmé de Te Deum, chanté moult bien a Nôtre Dame, le peuple oublia qu'il payait fort cher tout, et se retirait fort joyeux."*

From these fiestas, after a year and a half, the color red ended up being an insignia of adherence to the cause. Rosas's portrait, at first placed on the altars, later on became part of the outfit of every man, who had to wear it on his chest as a sign of "intense love for the person" of the Restorer. Lastly, from among these fiestas finally emerged the terrible Mazorca, a police corps of enthusiasts, federalists, whose job was, at first, to give malcontents enemas of chili peppers and turpentine, and later, this phlogistic treatment not sufficing, to cut the throats of anyone so indicated to them.

All America has mocked those famous fiestas of Buenos Aires and seen them as the height of a people's degradation, but I see in them only a political design, one most fruitful in results. How to incarnate in a republic that never had a king the idea of the personality of government? The red ribbon is a materialization of the terror that accompa-

Chronique du moyen âge. (Author's note from the first edition.) ["And the people, entranced by such spectacle, enthused by the Te Deum, sang very well in Notre Dame, the people forgot they would pay for it all very dearly, and they went away very happy" (trans. K. Ross).]

nies you everywhere, in the streets, in the bosom of the family; it must be thought about when dressing, when undressing, and ideas are always engraved upon us by association. Seeing a tree in the country reminds us of something we had a conversation about ten years before, when we passed nearby; imagine the ideas that the red ribbon brings along with it, and the indelible impressions that it must leave united with Rosas's image. Thus, in a communication of a highly placed official of Rosas, I have recently read "that it is an emblem their Government has ordered all its employees to wear, as a sign of conciliation and peace."[6] The words "Death to the savage, disgusting, filthy unitarists" are, to be sure, very conciliatory, so much so that only in exile, or in the grave, are to be found those who dare deny its effectiveness. The Mazorca has been a powerful instrument of conciliation and peace; if you do not think so, go see the results and search the earth for a city more reconciled and peaceful than Buenos Aires. Upon the death of Rosas's wife, which a brutal comment of his own had precipitated, he commanded that the honors of a captain general be paid to her and ordered a mourning period of two years in the city and the provincial countryside, which consisted of wearing a wide crepe band tied to one's hat with a red ribbon. Imagine a cultured city, men and boys dressed in European style, uniformed for two entire years with a red trim on their hats! Does it seem ridiculous to you? No! There is nothing ridiculous when everyone, without exception, participates in the extravagance, and above all, when the whip or the chili-pepper enemas are there to make you as serious as a statue if you get tempted to laugh. The night watchmen sang out every quarter hour: "Long live the illustrious Restorer! Long live Doña Encarnación Ezcurra![7] Death to the godless unitarists!" The sergeant, before company roll call, repeated the same words; the child, getting out of bed, greeted the day with the sacramental phrase. Less than a month ago, an Argentine mother staying at a Chilean inn said to one of her children, who awoke repeating aloud, "Long live the federalists! Death to the savage, disgusting unitarists!": "Quiet, son, don't say that here, it's not the custom; don't say it again, don't let them hear you!" Her fear was justified: they heard him! What politician has Europe produced who has been able to comprehend the means for creating the idea of the personality of a government head, or the long-term tenacity to incubate the idea for fifteen years, or who has used means more varied or more conducive to his objective? Nevertheless, we may console ourselves that Europe has supplied a model for the American genius. The Mazorca, with the same characteristics, composed of the same men, existed in France during the Middle Ages, at the time of the wars between the parties of the Armagnacs and the duke of Burgundy. In the *History of Paris*, written by G. Fouchare La Fosse, I find these singular details: "These instigators of the assassination, with the goal of having the Burgundians recognized everywhere, had already ordered that they wear on their clothing the cross of St. Andrew, the principal element of the coat of arms of Burgundy, and to tighten the bond within the party, they immediately thought of forming a Brotherhood under the protection of that same St. Andrew. Each member would wear as a distinctive emblem, besides the cross, a crown of roses. . . . A horrible confusion! The symbol of innocence and tenderness on the heads of the throat-cutters! . . . Roses and blood![8] . . . The odious society of the Cabochiens, that is, the horde of butchers and slaughterers, was loosed upon the city like a troop of hungry tigers, and these numberless executioners bathed themselves in human blood."*

In the place of the cross of St. Andrew, put the red ribbon; instead of the red roses, the red vest; instead of the Cabochiens, the *mazorqueros;* instead of 1418, the date of that society, 1835, the date of this one; instead of Paris, Buenos Aires; instead of the duke of Burgundy, Rosas, and you will have the copy made in our own times. The Mazorca, like the Cabochiens, was originally made up of the butchers and slaughterers of Buenos Aires.[9] How instructive is history! How it repeats itself time and again!

Another creation of that era was the opinion census. This was a truly original institution. Rosas ordered that a registry be compiled in the city and the countryside by the justices of the peace, in which was noted the name of each inhabitant, classifying him as unitarist, indifferent, federalist, or pure federalist. In the schools, the rectors were given this duty, and it was carried out everywhere with the most scrupulous attention to detail, checking it afterward and allowing for complaints arising from imprecision. These registries, collected later by the government, have served for seven years to supply throats to the tireless knife of the Mazorca.

The thought of gathering statistics on the opinions of an entire people, characterizing them according to significance, and with the registry at hand, spending ten years at the task of removing all the adverse numbers, destroying in the person the germ of hostility, without a

---

Histoire de Paris, vol. III, p. 176. (Author's note to the first edition.)

doubt is stunning in its audacity. History shows me nothing equal to it, except the classifications of the Inquisition, which distinguished heretical opinions as rude, offensive to pious ears, almost heresy, heresy, pernicious heresy, etc. But even so, the Inquisition did not make a registry of Spain to exterminate generations and individuals before they were denounced to the Holy Tribunal.

Since my idea is only to show the new order of institutions that supplanted the ones we were copying from Europe, I need to group the principal ones without regard to date. The execution we call shooting, of course, was substituted with that of cutting the throat. It is true that one morning forty-four Indians were shot in a city plaza, leaving all of them lying dead in this slaughter, for although savages, they were, in the end, men. But little by little, this was abandoned and the knife became the instrument of justice.

Where has this horribly extravagant man gotten such strange ideas of government? I will record some facts. Rosas comes from a family persecuted as "Goths" during the Revolution of Independence.[10] His education at home suffered from the hardness and stubbornness of the old, noble customs. I have already said that his mother, with a hard, gloomy character, made her servants kneel down to her right up until these last few years. Silence surrounded him during his childhood, and the spectacle of authority and servitude must have left lasting impressions on him. There was something extravagant about his mother's character, and this has been reproduced in Don Juan Manuel and his two sisters. Scarcely into puberty, he became insufferable to the family, and his father banished him to an *estancia*. Rosas, with some short breaks, has resided in the countryside of Buenos Aires for almost thirty years, and by 1824 he was already an authority consulted by the cattle-industry associations about matters regarding the *estancias*. He is the best horseman in the Argentine Republic, and when I say in the Argentine Republic, I suspect in the whole world, because not even equestrians or Arabs have to deal with the wild horses of the Pampas.

He is a prodigy of activity; he suffers from nervous attacks when life is so overwhelming that he needs to jump onto a horse and go racing through the Pampas, yelling uncontrollably, rolling around, until, finally, the horse exhausted and sweating rivers, he returns to his rooms, now fresh and ready for work. Napoleon and Lord Byron suffered from these fits, from these furors caused by an excess of life.

Rosas distinguished himself from early on in the countryside, for the vast business sowing leagues of wheat fields that he tackled and ran successfully, and above all, for the harsh administration, for the iron discipline that he introduced into his *estancias*. This was his masterpiece, his type of government, which he would try out later on in the city itself. One must understand the Argentine gaucho and his innate propensities, his inveterate habits. If, passing through the Pampas, you propose to give him an *estancia* with cattle that will make him a rich landowner, or if he is running to find the local lady doctor so that she might save his mother or his beloved wife whom he has left in agony, and an ostrich crosses his path, he will go after it, forgetting the fortune you offer him, his dying wife or mother. And he isn't the only one dominated by this instinct: even his horse whinnies, shakes its head, and pulls at the bit with impatience to go flying after the ostrich. If, ten leagues away from home, the gaucho finds his knife missing, he goes back to get it, even though he may be a block from where he was going, because for him the knife is like breathing, his very life. Very well then: On his *estancias*, which join together under different names from the Cerrillos hills to the Cachagualefú stream, Rosas has succeeded in having ostriches walk around in herds and even to stop fleeing when a gaucho approaches. That is how safely and peacefully they can graze on Rosas's lands, and this is so although by now they have been wiped out in all the adjacent countryside. As for knives, none of his peons ever carried one, despite the fact that the majority of them were murderers sought by the law. One time he had forgetfully placed his dagger in his waistband, and the overseer pointed it out to him; Rosas pulled down his own pants, and ordered them to give him the two hundred lashes which was the penalty imposed on his *estancia* for anyone carrying a knife. There are those who doubt this fact, which he himself admitted and made public, but it is authentic, as are the bloody extravagances and peculiarities that the civilized world has obstinately refused to believe for ten years. Authority above all, respect for commands, although they may be ridiculous or absurd; he will spend ten years in Buenos Aires and the whole Republic having people whipped and throats cut, until the red ribbon is part of the existence of an individual, like his very heart. In front of the whole world, with no accommodation whatsoever, he will repeat in every official communication, "Death to the disgusting, savage, filthy unitarists!" until the whole world learns and gets used to hearing this bloody cry without scandal, without a reply, and now we have seen a magistrate in Chile offer tribute and acquiescence to this fact, which after all interests no one.

Where, then, has this man learned the plan of innovation that he introduced into his government, with contempt for the common sense, the traditions, the conscience, and the immemorial practice of civilized peoples? May God forgive me if I am wrong, but this idea has consumed me for a while: on the *estancia* where he had spent his whole life, and from the Inquisition, in whose tradition he had been educated. The parish fiestas were an imitation of the cattle branding, which all the neighbors attended. The red ribbon he stuck onto every man, woman, and child was the brand by which the landowner recognized his cattle. The throat cutting with a knife, elevated to a method of public execution, came from the custom of cutting the throats of steers, shared by every man of the countryside. The successive imprisonment of hundreds of citizens, without any known reason and for long years, was the roundup in which the cattle were tamed, closing them up daily inside the corral. The whippings in the street, the Mazorca, the orderly massacres, were some other methods of breaking the city, finally leaving it like the tamest, most orderly cattle known.

This tidiness and order have distinguished the private life of Don Juan Manuel de Rosas, whose *estancias* were cited as models for the peons' discipline and the tameness of the cattle. If this explanation seems monstrous and absurd, give me another; show me the reason why there is such a frightening coincidence between the way he manages an *estancia*, its policies and administration, and the government, policies, and administration of Rosas. Even the respect he had back then for private property came from the fact that the gaucho governor is a property owner! Facundo respected property as if it were his life. Rosas has persecuted cattle thieves as obstinately as unitarists. His government has shown itself to be implacable against poachers of hides in the countryside, and hundreds of them have had their throats cut. This, without a doubt, is laudable; I am only explaining the origin of his antipathy.

But there was another part of society that had to be moralized and taught to obey, to get excited when it should get excited, to applaud when it should applaud, to be quiet when it should be quiet. With the possession of the Sum of Public Power, the Representative Assembly became useless, since the law emanated directly from the person of the chief of the Republic. However, appearances were maintained, and for fifteen years some thirty individuals have been reelected who keep up to date on business. But past tradition had assigned another role to the Assembly; there, Alcorta, Guido, and others had made heard, in the days of Balcarce and Viamonte, pronouncements of freedom and reproaches to the instigator of the disorder. He needed, then, to break with this past and give a serious lesson for the future. Dr. Don Vicente Maza, president of the Assembly and the Chamber of Justice, adviser to Rosas and the one who had contributed the most to his rise, saw one day that his portrait had been removed from the hall of the Tribunal by a detachment of the Mazorca. During the night, they broke the windowpanes of his house, where he had taken refuge. The next day he wrote to Rosas, in other times his protégé, his godson, protesting the strangeness of these proceedings and his innocence of any crime. On the night of the third day, he went to the Assembly, and was dictating his resignation to his scribe when the knife that cut his throat interrupted the dictation. The representatives started to arrive, the carpet was covered with blood, the body of the president still lay there. Señor Irigoyen proposed that the following day the greatest possible number of carriages should gather to properly accompany the illustrious victim to the cemetery. Don Baldomero García said: "I think that is fine, but . . . not so many coaches . . . what for?" General Guido entered and they informed him of the idea, to which he answered, fixing on them with wide eyes and staring: "Coaches? Accompaniment? Have the Police cart come and take him away right now." "That's what I was saying," García went on, "Why the coaches?" The next day's *Gaceta* announced that the godless Unitarists had assassinated Maza. A governor of an interior province, terrified, upon learning of this catastrophe said, "It's not possible that Rosas was the one who had him killed!" To which his secretary added: "And if he did do it, he must have had a reason"; with which all present agreed.

In fact, he did have a reason. His son, Colonel Maza, had plotted a conspiracy involving the whole army, and afterward Rosas said that he had killed the old father so as not to give him the grief of seeing his beloved son die.

But I still have to go into the vast area of Rosas's general policies with respect to the entire Republic. He now had his government; Facundo had died, leaving orphaned the eight provinces unified under his influence. The Republic marched visibly toward the unity of government to which it was condemned by its flat surface, its sole port. It was said to be federalist, they called it the Argentine Confederation, but everything was heading for the most absolute unity; this had been forming since 1831, from the interior, in appearance, practice, and influence. As soon as Rosas took over the government in 1835, he declared in a proclamation that the godless Unitarists had premeditatively murdered the illustrious General Quiroga, and that he proposed to punish such a frightful assault, which had deprived the federation of its most powerful pillar. "What!" said the poor Unitarists, their mouths dropping wide open upon reading the proclamation, "What! . . . Are the Reinafés Unitarists? Aren't they a creation of López, didn't they go into Córdoba pursuing Paz's army, aren't they in active, friendly contact with Rosas? Didn't Quiroga leave Buenos Aires at Rosas's request? Didn't a courier go on ahead of him, announcing his arrival to the Reinafés? Didn't the Reinafés organize beforehand the posse that was going to assassinate him? . . . " None of that; the godless Unitarists were the assassins, and woe to the one who doubted it! . . . Rosas sent to Córdoba for the precious remains of Quiroga, the carriage in which he was killed, and in Buenos Aires they gave him the most sumptuous funeral ever seen up to that time. The entire city was ordered to go into mourning. At the same time, he directed a circular to all provincial governments, in which he asked them to name him as arbitrating judge, to try the case and judge the godless Unitarists who had murdered Quiroga. He indicated the procedure by which they should authorize him, and in private letters he stressed the importance of the measure; he flattered, seduced, and pleaded with them. The authorization was unanimous and the Reinafés were deposed, and all those who had taken part, had knowledge, or been relevant to the crime were arrested and taken to Buenos Aires. One of the Reinafés escaped, and was caught in Bolivian territory; another crossed the Paraná and later fell into Rosas's hands, after having escaped abduction by a ship captain in Montevideo. Rosas and Dr. Maza tried the case at night, behind closed doors. Dr. Gamboa, who took some liberty on behalf of a subordinate prisoner, was declared a godless Unitarist by Rosas's decree. Finally, all the criminals who had been caught were judged, and a voluminous excerpt of the case was made public. Two years later, López had died of natural causes in Santa Fe, although the doctor sent by Rosas to treat him later received a house from the municipality, as payment for his service to the government. Cullen, López's secretary at the time of Quiroga's death, and who upon López's death became governor of Santa Fe by disposition of the late man's legal will, was deposed by Rosas and finally removed from Santiago del Estero, where he had taken refuge and to whose governor Rosas sent a sack of gold or a declaration of war if that friend did not turn over his friend. The governor preferred the gold; Cullen was turned over to Rosas, and upon stepping over the border into Buenos Aires, he found an armed party and an officer, who made him dismount from his horse and had him shot. The Buenos Aires *Gaceta* later published a letter from Cullen to Rosas, in which there were clear indications of the complicity of the government of Santa Fe in the assassination of Quiroga, and since the late López, said the *Gaceta,* had full confidence in his secretary, he was unaware of the atrocious crime the latter was planning. No one could answer, back then, that if López was unaware Rosas was not, because the letter was sent to him. Ultimately, Dr. Don Vicente Maza, secretary to Rosas and prosecutor of the prisoners, died also with his throat cut, in the Assembly hall. So within two years, Quiroga, his assassins, the judges of the assassins, and the instigators of the crime, all received the gag put on indiscreet revelations by the grave. Go now and ask who ordered Quiroga killed. López? No one knows. A major of the auxiliary forces, Muslera, once said in front of many people in Montevideo: "It's taken me until now to find out why General Rosas had me held prisoner and incommunicado for two years and five months. The night before my arrest I was at his house. His sister and I were on the sofa, while he paced the length of the room with visible signs of distress. 'Can you guess,' the lady said to me, 'why Juan Manuel is acting like this? It's because he sees me with this little green branch I have in my hands. Now you'll see,' she added, tossing it to the floor. In effect, Don Juan Manuel shortly stopped pacing, came over to us, and said to me in a friendly tone: 'And what are they saying in San Luis about Quiroga's death?' 'They say, sir, that Your Excellency is the one who had him killed.' 'Really? Rumor gets around. . . . ' He kept on pacing, then I said goodnight, and the next day I was imprisoned, and stayed there until the day that news arrived of the victory at Yungay, when I was set free along with two hundred others." Major Muslera also died fighting against Rosas, which has not kept the same thing he heard from being said up to this day.

But the common people have seen nothing more than a horrible crime in Quiroga's death and the trial of his assassins. History will see something else: in the first, the fusion of the Republic into a compact unit, and in the trial of the Reinafés, provincial governors, the action that constituted Rosas as chief of an absolute, unitarist government, which from that day and because of that act constituted the Argentine Republic. Rosas, invested with the power to judge another governor, established in the consciousness of the rest the idea of the supreme authority with which he was invested.

He tried the Reinafés for a proven crime, but then he immediately ordered that Rodríguez, the governor of Córdoba who succeeded the Reinafés, be shot without trial for not having obeyed all of his instructions. Right after that he shot Cullen, the governor of Santa Fe, for reasons only he knew, and ultimately he issued a decree in which he declared that no government of the other provinces would be recognized as valid without obtaining his *exequatur*. If there was any doubt left that he had assumed supreme command, and that the other governors were mere pashas to whom he might send a purple cord whenever they didn't carry out his orders, he issued another one, in which he derogated all the existing laws of the Republic from 1810 forward, although they might have been dictated by general congresses or some other competent authority, declaring also to be null and invalid everything that, in following and carrying out those laws, had been done until then. I ask: What legislator, what Moses or Lycurgus, went further with his attempt to remold a society according to a new plan? The 1810 revolution, by this decree, was left derogated. No law or agreement was left in force; the field for innovation, as clean as the palm of a hand, and the entire Republic subjugated, without even fighting one battle and without consulting with the caudillos. He extended the Sum of Public Power, with which he was invested only for Buenos Aires, to the whole Republic, because not only was it not said that what had been established was a unitarist system, of which Rosas's person was the center, but with greater determination than ever went the cry: Long live the federation; death to the unitarists! The epithet "unitarist" stopped being the emblem of a party, and now expressed all that was execrable: Quiroga's assassins were unitarists; Rodríguez was a unitarist; Cullen, a unitarist; Santa Cruz, who tried to establish a Peruvian-Bolivian confederation, a unitarist. The patience Rosas has shown in setting the meaning of certain words, and the tenacity to keep repeating them, is admirable. Long live the confederation! Long live the illustrious Restorer! Death to the savage unitarists! must have been seen written down in the Argentine Republic thirty million times in the last ten years, and neither Christianity nor Islam ever so multiplied their respective symbols, the cross and the crescent, to externally stereotype moral beliefs in material, tangible form. It was still necessary to refine that insult of unitarist. First it was unitarists, plain and simple; later on, the godless unitarists, thus favoring the concerns of the ultra-Catholic party that had seconded his rise. When he freed himself of that poor party, and the knife had also reached the throats of priests and canons, it was necessary to give up the name godless. Chance supplied the circumstances. The Montevideo newspapers started to call Rosas savage; one day, the Buenos Aires *Gaceta* appeared with this addition to the ordinary theme: death to the savage unitarists. The Mazorca repeated it, all the official communications repeated it, the governors of the interior repeated it, and its adoption was consummated. "Repeat the word *savage*," Rosas wrote to López, "until you are sick of it, until it bores you, until you tire of it. I know what I'm saying, my friend." Later, *filthy* was added; later, *disgusting*; later, finally, Don Baldomero García said in a communication to the Chilean government, which was used to open the trial of Bedoya, that that emblem and slogan were a sign of conciliation and peace, because the whole system comes down to mocking common sense. The unity of the Republic is realized by dint of denying it, and since everyone is saying "federation," of course there is unity. Rosas called himself the one in charge of foreign relations of the Republic, and only when the fusion was consummated and had become custom, some ten years later, in Chile Don Baldomero García exchanged that title for the one of supreme director of the affairs of the Republic.

This, then, is the unitarized Republic, entirely subject to Rosas's decision; the old question of the parties of the city, denaturalized; the meaning of words changed, and the regime of the cattle ranch introduced into the administration of the Republic that had been the most warlike and most enthusiastic for the cause of liberty and had made the most sacrifices to attain it. López's death delivered Santa Fe to him; that of the Reinafés, Córdoba; that of Facundo, the eight provinces along the Andes. To take possession of all of them, he only needed some personal gifts, some friendly letters, and some outlays from the treasury. The auxiliary forces camped in San Luis received a magnificent wardrobe, and their salaries began to be paid out of Buenos Aires funds. Father Aldao, in addition to more than one amount of money, started to receive his general's salary directly from Rosas, and General Heredia from Tucumán, who when Quiroga died had written to a friend of his, "Ah, my friend! You do not know what the Republic has lost with the death of Quiroga! What a future, what great thoughts for man! He wanted to establish the Republic and summon all the émigrés, so that they might contribute with their knowledge and learning to this great work!" General Heredia received arms and money to prepare a war against the godless unitarist Santa Cruz, and he forgot quite quickly about the grand picture that Facundo had developed for him in the conversations they had before his death.

An administrative measure that influenced the whole nation came to serve as a test and demonstration of this unitarist fusion and absolute dependency on Rosas. Rivadavia had established weekly mail services that sent out and brought back correspondence from the provinces to

Buenos Aires, and a monthly one to Chile and Bolivia, for which were named the two general travel routes established in the Republic. The world's civilized governments today take great care to increase, at immense cost, mail service not only from city to city, day to day, and hour to hour, but also in the very bosom of the big cities, establishing branch offices, and between all points on earth by means of steamship lines that cross the Atlantic or follow the coast of the Mediterranean, because the wealth of nations, the security of business speculations, all depend on the facility to obtain news. In Chile, every day we see demands from towns that mail services be increased, as well as the care the government takes to multiply them by sea or by land. Amid this worldwide general movement to accelerate communications between peoples, Don Juan Manuel Rosas, to better govern his provinces, eliminated mail services, which have not existed anywhere in the Republic for fourteen years. In their place, he established government couriers, which he dispatches when there is an order or some news to communicate to his subordinates. This horrible, ruinous measure nevertheless has produced, for its own system, the most useful results. Expectation, doubt, uncertainty are maintained in the interior; the governors themselves go three or four months without receiving a dispatch, without knowing except by hearsay what is happening in Buenos Aires. When a conflict has passed, when some advantage has been gained, then the couriers leave for the interior, carrying loads of *Gacetas,* reports, and bulletins, with a letter to the governor, his friend and comrade, announcing that the savage unitarists have been defeated, that divine Providence is watching over the preservation of the Republic.

In 1843 it so happened that in Buenos Aires flour had an exorbitant price and the interior provinces were ignorant of this. Some people, who had private news from their correspondents, sent shipments that left them with huge profits. Then the provinces of San Juan and Mendoza, en masse, started speculating in flour. Thousands of loads crossed the Pampas, arrived in Buenos Aires, and found . . . that two months before prices had gone down so much that they didn't even cover shipping costs. Later, rumor went around in San Juan that flour had gone up in Buenos Aires; the farmers raised prices; offers increased; wheat was bought in exorbitant quantities; it accumulated in several hands, until finally a mule driver who arrived at the market discovered that there had been no change whatsoever, and she left her load of flour because there were no buyers at all. Imagine, if you can, towns set at immense distances, being governed in this manner!

Even in these last few years, the consequences of his outrages have helped him consummate his unitarist work. The government of Chile, scorned for its complaints about the wrongs inflicted on its subjects, thought it opportune to cut commercial relations with the provinces of the Cuyo region. Rosas applauded the measure and kept quiet. Chile was providing something he himself hadn't dared to attempt, which was to close all commercial routes that didn't go through Buenos Aires. Mendoza and San Juan, La Rioja and Tucumán, which supplied cattle, flour, soap, and other valuable industries to the provinces of northern Chile, have abandoned that business. One envoy has come to Chile that waited six months in Mendoza until the Andes route shut down, and that for three months, as of now, has not said a word about opening trade.

With the Republic organized under a communications plan so rich in results, Rosas tightened the organization of his power in Buenos Aires, putting it on a lasting basis. He had thrust the countryside upon the city; but, abandoning the *estancia* for the Fort, needing to moralize that same countryside as a landowner and to erase the path down which other campaign commanders could follow his footsteps, he dedicated himself to raising an army that grew day by day, which was supposed to maintain the obedience of the Republic and take the standard of the holy cause to all the neighboring peoples.

The army wasn't the only force that had substituted for the adhesion of the countryside and the public opinion of the city. Two different peoples, two diverse races, came to his aid. There exists in Buenos Aires a multitude of blacks, from the thousands taken by privateers during the war with Brazil. They form associations according to the African peoples to which they belong, have public meetings, a municipal fund, and a strong esprit de corps, which supports them amid the whites.

The Africans are known by all travelers as a warlike race, full of imagination and fire, and although fierce when they are excited, docile, loyal, and attached to the master or the one who employs them. The Europeans who penetrate the African interior take blacks into their service who defend them from other blacks and who expose themselves to great danger on their behalf.

Rosas shaped public opinion and a strong group of followers for himself within the black population of Buenos Aires, and he entrusted his daughter Doña Manuelita with this part of his government. The influence that black women had with her, her favor with the government, has always been limitless. A young man from San Juan was in Buenos Aires when Lavalle was approaching in 1840; anyone leaving the city limits would receive the death penalty. An old black woman, who in other times had belonged to his family and had been sold in Buenos Aires, recognized him; she learned he was being detained. "Little master," she said to him, "why didn't you let me know? I'm going to get you a passport right away." "You?" "Me, little master; Señorita Manuelita won't say no to me." Fifteen minutes later, the black woman returned with a passport signed by Rosas, with orders for the soldiers to let him leave freely.

The blacks, won over to the government in this way, put into Rosas's hands zealous espionage within the bosom of every family, through servants and slaves, and in addition provided him with excellent, incorruptible soldiers of another language and a savage race. When Lavalle neared Buenos Aires, the Fort and Santos Lugares, lacking soldiers, were full of enthusiastic black women dressed as men to fill out the forces. The adhesion of blacks gave Rosas's power an indestructible base. Happily, continual wars have now exterminated the masculine part of this population, who found their own homeland and its form of government in the master whom they served. To intimidate the countryside, he brought into the southern forts some savage tribes whose caciques were under his command.

With these principal points secured, time would consolidate the work of the unitarist organization that crime had started and that deception and astuteness sustained. The Republic thus reconstructed, the federalism of the provinces suffocated, and because of persuasion, self-interest, or fear, all its governments obeying the impulse they received from Buenos Aires, Rosas needed to go beyond the limits of his state, to show off outside it, to exhibit in public view the work of his intelligence. What good did it do him to absorb the provinces, if in the end he was going to remain, like Dr. Francia, with no luster abroad, with no contacts or influence over neighboring peoples? The strong unity given to the Republic was only the firm base he needed to launch himself and prove himself in a higher theater, because Rosas was conscious of his own worth and expected everlasting fame.

At the invitation of the government of Chile, he took part in the war the latter state was waging against Santa Cruz. What motives made him embrace with such fervor a faraway war that had no history for him? A fixed idea that had dominated him since long before taking over the supreme government of the Republic, namely, the reconstruction of the old viceroyalty of Buenos Aires. It wasn't that he imagined taking control of Bolivia then, but rather, with issues pending regarding national borders, he demanded the province of Tarija. Time and circumstances would give him the rest. On the other bank of the Río de la Plata, there was also a dismantling of the viceroyalty: the Oriental Republic. There Rosas found ways to establish his influence with the Oribe government, and while he couldn't get the press to stop attacking him, he at least succeeded in getting the peaceful Rivadavia, the Agüeros, Varelas, and other notable unitarists expelled from Oriental territory. From then on, Rosas's influence came more and more into play in that Republic, until finally ex-president Oribe became one of Rosas's generals, and the Argentine immigrants joined with the nationals in posing resistance to this conquest, disguised with specious names. Later on, when Dr. Francia died, Rosas refused to recognize the independence of Paraguay, always thinking about his favorite idea: the reconstruction of the old viceroyalty.

But all these manifestations of the Argentine confederation weren't enough to show him in all his glory. He needed a vaster field, more powerful antagonists, more burning issues, a European power, finally, with which he could have it out and show what an original American government really is, and this time fate did not shy away from offering it to him.

France maintained in Buenos Aires, in the capacity of consular envoy, a young man with heart, capable of ardent sympathy for civilization and liberty. M. Roger was in contact with the literary youth of Buenos Aires, and he watched, with the indignation of a young, French heart, the immoral acts, the subversion of all principles of justice, and the enslavement of a people he held in high esteem. I do not wish to enter into an appraisal of the ostensible motives that motivated the French blockade, but rather the causes that had been preparing a coalition between Rosas and the envoys of the European powers. The French, above all, had distinguished themselves since 1828 in their decided enthusiasm for the cause supported by the old unitarists. M. Guizot has said before Parliament that his fellow citizens are very meddlesome. I will not put such competent authority into doubt; all I will assert is that, among us, the French residents always showed themselves to be French, Europeans, and men with heart. If later, in Montevideo, they have done what they did in 1828, this could prove that they are meddlesome at all times, or perhaps that there is something about the political questions of the Plata that affects them directly. However, I do not understand how M. Guizot imagines that in a Christian country, where French residents have their children and their future and expect to make their definitive homeland, they are going to watch with indifference while a system of government that destroys all guaranteed rights of civilized societies— and abjures all the traditions, doctrines, and principles that tie that country to the great European family—is built and consolidated. If the scene were in Turkey or Persia, I understand very well that foreigners getting into the arguments of the inhabitants would be overly meddlesome; among us, and when the issues are of the type being aired there, I find it very difficult to believe that the same M. Guizot maintains calm enough not even to wish for the triumph of that cause that is most in agreement with his education, customs, and European ideas. Whatever the reason might be, what is certain is that the Europeans, of whatever nation they may be, have warmly embraced one party, and for this to happen very profound social causes must militate to overcome the natural egotism of the foreigner; the Americans themselves have always shown more indifference.

Rosas's *Gaceta* complains to this day about the purely personal hostility of Purvis and other European envoys who favor Rosas's enemies, even against the express orders of their governments. These personal antipathies of civilized Europeans, more than the death of Bacle, prepared the way for the blockade. The young Roger tried to put France's weight into the balance in which the civilized, European party that Rosas was destroying didn't weigh enough, and M. Martigny, as passionate as he, seconded him in that work, more worthy of that ideal France that French literature has made us love than of the true France, which today goes dragging itself after all sorts of base deeds, with no lofty thoughts.

A disagreement with France, for Rosas, was perfectly ideal for his government, and it would be hard to say who made the quarrel more bitter: whether M. Roger with his complaints and his desire to make that barbarous tyrant fall, or Rosas, motivated by his grudge against foreigners and their institutions, dress, customs, and ideas of government. "This blockade," said Rosas, rubbing his hands with happiness and enthusiasm, "is going to take my name over the whole world, and America will see me as the defender of its independence." His predictions have gone further than he could have expected, and without a doubt neither Mehemet Ali nor Abdel Kader today enjoys a fame on earth more talked about than his. As for defender of American independence, a title he has assumed for himself, today the enlightened men of America are beginning to dispute it, and perhaps the facts sadly are coming to show that only Rosas could have thrown Europe upon America and forced it to intervene in the problems stirring on this side of the Atlantic. The declared triple intervention was the first that had taken place in the new American states.

The French blockade was the public channel by which the feeling properly called Americanism came to manifest itself without disguise. Everything barbarous about us, everything that separates us from cultured Europe, has emerged since then in the Argentine Republic, organized into a system and ready to make us an entity apart from peoples of European ancestry. Alongside the destruction of all the institutions we tried everywhere to copy from Europe, went the persecution of the tailcoat, fashion, sideburns, tight trousers, elegant hairstyles, and vest cuts. This European outward appearance was substituted by loose, wide pants, red vests, short jackets, and ponchos, as eminently national, American dress, and this same Don Baldomero García who today brings to us in Chile that "Death to the savage, disgusting, filthy unitarists" as "a sign of conciliation and peace," was thrown out of the Fort by force one day when, as magistrate, attending a hand-kissing reception, he had the disgusting, filthy savagery to appear in a tailcoat.

From then on, the *Gaceta* cultivated, expanded, stirred, and developed in its readers a feeling of hatred for Europeans, contempt for the forces that wanted to conquer us. The French, it called mangy, and puppeteers; Louis Philippe, a pig keeper, a unitarist; and European policy, barbarous, disgusting, brutal, bloody, cruel, inhuman. The blockade started, and Rosas selected a means for resisting it worthy of a war between him and France. He took away the salaries of university professors and from the primary schools for girls and boys, the generous donations Rivadavia had assigned to them. He closed all charitable institutions; crazy people were thrown into the streets, and the neighbors took on the task of locking those wretched, dangerous people up in their homes. Was there not exquisitely penetrating insight in these measures? Was not a true war being made on France, which led Europe in knowledge, by attacking it through public education? Rosas's address announces every year that the zeal of the citizens maintains public institutions. Barbarian! It is the city that tries to save itself from being turned into the Pampas, if it abandons the education that ties it to the civilized world! And in fact, Dr. Alcorta and other young men have given lessons for free in the university for many years, so that courses of study will not be closed; schoolteachers continue to teach and ask the students' fathers for a donation to live on, because they want to continue giving lessons. The Beneficent Society secretly visits homes, looking for subscriptions; it improvises resources to support the heroic lady teachers, who, as long as they do not die of hunger, have vowed not to close their schools, and on May 25 every year present their thousands of students, girls dressed in white, to show their achievement in public examinations. . . . Oh, hearts of stone! Still you ask us why we fight!

With this, I would consider ended the life of Facundo Quiroga, and the consequences deriving from it in the historical events and politics of the Argentine Republic, if, as a conclusion to these notes, it were not still left for me to appraise the moral consequences that the struggle of the pastoral countryside with the cities has brought, and the results, sometimes favorable, sometimes adverse, that it has produced for the future of the Republic.

CHAPTER XV

Present and Future

Après avoir été conquérant, après s'être déployé tout entier, il
s'épuise, il a fait son temps, il est conquis lui-même; ce jour-la il
quitte la scène du monde, parce qu'alors il est devenu inutile à
l'humanité.

Cousin[1]

France's blockade had lasted for two years, and the "American" government, inspired by "American" spirit, was facing off with France, European principles, European pretensions. The social results of the French blockade, however, had been fruitful for the Argentine Republic, and served to demonstrate in all their nakedness the current state of mind and the new elements in the struggle, which were to ignite a fierce war that can end only with the fall of that monstrous government. Rosas's personal government continued its ravages in Buenos Aires, its unitarist fusion in the interior provinces, while abroad it presented itself as gloriously facing off with the pretensions of a European nation and reclaiming American power against every attempted invasion. Rosas had proven, so it was said all over America and is still being said today, that Europe is too weak to conquer an American state that wants to uphold its rights.

Without denying this unquestionable truth, I believe what Rosas made manifest is the crass ignorance in which Europe exists regarding European interests in America, and the true means of making those interests prosper without diminishing American independence. Additionally, in these last years the Argentine Republic owes a debt to Rosas for having filled the civilized world with its name, its struggles, and a discussion of its interests, and for having put it into more immediate contact with Europe, forcing learned men and politicians there to commit to the study of this transatlantic world, which is destined to play such an important role in the future world. I am not saying that today those men are much more advanced in their knowledge, but rather that they are now in the process of learning, and that in the end the truth will be known. The French blockade, seen in its material aspects, was an obscure event that led to no historical outcome; Rosas ceded his claims, France let its warships rot in the waters of the Plata: this was the whole story of the blockade.

The implementation of Rosas's new system brought a singular result, namely, that the population of Buenos Aires had fled and gathered in Montevideo. It is true that on the left bank of the Plata remained the women, the materialistic men, those who gnaw their bread under the rule of any tyrant, the men, that is, for whom the importance of liberty, civilization, and dignity of the homeland comes after that of eating and sleeping. But all that limited portion of our society, and of all human societies, for whom living under a rational government and preparing its future destiny count for something in the dealings of life was gathered in Montevideo, where, in any case, because of the blockade and the lack of personal security, Buenos Aires commerce and the principal foreign companies had transferred business.

So the old Unitarists were in Montevideo, with all the personnel of the Rivadavia administration, its supporters, eighteen generals of the Republic, its writers, ex-congressmen, etc. Also there were the Federalists of the city, who emigrated from 1833 on; that is to say, all the notable people hostile to the 1826 Constitution, expelled by Rosas, with the nickname of *lomos negros*. Later came the abettors of Rosas who had not been able to watch their handiwork without horror, or who, sensing the exterminating knife coming near them, had tried to save their lives and the homeland, like Tallien and the Thermidorians, by destroying the very thing they had created.[2]

Lastly, a fourth element had gathered in Montevideo that was neither unitarist, nor federalist, nor ex-Rosista, and had no affinity with any of them, made up of the new generation that had reached manhood amid the destruction of the old order and the implantation of the new. As Rosas has been so careful and so determined to make the world believe that his enemies today are the Unitarists of 1826, I think it opportune to enter into some detail about this latest face of the ideas agitating the Republic.

The numerous young people that the Colegio de Ciencias Morales, founded by Rivadavia, had gathered together from all the provinces, whom the university, the seminary, and the many educational establishments that used to teem in that city—which at one time had the naïveté to call itself the Athens of America—had prepared for public life, found themselves without a forum, a press, a platform; without that public life, without a theater, in sum, in which to test the strengths of a young intelligence full of activity.[3] In addition, the close contact established with Europe by the Revolution of Independence, commerce, and the Rivadavia administration, so eminently European, had thrown Argentine youth into studying political and literary movements in Europe, and above all in France. Romanticism, eclecticism, socialism—all those diverse systems of ideas had devoted followers—and the study of social theories was carried out in the shadow of a despotism most hostile to all development of ideas. Dr. Alsina, giving classes in the university on legislation, after explaining what despotism was, added this final phrase: "In sum, gentlemen: do you want to have an exact idea of what despotism is? There you have the government of Don Juan Manuel Rosas with extraordinary powers." A deluge of clapping, sinister and threatening, drowned out the voice of the courageous professor.

Finally, those young people who hid with their European books to study in secret, with their Sismondi, their Lerminier, their Tocqueville, their *Revue des Deux Mondes*, their *Britannica* and *Revue Encylopédique*, their Jouffroy, their Cousin, their Guizot, etc., etc., questioned, agitated, communicated, and finally joined together, but not deliberately, without knowing exactly why, carried along by an impulse they thought was purely literary, as if letters ran the risk of being lost in that barbarous world, or as if good doctrine, persecuted above the surface, had to go hide in the underground refuge of the catacombs to emerge compact and strengthened for the fight with power.

The Salón Literario of Buenos Aires was the first manifestation of this new spirit.[4] Some periodical publications, some treatises in which appeared still badly digested European doctrines, were its first attempts. Until that point there were no politics, no parties; there were still many young men who, with the prejudice of French historical doctrine, thought that Rosas, his government, his original system, his reaction against Europe, were a national, American manifestation, in sum, a civilization, with its peculiar characteristics and forms. I will not enter into an appraisal of the real importance of these studies, or the incomplete, presumptuous, and even ridiculous phases that literary movement presented. They were tests of inexpert and juvenile strength that would not merit recall were they not the precursors of a movement more fruitful in results. From the bosom of the Salón Literario broke off a group of intelligent leaders, who, meeting in secret, proposed the formation of a Carbonaria that would spread, throughout the Republic, the basis for a civilized reaction against the barbarous government that had triumphed.[5]

Fortunately, I have at hand the original document of this association, and I can count with satisfaction the names who subscribed to it. The ones who bear those names are disseminated today over Europe and America, except for some who have paid their debt to the homeland with a glorious death on the battlefield. Almost all those who survive are today distinguished men of letters, and if one day intellectual powers come to play a part in the running of the affairs of the Argentine Republic, many, and very versatile instruments will be found in this pleiad of refugees, long prepared by talent, study, travel, misfortune, and the spectacle of the errors and mistakes they themselves have either witnessed or committed.

"In the name of God," says the document, "of the Homeland, of the Heroes and Martyrs of American independence; in the name of the blood and the tears uselessly spilled in our civil war, each and every one of the members of the association of this generation of Argentine youth:

BELIEVING

That all men are equal,
That all are free, that all are brothers, equal in rights and obligations,
Free in the exercise of their faculties for the good of all,
Brothers in the march to win that good and to fulfill human destiny;

BELIEVING

In the progress of humanity, having faith in the future,
Convinced that union constitutes strength,
That neither fraternity nor union can exist without the bond of
    principles,
And desiring to consecrate their efforts to the liberty and happiness of
    their homeland and to the complete regeneration of Argentine
    society;

SWEAR

1. to contribute, with their minds, their goods, and their hands, to the realization of the principles formulated in the symbolic words that form the basis of the pact of the alliance;

2. swear not to desist in the enterprise, whatever may be the dangers that threaten every one of the members;

3. swear to uphold them at any cost and to use all means at hand to spread and propagate them;

4. swear mutual fraternity, close unity, and perpetual silence concerning whatever might compromise the existence of the Association.

The "Symbolic Words," despite the emblematic obscurity of that term, were only the political creed recognized and professed by the Christian world, with the sole addition that associated members would disregard the ideas and interests that before had divided unitarists and federalists, with whom they could now harmonize since common misfortune had united them in exile.[6]

While these new apostles of the Republic and of European civilization were preparing to put their vows to the test, Rosas's persecution was now reaching them, young men with no political background, after having gone through his own partisans, through the Federalist *lomos negros,* and through the old Unitarists. It was necessary for them to save, then, along with their lives, the doctrines they had so sensibly formulated, and Montevideo saw arrive, one after another, hundreds of young men who abandoned their families, their studies, and their businesses to go search the eastern shore of the Plata for the support to topple, if they could, that dismal power who made himself a parapet of bodies and had for advance troops a legally constituted horde of assassins.

I have had to go into these details to characterize a great movement operating in Montevideo at that time, one which has scandalized America, giving Rosas a powerful moral weapon to strengthen his government and its "American" principles. I speak of the alliance of Rosas's enemies with the French who were blockading Buenos Aires, which Rosas has eternally thrown back at the Unitarists like an insult. But to honor historical truth and justice, I must declare, now that the occasion presents itself, that the true Unitarists, the men who figured prominently until 1829, were not responsible for that alliance. Those who committed that crime of lèse-Americanism, those who threw themselves into the arms of France to save European civilization, its institutions, customs, and ideas on the banks of the Plata, were the young men, in a word: us! I know very well that in the American nations Rosas finds his echo on this delicate point even among liberal, eminently civilized men, and that for many it is still an insulting error for the Argentines to have associated with foreigners to bring down a tyrant. But each man must rest on his convictions, and not back down from justifying himself with what he firmly believes and upholds in word and deed. So then, I will say in defiance of whomever it may be, that the glory belonged entirely to us of having understood that there was an intimate alliance between the enemies of Rosas and the civilized powers of Europe. The most eminent Unitarists, like the Americans, like Rosas and his satellites, were too prejudiced with the idea of nationality that is the patrimony of man since the savage tribes, which makes him look with horror at the foreigner. Among the Castilian people, this sentiment has gone so far as to turn into a brutal passion, capable of the greatest and guiltiest excesses, capable of suicide. The youth of Buenos Aires took with them this fertile idea of a fraternity of interests with France and England; they took a love for European peoples, associated with a love for the civilization, institutions, and letters that Europe had bequeathed to us and that Rosas was destroying in the name of America, substituting another mode of dress for European dress, other laws for European laws, another government for European government. This youth, impregnated with the civilizing ideas of European literature, was going to look to Rosas's European enemies for their ancestors, their fathers, their models, and support against America as presented by Rosas, barbarous like Asia, despotic and bloody like Turkey, persecuting and disdaining intelligence like Mohammedism. If the outcome hasn't corresponded to their expectations, the fault wasn't theirs; nor can those who criticize them for that alliance boast of having done better, either. For if the French finally did make a pact with the tyrant, that didn't mean they made any attempts against Argentine independence, and if they occupied Martín García Island for a moment, they soon summoned an Argentine leader to take it over. The Argentines, before associating themselves with the French, had demanded public declarations from the blockaders that they would respect Argentine territory, and had solemnly obtained them.

Meanwhile, the idea that the Unitarists fought so hard in the beginning—and that they called a betrayal of the homeland—spread, dominating and subjugating even them, and today it grows all over America and takes root in hearts and minds.

In Montevideo, then, France and the European Argentine Republic joined to bring down the monster of Americanism, son of the Pampas. Unfortunately, two years were lost in discussions, and when the alliance was signed, the problem in Oriente required the naval power of France, and the Argentine allies were left alone in the thick of it. In addition, unitarist prejudices prevented adoption of true military and revolutionary means for working against the tyrant, and the efforts that were attempted slammed into other elements that had been allowed to become more powerful. M. Martigny, one of the few Frenchmen who, having lived a long time among Americans, knew how to understand their interests and those of France in America, a sincere Frenchman who deplored every day the excesses, prejudices, and errors of those same Argentines whom he wanted to save, said of the old Unitarists: "They are the French émigrés of 1789; they have neither forgotten nor learned anything." And indeed, defeated by the *montonera* in 1829, they thought the *montonera* was still an element of the war and did not want to form a regular army; dominated at that time by the pastoral countryside, they now thought it useless to take control of Buenos Aires; with insurmountable prejudices against the "gauchos," they still saw them as their born enemies, nevertheless parodying their war tactics, their cavalry hordes, and even their uniforms.

A radical revolution, however, had been taking place in the Republic, and understanding that in time would have been enough to save it. Rosas, elevated to power by the countryside and scarcely secure in his government, had dedicated himself to taking away all its power. Through poison, through betrayal, through the knife he had killed all the campaign commanders who had aided his rise and substituted in their place men without ability, without reputation, armed, nevertheless, with the power to kill without accountability. In addition, the atrocities for which Buenos Aires was the bloody theater had made an immense multitude of citizens flee to the countryside; and mixing with the gauchos, they were slowly working a radical fusion between the men of the country and those of the city. Common misfortune joined them together; all of them execrated that monster who thirsted for blood and crime, bonding them forever in a common vow. The countryside, then, had stopped belonging to Rosas, and his power, lacking both this base and that of public opinion, had come to rely on a horde of disciplined assassins and on a regular army. Rosas, more shrewd than the Unitarists, had taken control of the weapon that they had abandoned gratuitously: the infantry and the cannons. Since 1835, he had disciplined his soldiers rigorously, and every day a squadron dismounted to swell out the battalions.

This didn't mean that Rosas could rely on the spirit of his troops, just as he couldn't rely on the countryside or on the city dwellers. Daily, conspiracies wove threads coming from diverse focuses, and the unanimity of that plan, because of the very profusion of its resources, made it almost impossible to carry out anything. Ultimately, the majority of its leaders and all the regular corps were implicated in a plot led by the young Colonel Maza, who, having Rosas's fate in his hands for four months, lost precious time in communicating with Montevideo and revealing his plans. Finally, what had to happen happened: the conspiracy was discovered and Maza died, taking with him the secret of the complicity of a majority of the leaders who today continue in Rosas's service. Later on, despite this opposition, a mass uprising in the countryside broke out, led by Colonel Cramer, Castelli, and hundreds of peaceful landowners. But even this revolution came out badly, and seven hundred gauchos went through the anguish of abandoning their Pampas and their horses and embarking to go on elsewhere with the war. The Unitarists had control of all these immense elements, but their prejudices didn't allow them to take advantage of them. Before all else, they asked that those new forces of the present be subordinated to old names of the past. They could only conceive of a revolution under the orders of Soler, Alvear, Lavalle, or another reputation of classic glory; and meanwhile, what had happened in France in 1830 happened in Buenos Aires, namely, that all the generals wanted a revolution but they lacked heart and guts. They were worn out, like those hundreds of French generals who, in those July days, reaped the results of the courage of a people whom they had refused to help triumph with their own swords. We lacked the young men of the École Polytechnique, who could have led a city, which needed only a voice to lead it into the streets to break up the Mazorca and evict the cannibal.[7] These attempts failing, the Mazorca took on the easy task of flooding the streets with blood and chilling the spirits of those who survived, through criminal acts.

The French government finally sent M. Mackau to end the blockade "at all costs," and with M. Mackau's knowledge of American issues a treaty was signed that left to Rosas's mercy the army headed by Lavalle, which at that very moment was reaching the outskirts of Buenos Aires, thus ruining the profound sympathy of the Argentines for France, and of the French for the Argentines; because Franco-Argentine fraternity was cemented on a profound affection from people to people, and on such commonality of interests and ideas, that even today, after the madness of French policy, in three years it has not been able to peel from the walls of Montevideo the heroic foreigners who have clung to them, like the last entrenchment of European civilization left within the limits of the Plata.[8] Perhaps this blindness of the French ministers has been useful to the Argentine Republic. A disenchantment of this kind was needed to get us to know France as power, France as government, very different from that ideal and beautiful, generous and cosmopolitan France that has shed so much blood for liberty and that since 1810 has made us love its books, its philosophers, its journals. The policy drawn for the French government by all its publicists—Considerant, Damiron, and others sympathetic to progress, liberty, and civilization—could have been put into effect in the Río de la Plata area without rocking Louis Philippe's throne, which they have tried to mint with the slavery of Italy, Poland, and Belgium; and France would have reaped, in influence and sympathy, what it did not get from its poor Mackau treaty, which consolidated a power by nature hostile to those European interests that can prosper in America only under the protection of civilizing and free institutions. I say the same thing with respect to England, whose policy in the Río de la Plata would cause suspicion that it has the secret design of allowing to weaken, under Rosas's despotism, the spirit that rejected it in 1806, so as to try its luck again when a European war or another great event leaves the land abandoned to pillage; and then to add this possession to the concessions necessary for a treaty to be signed, like the definitive one of Vienna in which Malta, Capetown, and other territories were ceded to it and acquired by the stroke of a pen. For how would it be possible to conceive otherwise, unless the ignorance of the American situation in which Europeans live was the excuse? How would it be possible to conceive, I mean, that England, so careful in shaping markets for its manufactured goods, has been watching calmly for twenty years, if not secretly contributing to the annihilation of all civilizing principles on the banks of the Plata, and, every time it has seen him sway, has given a hand to help the ignorant little tyrant who has put a bar across the river, so that Europe may not penetrate into the heart of America to take out the riches it encloses, wasted by our lack of skill? Why tolerate the implacable enemy of the "foreigners," who, with their immigration under the wing of a government sympathetic to Europeans and protective of individual security, in these last twenty years would have populated the coasts of our immense rivers and accomplished the same wonders that have been consummated in less time on the banks of the Mississippi? Does England want consumers, no matter what the government of a country may be? But what are six hundred thousand poor gauchos without industry and without needs going to consume under a government that, by extinguishing European customs and tastes, necessarily decreases the consumption of European products? Are we to believe that England does not recognize its interests in America to such a degree? Has it wanted to use its powerful hand so that a state like the one engendered in the north will not rise up in South America? What an illusion! That state will rise up despite them, although every year they may cut off its shoots, because the greatness of the state is in the grassy Pampas, in the tropical products of the north, and in the great system of navigable rivers whose aorta is the Plata. In any case, we Spaniards are neither navigators nor industrious men, and Europe will provide us for long centuries with her wares in exchange for our raw materials, and they and we will win in the exchange. Europe will put the oar in our hands and will tow us upstream until we have acquired a taste for navigation.

It has been repeated in all the European press, by Rosas's order, that he is the only one capable of governing the semibarbarous peoples of America. I pity not so much America, so deeply offended, as I do the poor hands that have let themselves be led to print those words. It is very curious that the only man capable of governing would be the one who hasn't been able to obtain a day of rest, and who, after having destroyed, debased, and bloodied his homeland, finds that at a time when he had planned to reap the triumph of so many crimes, he is entangled with three American states, Uruguay, Paraguay, and Brazil, and that Chile and Bolivia, with which he has all the outward signs of a state of war, are still there at his rear guard. Because, for all the precautions that the government of Chile may take so as not to incur the ill will of the monster, ill will is there in the intimate way of being of both peoples, in the institutions that rule them, the diverse tendencies of their policies. To know what Rosas wants from Chile, it is enough to look at the state Constitution, and there you have the war. Surrender the Constitution to him, either directly or indirectly, and peace will follow, that is, you will be conquered for the "American" government.

Europe, which for ten years has been distancing itself from contact with the Argentine Republic, today sees itself summoned by Brazil so that it may protect that country against the distress caused by proximity to Rosas. Will it not answer this call? It will answer later, fear not; it will answer when the Republic itself comes out of the daze in which it has been left by the thousands of murders that have terrified it, because murders do not constitute a state; it will answer when Uruguay and Paraguay ask that the treaty made between the lion and the lamb be respected; it will answer when half of South America finds itself disrupted by the madness brought on by the subversion of all principles of morality and justice. The Argentine Republic today is organized into a war machine that cannot stop acting without overturning the power that has absorbed all social interests. Having ended in the interior, the war has now gone abroad. Ten years ago Uruguay did not suspect that it would have to deal with Rosas; Paraguay did not imagine it five years ago; Brazil did not fear it two years ago; Chile still does not suspect it; Bolivia would see it as ridiculous; but it will come, because of the nature of things, because this does not depend on the will of peoples or governments, but rather on the conditions inherent to any social phase. Those who expect that the same man will first be the scourge of their people and then the healer of their woes; the destroyer of institutions that are sanctioned by civilized humanity and then the organizer of society, know very little history. God does not proceed that way, one man, one era for each phase, for each revolution, for each advance.

It is not my aim to trace the history of this reign of terror that lasts from 1832 to 1845, a circumstance that makes it unique in the history of the world. The details of all its frightful excesses do not enter into the plan of my work. The history of human misfortune and of the excesses to which a man can surrender himself when he enjoys unbridled power will swell with horrible, strange facts from Buenos Aires. I have only wished to depict the origins of this government, and to tie them to the causes, characters, customs, and national features that, even from 1810, were fighting to get ahead and take control of society. I have wished, besides this, to show the results and the consequences brought about by that frightful subversion of all the principles upon which human societies rest. There is a vacuum in the Rosas government that for now I cannot fathom, but that has been hidden up to this point by the vertigo that has made society go mad. Rosas does not administer; he does not govern, in the official sense of the word. Closed up for months in his house, without letting anyone see him, he alone runs the war, the intrigues, the espionage, the Mazorca, all the diverse mechanisms of his dark policy; anything that is not of use for the war, anything that is not detrimental to his enemies, is not part of his government, does not enter into his administration.

But do not imagine that Rosas hasn't succeeded in making the Republic he tears to pieces go forward; no, he is a great and powerful instrument of Providence, which accomplishes everything important for the future of our homeland. Let us see why. Before him and before Quiroga, federalist spirit existed in the provinces, in the cities, in the Federalists, and in the Unitarists themselves. He extinguished it, and organized for his own benefit the unitarist system that Rivadavia wanted for the benefit of all. Today, all those measly caudillos of the interior—degraded, debased—tremble with fear of displeasing him and do not take a breath without his consent. The Unitarists' idea has been carried out; only the tyrant is unneeded. The day that a good government is established, it will find local resistance conquered and everything in place for the union.

The civil war has taken Buenos Aires natives to the interior and provincial inhabitants from their own provinces to others. People have met each other, studied each other, and gotten closer to each other than the tyrant would have wished; that is the reason for his care in taking away mail service, in breaking off correspondence, and in keeping everyone under watch. A union is intimate.

Before, two diverse societies existed: the cities and the countryside. The countryside having taken over the cities, the gauchos have become citizens and have sympathized with the cause of the cities. With the depopulation of its old centers—La Rioja, San Luis, Santa Fe, and Entre Ríos—the *montonera* has disappeared, and today the gauchos of the first three run around the Llanos and the Pampas, supporting Rosas's enemies. Does Rosas abhor foreigners? Foreigners take sides in favor of American civilization, and for three years they mocked his power in Montevideo and showed the whole Republic that Rosas is not invincible and that he can still be fought. Corrientes rearmed itself, and under the orders of the most able and most European general the Republic has, it is now preparing to begin the struggle in good form, because all the past errors are more lessons for the future. What Corrientes has done, all the provinces must do sooner or later, because their life and their future depend on it.

Did he deprive his fellow citizens of all their rights and strip them of all guarantees? Very well: not being able to do the same with foreigners, the latter are the only ones who walk safely in Buenos Aires. Every contract that a native son needs to sign he puts under the signature of a foreigner, and there is no society, there is no business in which foreigners do not take part. And so rights and guarantees do exist in Buenos Aires—under the most horrible despotism. "What a good servant this Irishman seems to be!" someone passing through Buenos Aires said to the man's employer. "Yes," the latter replied, "that's why I have taken him on: because I am assured of not being spied on by my servant, and because he signs all my contracts. Here, only these servants have safe lives and property."

Did the gauchos, the common people, and the *compadritos* elevate him? Well, he will extinguish them, his armies will devour them. Today there is no milkman, servant, baker, peon, farmhand, or cattle herder who is not German, English, Basque, Italian, or Spanish, because so many men have been consumed in ten years, so much human flesh is needed by Americanism, that in the end the American population gets used up, all going into the regiments that grapeshot thins out from sunup to sundown. There is no corps today on the Montevideo front that still has left one soldier and two officers of those who formed it from the start. The Argentine population is disappearing, and the foreign one takes its place amid the cries of the Mazorca and the *Gaceta*: Death to the foreigners! Just as unity is attained by crying: Death to the unitarists! Just as the federation has died crying: Long live the federation!

Does Rosas not wish the rivers to be navigated? Very well: Paraguay takes up arms so that it will be permitted to navigate them freely. It joins with Rosas's enemies, with Uruguay, England, and France, who all want free traffic to be allowed so as to exploit the immense wealth of the heart of America. Bolivia will join this movement, like it or not, and Santa Fe, Córdoba, Entre Ríos, Corrientes, Jujuy, Salta, and Tucumán will second it when they understand that all their interests, all their future greatness depend on these rivers on whose banks today they sleep rather than live, taking away and bringing in the wealth of commerce that today only Rosas exploits with the port, whose possession gives him millions to the impoverishment of the provinces. The issue of free navigation of the rivers that flow into the Plata is today at once a European, American, and Argentine issue, and because of it Rosas has war abroad and at home until he falls and the rivers are freely navigated. In this way, what was not attained from the Unitarists who gave importance to navigation of the rivers is attained today because of the stupidity of the gaucho from the Pampas.

Has Rosas persecuted public education and harassed and closed the schools, the university, and expelled the Jesuits?

It doesn't matter: the schools of France, Chile, Brazil, North America, England, and even Spain count hundreds of Argentine students in their bosom. They will later return, to form in their homeland the institutions they see shining in all those free states, and will put their shoulders into bringing down the semibarbarous tyrant. Does he have a mortal antipathy to the European powers? Very well, the European powers need to be well armed and strong in the Río de la Plata, and while Chile and the other free states of America have only a consul and a foreign warship on their shores, Buenos Aires has to host second-rate envoys and foreign squadrons guarding their interests and containing the excesses of the untamed, unbridled steed who is the head of state.

Does he castrate, cut to pieces, slit the throats of his enemies, to end the war with just one blow and one battle? Very well: by now he has given twenty battles, has killed twenty thousand men, has covered the whole Republic with blood and frightful crimes, has depopulated the country and the city to swell out his followers, and after ten years of triumph, his precarious position is the same. If his armies do not take Montevideo, he succumbs. If they take it, he still has General Paz with fresh armies; still has a virgin Paraguay, still has the empire of Brazil, still has Chile and Bolivia, which will finally explode; still has Europe, which will restrain him; still has, in the end, ten years of war, of depopulation and poverty for the Republic, or else to succumb; there is no solution. Will he triumph? But all his followers will have perished, and another population and other men will refill the vacuum they leave. The emigrants will return to reap the fruits of their triumph.

Has he chained the press and put a gag on thinking, so that it will not discuss the homeland's interests, so that it will not instruct or illuminate, so that it will not reveal the horrendous crimes he has committed and that no one wants to believe, since they are so frightful and unprecedented? Fool! What have you done? The cries you want to choke by cutting the throat, so that the voice will escape through the wound and not get to the lips, resound today around the world. The presses of Europe and America keep calling you the execrable Nero, the brutal tyrant. All your crimes have been recounted, your victims find partisans and sympathy everywhere, and vengeful cries reach right to your ears. Today all the European press discusses Argentine interests as if they were their own, and Argentina's name, to your dishonor, is on the lips of all civilized peoples. Today the discussion in the press is everywhere, and to counter your infamous *Gaceta* with the truth, there are a hundred newspapers that from Paris and London, from Brazil and Chile, from Montevideo and Bolivia, fight you and publish your evils. You have attained the fame to which you aspired, without a doubt; but in the misery of exile, in the obscurity of private life, those you have proscribed would not change a single hour of their idleness for the hours that give you your frightful celebrity, for the stabbing you get from all sides, for the reproaches you bring upon yourself for having done so much useless evil. The American, the enemy of the Europeans, condemned to cry in French, in English, and in Castilian: Death to the foreigners! Death to the unitarists! Hah! Is it you, wretch, who knows you are dying, and swears in the languages of those foreigners, and in the press, which is the weapon of those unitarists? What American state has seen itself condemned, like Rosas, to compose its official excuses in three languages, so as to respond to the press of all nations, American and European, at the same time! But where can your infamous diatribes go where the execrable motto:

Death to the savage, disgusting, filthy unitarists! does not reveal the bloody and pagan hand that writes them?

So in this way, what would have been an obscure discussion, of interest only to the Argentine Republic, is now one for all America and Europe. It is an issue for the Christian world.

Has Rosas persecuted politicians, writers, and men of letters? Then look at what has happened. The political doctrines that nourished the Unitarists up to 1829 were incomplete and insufficient for establishing a government and freedom; the Pampas stirred, and that was enough to make their edifice, based on sand, fall to the ground. This inexperience and lack of practical ideas were remedied by Rosas, in the minds of all, with the cruel and instructive lessons that his frightful despotism gave them. New generations have come up, educated in that practical school, who would know how to cut off the avenues through which unbridled geniuses like Rosas's might one day threaten to overflow again. The words tyranny, despotism, so discredited in the press because of the abuse to which they are put, in the Argentine Republic have a precise meaning, awaken in the mind a painful memory; they make bleed, when pronounced, all the wounds they have made in fifteen years of frightful remembrance. His red ribbon, with which he has taken terror and the idea of slaughter into the very heart of his vassals today, will later on serve as a national curiosity that we will show to those who visit our shores from remote countries.

The studious youths whom Rosas has persecuted have spread out all over America, examining its diverse customs, penetrating the intimate life of its peoples, studying its governments, and seeing the mechanisms that in some places maintain order without detriment to liberty and progress, noting in others the obstacles that oppose good organization. Some have traveled in Europe, studying law and government; others have resided in Brazil, some in Bolivia, some in Chile, and then some others have covered half of Europe and half of America. They bring an immense treasure of practical knowledge, of experience and valuable data, that one day they will put at the service of the homeland, which will gather in its bosom those thousands of exiles who today are disseminated throughout the world, waiting for the hour to come for the fall of an absurd, insupportable government that has not yet ceded to the impulse of the many forces that must, of necessity, bring its destruction.

And as for literature, today the Argentine Republic is a thousand times richer than it ever was in writers able to depict an American state. If, after all I have shown, any doubt were left that the current struggle of the Argentine Republic is one only of civilization and barbarism, proof enough would be that not one writer, one poet of the many that young nation possesses, is on Rosas's side. Montevideo has witnessed for three consecutive years the literary jousts of May 25, a day on which scores of poets, inspired by passion for the homeland, have challenged one another for laurels.[9] Why has poetry abandoned Rosas? Why does the soil of Buenos Aires, in other times so fertile in songs and poems, today not even produce rhapsodies? There exist abroad four or five associations of writers who have undertaken a compilation of data to write the history of the Republic, so full of events, and the pile of materials they have gathered from all points in America is truly amazing: manuscripts, printed matter, documents, old chronicles, diaries, travelogues, etc. Europe one day will be amazed when such rich materials come to public light and swell the voluminous collection, of which Angelis has not published more than a small portion.[10]

How much, then, those Argentine people will reap on the day, now not so remote, when spilled blood drowns the tyrant! How many lessons! How much acquired experience! Our political education is consummated! All the social issues aired—federation, unity, freedom of religion, immigration, navigation of the rivers, political authority, liberty, tyranny—everything has been said between us, everything has cost us torrents of blood. A wish for authority is in all hearts, at the same time that Rosas, with his atrocities, has deeply inculcated the need to contain the arbitrariness of power. Now all that remains for us to do is what he has not done and repair what he has destroyed.

Because he, in fifteen years, has not taken one administrative measure to favor domestic commerce and the nascent industry of our provinces, the people will devote themselves assiduously to the development of their means of wealth, their routes of communication, and the new government will consecrate itself to reestablishing mail service and securing the roads that nature opens all throughout the Republic.

Because for fifteen years he has refused to secure the southern and northern borders by means of a line of forts, since this work and this good, done for the Republic, would give him no advantage at all over his enemies, the new government will situate a permanent army in the south and will secure territories to establish military colonies, which in fifty years will be flourishing cities and provinces.

Because he has persecuted European influence and been hostile to foreign immigration, the new government will establish large associations to begin settlements and to distribute them along fertile territories on the banks of the immense rivers; and in twenty years, what has happened in North America in the same amount of time will happen here: cities, provinces, and states have been raised in deserts where, not long before, herds of wild bison grazed. Because today the Argentine Republic finds itself in the same situation as the Roman senate, which by decree ordered that five hundred cities be raised at once, and the cities rose at its call.

Because he has placed an insurmountable barrier to the free navigation of our inland rivers, the new government will promote a preference for river navigation. Thousands of ships will go upriver to extract the riches that today have neither value nor an outlet, all the way to Bolivia and Paraguay, enriching along the way Jujuy, Tucumán and Salta, Corrientes, Entre Ríos and Santa Fe, which will turn into rich and beautiful cities like Montevideo, like Buenos Aires. Because he has squandered the huge income of the port of Buenos Aires, and for fifteen years has spent the forty million pesos it produces on carrying out his madness, the port will be declared national property, so that its income will be devoted to promoting the good of the whole Republic, which has a right to that port to which it is a tributary.

Because he has destroyed the schools and taken funding away from them, the new government will organize public education throughout the Republic, with adequate funds and with a special ministry, as in Europe, as in Chile, Bolivia, and all civilized countries; because knowledge is wealth, and a people that vegetates in ignorance is poor and barbarous, like those of the coast of Africa, or the savages of our Pampas.

Because he has put the press in chains, not permitting any newspapers other than those he has designated to vomit blood, threats, and demands for death, the new government will extend throughout the

Republic the benefit of the press, and we will see a teeming of textbooks and publications dedicated to industry, literature, the arts, and all the workings of the mind.

Because he has persecuted to death all enlightened men, allowing only his whim, his madness, and his thirst for blood to govern, the new government will surround itself with all the great men the Republic possesses, who today are spread all over the world, and with the combination of all those lights will do good for everyone in general. Intelligence, talent, and knowledge will be called upon again to direct public destiny, as in all civilized countries.

Because he has destroyed the guarantees that among Christian peoples assure citizens their life and property, the new government will re-establish representative laws, and will assure forever the rights of every man not to be disturbed in the free exercise of his intellectual faculties and his activity.

Because he has made crime, murder, castration, and the cutting of throats a system of government; because he has developed all the evil instincts of human nature so as to create his accomplices and partisans, the new government will make justice, the accepted law of civilized peoples, the means for correcting public crimes, and will work to stimulate the noble and virtuous passions that God has put in the heart of man for his happiness on earth, making them the steps by which one may ascend and influence public affairs.

Because he has profaned the altars, putting his infamous portrait on them, because he has cut the throats of priests, mistreated them, or made them leave their homeland, the new government will give religious observance the dignity it deserves, and will raise religion and its ministers to the level necessary for them to moralize the people.

Because he has cried "Death to the savage unitarists!" for fifteen years, making people believe that a government has the right to kill those who do not think as it does, branding a whole nation with a slogan and a ribbon so that it will be believed that the one who wears the brand thinks as they order him with a whip to think, the new government will respect diverse opinions, because opinions are not deeds or crimes, and because God has given us reason that distinguishes us from beasts, free to judge according to our own free will.

Because he has been provoking quarrels continually with neighboring and European governments; because he has deprived us of commerce with Chile, has bloodied Uruguay, incurred the hatred of Brazil, brought upon himself a French blockade, taunts from the North American navy, harassment from that of England, and gotten himself into a labyrinth of interminable wars and reclamations that will only end in the depopulation of the Republic and the death of all his partisans, the new government, friend of European powers, congenial to all American peoples, will untie at one blow this tangle of foreign relations, and will establish tranquillity at home and abroad, giving each his rights, and marching down the same routes of conciliation and order by which all other cultured peoples march.

Such is the task we have yet to realize in the Argentine Republic. It may be that so many good results will not be obtained right away, and that after so radical a subversion as the one Rosas has carried out, it may still take a year or more of wavering to get society back into its true balance. But, with the fall of that monster, we will at least start down the road leading to such a beautiful future, rather than getting further and further away every day under his disastrous impulse, and moving backward by giant steps into barbarism, demoralization, and poverty. Peru, no doubt, suffers the effects of its internal upheavals, but still its sons have not left for decades by the thousands, to wander through neighboring countries; no monster has risen up who surrounds himself with bodies, suffocates all spontaneity and all virtuous feeling. What the Argentine Republic needs above all, and what Rosas will never give, because it is no longer his to give, is that the lives, the property of men, not hang on an indiscreetly pronounced word, on the whim of the ruler. Given these two bases, security of life and of property, the form of government, the political organization of the state, will come from time, events, circumstances. There is probably no people in America with less faith in a written pact, in a constitution, than the Argentines. Illusions are gone now; the Constitution of the Republic will be made imperceptibly, from within, without anyone having proposed it. Unitarist, federalist, or both, it must emerge from consummated deeds.

Nor do I think it impossible that upon Rosas's fall order will immediately follow. As great as it may seem from a distance, the demoralization that Rosas has engendered is not so great. The crimes which the Republic has witnessed have been official ones, mandated by the government; no one has been castrated, persecuted, or had his throat cut without the express order to do so. Besides, the people always perform reactively; the state of distress and alarm in which Rosas has had them for fifteen years will necessarily be followed by calm. Because so many and such horrible crimes have been committed, the people and the government will flee from committing even one, so that the ominous words

Mazorca! Rosas! will not be buzzing in their ears like vengeful furies. Because the exaggerated pretensions of liberty that the Unitarists entertained have brought such calamitous results, from now on politicians will be prudent in their proposals, parties measured in their demands. Besides, to believe that a people can become criminal, and that the lost men who murder when there is a tyrant who impels them to do so are at base evil, is to know very little about human nature. Everything depends on the prejudices that are dominant at certain moments, and the man who today sates himself on blood, because of fanaticism, was yesterday an innocent follower and tomorrow will be a good citizen— once the excitation that induced him to crime disappears. When the French nation fell in 1793 into the hands of those implacable terrorists, more than a million and a half French people were tired of blood and crimes, and after the fall of Robespierre and the Terror, only sixty of the best-known evil men had to be sacrificed along with him to return France to its customs of tameness and morality, and the same men who had perpetrated such horrors were later useful and moral citizens. Even in Rosas's partisans, in the *mazorqueros* themselves, underneath the criminal exterior there are virtues that one day should be rewarded. Thousands of lives have been saved by the warnings that the *mazorqueros* secretly gave to the victims they had been commanded to immolate.

Independent of these general motives for morality that belong to the human species at all times and in all countries, the Argentine Republic has elements of order that many countries in the world lack. One of the obstacles that blocks the calming of tempers in convulsive countries is the difficulty of calling public attention to new objectives that will remove that attention from the vicious circle of thought in which it exists. The Argentine Republic, fortunately, has so much wealth to exploit, so much novelty with which to attract people's spirits after a government like that of Rosas, that it would be impossible to upset the calm necessary to arrive at new goals. When there is a cultured government concerned with the interests of the nation, how many enterprises, how much industrial movement! The pastoral peoples, busy propagating the merino sheep that produce millions and occupy thousands of men at every hour of the day; the provinces of San Juan and Mendoza, dedicated to raising silkworms, which, with government support and protection, within four years will lack enough workers for the agricultural and industrial tasks they require; the provinces of the north, devoted to the cultivation of sugarcane, of the indigo that is spontaneously produced; the river banks with free navigation that would give movement and life to the industries of the interior. Amid this movement, who will wage war? To achieve what? Only if there is a government as stupid as the present one, which treads on all these interests and instead of giving men work puts them in the army to wage war in Uruguay, Paraguay, Brazil, in sum, everywhere.

But the principal element of order and morality upon which the Argentine Republic relies today is the immigration of Europeans, who on their own, and in spite of the lack of security offered, crowd day by day into the Plata. If there were a government capable of directing their movement, this alone would be enough to cure in ten years, at most, all the homeland's wounds made by the bandits, from Facundo to Rosas, who have dominated it. I will show how. There emigrate annually from Europe at least half a million men per year, who, possessing industry and training, go out to seek their fortune and settle where they find land to own. Until 1840, these emigrants headed principally for North America, which has been covered with magnificent cities and filled with an immense population thanks to immigration. At times the mania to emigrate has been such that entire towns in Germany have been transported to North America, with their mayors, priests, schoolteachers, etc. But what has finally happened is that in the coastal cities, the increase in population has made life as difficult as in Europe, and the immigrants have found there the discomfort and misery they were fleeing. Since 1840, one can read notices in the North American newspapers warning of the problems that immigrants find, and the American consuls publish the same warnings in the newspapers of Germany, Switzerland, and Italy, so that no more will emigrate. In 1843, two ships loaded with men had to return to Europe with their load, and in 1844 the French government sent to Algeria twenty-one thousand Swiss who had been going, in vain, to North America.

That flow of immigrants that no longer finds advantages in the north has begun to sail the coast of America. Some head for Texas, others to Mexico, whose unhealthy coasts reject them; the immense littoral of Brazil does not offer them great advantages because of the work of black slaves that removes value from production. So they have to make landfall in the Río de la Plata, whose mild climate, fertile earth, and abundance of means for subsistence attracts and keeps them. Since 1836, thousands of immigrants began arriving in Montevideo, and while Rosas dispersed the native population of the Republic with his atrocities, Montevideo grew in one year to become a flourishing and rich city, more beautiful than Buenos Aires and fuller with movement and commerce. Now that Rosas has taken destruction to Montevideo, because that damned genius was born only to destroy, the immigrants crowd into Buenos Aires and take the place of the population the monster has killed daily in the armies, and already this year he proposed to the Assembly that the Basques be snared to replace his decimated troops.

The day, then, that a new government directs toward goals useful to the nation the millions that today are spent waging disastrous and useless wars and paying criminals, the day that throughout Europe it is known that the horrible monster who today desolates the Republic and daily shouts "Death to the foreigners!" has disappeared—that day an industrious European immigration will head en masse to the Río de la Plata. The new government will take charge of distributing it through the provinces; the engineers of the Republic will draw up, in all the suitable places, plans for cities and towns that will be constructed to house it, and fertile plots of land will be adjudicated to it; and in ten years all the river banks will be covered with cities, and the Republic will double its population with active, moral, and industrious inhabitants. These are not chimeras; it is enough to want this, and for there to be a less brutal government than the present one, to achieve it.

In 1835, 500,650 souls emigrated to North America. Why wouldn't one hundred thousand per year emigrate to the Argentine Republic, if the horrible fame of Rosas weren't threatening them? Very well then: one hundred thousand per year would make in ten years a million industrious Europeans disseminated throughout the Republic, teaching us to work, exploiting new riches, and enriching the country with their property; and with a million civilized men, civil war is impossible, because those who would desire it would be fewer. The Scottish colony Rivadavia founded in southern Buenos Aires is the evidence that proves this: it has suffered from the war but has never taken part in it, and no German gaucho has abandoned his work, his dairy, or his cheese making to go running around the Pampas.

I believe I have demonstrated that the revolution in the Argentine Republic is now finished, and that only the existence of the execrable tyrant it engendered blocks it from beginning, this very day, an uninterrupted career of progress that some American peoples could very soon be envying. The struggle of the countryside with the cities has ended; hatred for Rosas has reunited these two elements. The old Federalists and the old Unitarists, like the new generation, have been persecuted by him and have united. Ultimately, his very brutality and unbridledness have led him to commit the Republic to a foreign war in which Paraguay, Uruguay, and Brazil would necessarily make him succumb, if Europe itself were not obligated to come collapse that scaffolding of bodies and blood that supports him. Those who still entertain biases against foreigners can answer this question: when an outlaw, a maniac, or a frenzied madman takes power over the government of a people, should all other governments tolerate him and let him destroy as he pleases, murder without pity, and keep all the neighboring countries in a commotion for ten years?

But the remedy will not come to us only from abroad. Providence has granted that, as the bloody drama of our revolution reaches its outcome, the party defeated so many times and a people so downtrodden find themselves with weapons in their hands and the ability to make the victims' moans be heard. The heroic province of Corrientes today has six thousand veterans that by now should have begun a campaign under the orders of the victor of La Tablada, Oncativo, and Caaguazú, the *boleado*, one-armed Paz, as Rosas calls him. How many times this furious man, who has sacrificed so many thousands of victims uselessly, must have bit and bloodied his lips in rage, recalling that he held prisoner for ten years and did not kill that same one-armed *boleado* who today prepares to punish his crimes! Providence must have wanted to give him this torment of damnation, making him the jailer and guardian of the one who was destined from on High to avenge the Republic, humanity, and justice.

May God protect your arms, honored General Paz! If you save the Republic, there will never have been a glory like yours! If you succumb, no curse will follow you to the grave! The people will join your cause, or later they will deplore their blindness and their debasement!

Glossary of Historical Names

ALCORTA, DIEGO (1801–42): Physician, teacher, and legislator during the Rosas period.

ALDAO, FRANCISCO (1787–1829): Independence fighter and caudillo. Enlisted with San Martín and crossed the Andes with Las Heras. Defeated by Quiroga in 1820, he rejoined San Martín and Bolívar.

ALDAO, JOSÉ (1788–1829): Independence fighter and caudillo brother of Francisco and José Félix.

ALDAO, JOSÉ FÉLIX (1775–1845): Independence fighter and caudillo. An ordained priest, he became a soldier in San Martín's army, eventually reaching the grade of colonel when he entered Lima. Originally a liberal, he became a federalist fighting on the side of Quiroga. Governor of Mendoza and supporter of Rosas.

ALSINA, ADOLFO (1829–77): Argentine statesman who fled as a child with his family to Montevideo due to persecution by Rosas. Returned after Rosas fell, working in the foreign ministry of the provisional government and holding several other posts.

ALSINA, VALENTÍN (1802–69): Argentine statesman and jurist. Father of Adolfo Alsina. Took part in Lavalle's revolution of 1828 and fought against Rosas in Montevideo. Governor of Buenos Aires after the fall of Rosas (1852).

ALVARADO, RUDECINDO (1792–1872): Independence fighter. Fought with Díaz Vélez and Belgrano and was part of San Martín's Andean army. Governor of Mendoza and Salta. Exiled by Rosas, but returned later and became war minister after Rosas's defeat.

ALVEAR, CARLOS MARÍA DE (1789–1852): Soldier and diplomat and one of the initiators of the Wars of Independence. Chief of the army of Buenos Aires and later of the army of the siege of Montevideo. Named general in chief of the army of Peru but was opposed by the other generals and returned to Buenos Aires. Was minister of war in the Lavalle administration and plenipotentiary minister under Rosas. He died in the United States in his post as Argentine representative.

ANCHORENA, TOMÁS MANUEL DE (1783–1847): Argentine Federalist and functionary. Secretary to Belgrano in Peru. Escaped to Montevideo after the triumph of Lavalle. Foreign minister under Rosas. One of Argentina's biggest landowners, from a powerful *porteño* family.

ARENGREEN, JUAN (?–1831): Swedish soldier. Fought in the Argentine army against Brazil (1827). Fought with Paz in 1828 and with Lamadrid against Quiroga in 1831.

ARTIGAS, JOSÉ GERVASIO (1764–1850): Uruguayan general and independence hero. Caudillo of the independence. As a federalist he was protector of the Banda Oriental. Fought against the Portuguese (1817) and was forced to retreat to Paraguay, where he lived in exile until his death.

BALCARCE, RAMÓN GONZÁLEZ (1773–1836): Military leader and independence fighter. Fought the English, 1806–7. Fought with Belgrano and participated in the Battle of Tucumán. Served as minister of war under Dorrego and later under Rosas. Elected governor of Buenos Aires 1832 but was ousted by Rosas supporters.

BARCALA, LORENZO (1795–1835): Argentine soldier and son of African slaves. Fought against Brazil and in the independence movement. Was with Paz in 1829 in Córdoba and passed over to Lamadrid. Taken prisoner by Quiroga but spared. Tried to topple Aldao in 1835 and was executed.

BÁRCENA, MANUEL DE LA (?–1846): Fought on the side of Bustos and was taken prisoner by Paz but escaped to join Quiroga. Fought against Lavalle and Lamadrid. Joined the army of Rosas and then that of Oribe in 1841. Died in the siege of Montevideo.

BARRIOS, IGNACIO (1785–1867): Independence fighter. Fought in the Banda Oriental. Served with Benavides, Soriano, Soler, Rondeau, and Artigas. Marched with San Martín to Peru. Joined Lavalleja and served under President Rivera.

BELGRANO, MANUEL (1770–1820): Colonial royal official, hero of the independence, and Argentine general. Member of the first governing junta. Fought against the English, 1806–7. Directed the unsuccessful Paraguay campaign (1811) and defeated the Spaniards at Tucumán (1812) and Salta (1813).

BENAVIDES, NAZARIO (1805–58): Caudillo from San Juan. Joined Quiroga in 1829. Fought with Felipe Aldao in the desert (1833). Executed Barcala in 1835. Fought on various occasions against the unitarists. Governor of San Juan. Fought on the side of Rosas against Urquiza but later passed over to Urquiza's side. Imprisoned and murdered in 1858.

BENTHAM, JEREMY (1748–1832): English philosopher and economist. Chief proponent of utilitarianism. Thought that every man should seek what he saw as his own advantage without hindrance, his credo being "The greatest happiness for the greatest number." Friend of Rivadavia.

BOLÍVAR, SIMÓN (1783–1830): Venezuelan general and statesman known as the Liberator. Best-known figure of the Latin American independence movement. Liberator of Venezuela and Colombia. Met with San Martín in Guayaquil, where the latter renounced power in favor of Bolívar. Entered Lima in 1823 and ended Spanish domination at the Battle of Junín (1824). Disillusioned at the eventual separation of what had been Gran Colombia, he renounced power in 1830 and died that same year.

BRIZUELA, TOMÁS (?–1841): Figure in the civil wars from La Rioja. Fought against Lamadrid. Former colleague of Quiroga. Took power in La Rioja allied to Rosas, but pronounced against him in 1840. Led the coalition of the north against Rosas until his death in 1841.

BUSTOS, JUAN BATISTA (1779–1830): Large landowner from Córdoba province. Fought against the English, 1806–7. Independence fighter in Peru. Overthrown as governor of Córdoba by Paz, he joined Quiroga at the Battle of La Tablada (1829).

CARRIL, SALVADOR MARÍA DEL (1798–1883): Jurist and statesman. As governor of San Juan he undertook a construction campaign and reforms following the Rivadavia model. Minister of finance under Rivadavia. Served as one of the chief advisers to Lavalle after Dorrego was elected governor. Went into exile at the defeat of Lavalle and returned with him to fight Rosas in 1839.

CASANOVA, SIXTO (1802–52): Independence fighter who served under Güemes. Was taken prisoner several times in the Wars of Independence. After 1824 he fought the Indians under Lavalle. As a colonel in 1835 he headed the investigation of the assassination of Quiroga. He captured Santos Pérez, who later escaped. Casanova sided with Lamadrid and the Unitarists but later changed over to the side of Oribe.

CASTELLI, JUAN JOSÉ (1764–1812): One of the initiators of the Wars of Independence and a friend of Belgrano. Was the spokesman of the first governing junta and brought the revolution to the interior of the country. He began the revolutionary propaganda in Bolivia but was tricked by a royalist general and was defeated. On his return to Buenos Aires he was tried and died in 1812.

CASTRO BARROS, PEDRO IGNACIO DE (1777–1849): Argentine priest, patriot, and writer; signer of the Declaration of Independence. Rector of the University of Córdoba, delegate to the congress of Tucumán, and friend of General Paz. An extremely religious man, he opposed the reforms of Carril and Rivadavia. When Paz was captured in 1831, he went into a ten-year exile in Uruguay and spent his remaining years in Chile.

CERNADAS, JUAN JOSÉ (?–1865): Jurist in Buenos Aires who was active in Dorrego's Federalist party. Emigrated to Montevideo during the Rosas regime and attacked the dictator through his writing.

CHENAUT, INDALECIO (1808–71): Colonel of the armies of the Republic. Served under Lavalle and Paz. Jailed as a unitarist after the defeat of Paz, he rejoined him in 1833.

COLINA, BERNARDO JOSÉ ANTONIO DE LA (1759–?): Priest and doctor of theology in Buenos Aires. Voted for independence in 1810. Continued working for independence and helped to establish the public library.

COLOMBRES, JOSÉ EUSEBIO (1778–1859): Priest and supporter of the independence movement. Best known as the organizer and founder of the Argentine sugar industry.

CONSTANT, BENJAMIN (1767–1830): Franco-Swiss novelist and political writer. *Adolphe* (1816) is considered a forerunner of the modern psychological novel.

CRAMER, AMBROSIO (1792–1839): Independence fighter. Organized a battalion and crossed the Andes with the Army of the Andes. Returned to Buenos Aires and assisted Belgrano in Tucumán. Died fighting against Rosas.

CULLEN, DOMINGO (1791–1839): Counselor and brother-in-law of Estanislao López. Became governor of Santa Fe after López died, but was not recognized by Rosas. Executed by Rosas after Ibarra surrendered him.

DÁVILA, NICOLÁS (1786–1876): Independence fighter in the Andes with San Martín. Governor of La Rioja, 1820–23.

DÍAZ VÉLEZ, EUSTAQUIO (1790–1856): Independence fighter. Fought the English before the independence and under Belgrano in the Battle of Tucumán. He later replaced Balcarce as interim governor of Buenos Aires. He supported the revolution of the south in 1839 and was taken prisoner. He eventually emigrated to Montevideo and returned after the fall of Rosas.

DORREGO, MANUEL (1787–1829): Argentine independence fighter and participant in the civil wars. Fought under Belgrano in the Army of the North. Opposed the directorate and was exiled in 1817. Governor of Buenos Aires (1820 and 1827). Leader of the Buenos Aires Federalists. His recognition of Uruguayan independence sparked a revolt led by Lavalle. Dorrego and Rosas opposed Lavalle but were defeated. Dorrego was captured and executed by Lavalle.

ECHEVERRÍA, ESTEBAN (1805–51): Argentine romantic poet and writer. His story *El matadero* (1840) is an indictment of the brutality of the Rosas regime.

FERRÉ, PEDRO (1788–1867): Political figure and governor of Corrientes. Federalist who fought against Rosas. Exiled to Brazil. Later returned and became a senator.

FRANCIA, JOSÉ GASPAR RODRÍGUEZ (1766–1840): Paraguayan dictator. Was the supreme and unquestioned authority in Paraguay for nearly thirty years.

FUNES, GREGORIO (1749–1829): Churchman, statesman, and historian. After completing his studies in Spain he became dean of the cathedral of Córdoba and rector of the university (1808). Became spokesman for the interior provinces in the Buenos Aires junta. Joined liberal churchmen in support of Rivadavia's ecclesiastical reforms.

GAMBOA, MARCELO (1793–1861): Jurist. Defended the Reinafé brothers in their trial for the assassination of Quiroga.

GARCÍA, BALDOMERO (1799–1870): Jurist. Wrote the manifesto of the Santa Fe convention of 1829. Plenipotentiary minister to Chile in 1844. Member of the Supreme Court in 1854. His visit to Chile stimulated Sarmiento to write *Facundo*.

GARCÍA, MARTÍN (1801–73): Doctor and professor of medicine after the reorganization of the university which took place after Rosas.

GARCÍA ZÚÑIGA, VICTORIO (1777–1834): Patriot elected deputy in 1820. Presided over the provincial legislature of Buenos Aires in 1827.

GODOY CRUZ, TOMÁS (1791–1852): Patriot and legislator, signer of the Declaration of Independence. Established Argentina's first gunpowder factory. He had close contact with San Martín. Governor of Tucumán, 1820–22 and 1830. Emigrated to Chile after Quiroga's invasion of 1831.

GÜEMES, MARTÍN MIGUEL DE (1785–1821): Argentine general and caudillo from Salta, hero of the independence. Fought the English, 1806–7. Fought in Peru in Balcarce's army, and took part in the siege of Montevideo. Known as the caudillo of the gauchos, he was border captain, governor of the province, and liaison between the province and the nation.

GUIDO, TOMÁS (1788–1866): Independence fighter. Field adjunct to San Martín, whom he accompanied to Peru where he was named general, and military and political chief of Lima. Collaborated in the independence with Bolívar and Sucre. Known as an excellent orator and writer.

GUIZOT, FRANÇOIS (1787–1874): French statesman and historian, was first minister to King Louis Philippe from 1840 to 1848. Guizot was elected to the Chamber of Deputies in January 1830, and when the revolution of 1830 forced King Charles X to abdicate, he joined other opposition deputies in bringing Louis Philippe to the throne. In the 1830s he served in several ministries; his most notable achievement in this period was drafting and winning parliamentary approval of the School Law of 1833, the founding statute of the French public primary education system. As a historian Guizot won widespread acclaim.

GUTIÉRREZ, CELDONIO (1804–80): Independence fighter, caudillo, and governor of Tucumán. A Rosas supporter, he was active in suppressing the Unitarists. Known for his reforms and reorganization and public works campaign.

HEREDIA, ALEJANDRO (1788–1838): Governor of Salta and Tucumán and leader in the northern provinces in the 1830s. Commander of the Argentine forces against the confederation of the Andes. Murdered in 1838.

HUIDOBRO, JOSÉ RUIZ (1802–42): Military commander under Quiroga. Purged by Rosas but later reinstated in the Federalist forces.

IBARRA, JUAN FELIPE (1787–1851): Military leader and caudillo of Santiago del Estero. Federalist. Fought in Upper Peru and in the Battle of Tucumán. When Santiago del Estero declared its independence from Tucumán, Ibarra became the first governor (1820). He controlled the province until his death. A supporter of Rosas, he maintained friendly relations with Quiroga.

LAMADRID, GREGORIO ARÁOZ DE (1795–1857): General, active in the independence and in the period of civil wars. Served in the north during the independence and became an aide to San Martín in Tucumán. Fought with the directorate against the caudillos López and Ramírez. Intervened in the civil war in Tucumán on the unitarist side. Was defeated and wounded by Quiroga at Tala and went into exile. He returned to Buenos Aires in 1828 and joined the unitarist forces of Paz. He took over on Paz's capture and retired to Tucumán. Defeated again by Quiroga in 1831, he went into exile in Bolivia. On his return seven years later he became a leading general under Rosas. He later changed sides and joined Lavalle's overthrow attempt, but they were defeated by the Federalist armies. Lamadrid fled to Chile, where he was aided by Sarmiento. He later participated in the defeat of Rosas at Caseros as commander in Urquiza's army.

LAPRIDA, FRANCISCO NARCISO DE (1786–1829): Signer of the Declaration of Independence. Close friend of San Martín, he helped build the Army of the Andes. Was a supporter of Rivadavia's centralist constitution. He was killed fighting Quiroga in Mendoza.

LAS HERAS, JUAN GREGORIO DE (1780–1866): Independence hero, assistant to San Martín, political figure. Fought against the English, 1806–7, and in the independence wars in Chile. Resigned his command and returned to Buenos Aires in 1823; became governor in 1824, continuing the reforms of Rivadavia. After leaving public life in 1826, he emigrated to Chile.

LAVALLE, JUAN GALO (1797–1841): Argentine general, hero of the independence and of the war with Brazil, anti-Federalist leader. Participated with San Martín in Chile and Peru and fought in Brazil at the Battle of Ituzaingó (1827), under Alvear. Ordered the execution of Dorrego after leading a revolt against his government, and was governor of Buenos Aires (1828). Defeated by Rosas and López in 1829. Signed a pact with Rosas but was forced into exile due to growing sentiment that Dorrego's execution had been an act of treason.

LAVALLEJA, JUAN ANTONIO (1786–1853): Uruguayan general who later emigrated to Argentina to serve under Rosas. Leader of the expedition of the Treinta y Tres Orientales (Famous thirty-three), who crossed into Uruguay and recruited a large force to fight Brazil. Succeeded Alvear as commander of the army, causing a revolt. Later led the Uruguayan "Blancos" (the party supporting Oribe, whose opposition was the "Colorados" party) and was supported by Rosas. Took part in the siege of Montevideo (1843–51).

LINIERS, SANTIAGO DE (1753–1810): Named viceroy of the Río de la Plata in 1807, after defending Buenos Aires against the English invasion in 1806. Opposed the 1810 May revolution and was executed in Córdoba.

LOMÉNIE DE BRIENNE, ETIENNE-CHARLES DE (1727–94): French cleric and minister of finance when the French Revolution broke out. He resigned in 1788. Made cardinal the same year and died in prison during the Reign of Terror.

LÓPEZ, ESTANISLAO (1786–1838): Independence fighter, caudillo of Santa Fe, participant on the federalist side in the civil wars. Fought the British in 1806 and as one of Belgrano's border fighters in 1810. Led his men in a revolt against Buenos Aires in 1816. He returned to Santa Fe where he ruled until his death, fighting in various alliances against Buenos Aires control. The directorate was brought down in 1820 with López's victory over Rondeau at Cepeda. Joined forces with Rosas to defeat Lavalle after the fall of Dorrego. As governor of Santa Fe, he participated in the Federal Pact of 1831. After the defeat of Paz at the hands of Quiroga, troubled relations between López and Quiroga allowed Rosas to assume national leadership.

MANSILLA, LUCIO NORBERTO (1792–1871): Hero of the independence and the Anglo-French blockade. Fought against the English, 1806–7, in the Banda Oriental, and in the Army of the Andes. Acted as liaison between Buenos Aires and the interior caudillos. Helped Ramírez against Artigas and then wrested Entre Ríos from Ramírez's successor. He supported national organization and Rivadavia. Fought in the war with Brazil. Married Juan Manuel Rosas's sister. Father of Lucio V. Mansilla, author of the 1870 essay *Una excursión a los indios ranqueles* (A visit to the Ranquel Indians).

MARTÍNEZ, ENRIQUE (1789–1870): Hero of the Wars of Independence. Fought the English (1806–7), against Montevideo (1814), and joined the Army of the Andes (1815). Fought in the liberation of Chile and in Peru under San Martín and Bolívar. Was Balcarce's minister of war and led a group of landowners opposing Rosas. Fled to Montevideo in 1835 and there supported Rivera.

MAZA, MANUEL VICENTE (1779–1839): Jurist and political figure. Was a close associate of Rosas, playing an active role in his government. Was the judge at the trial which convicted the Reinafé brothers of Quiroga's murder. Assassinated while writing to Rosas to ask for clemency for his son RAMÓN (1810–39), who was accused of a conspiracy against Rosas and shot a few hours after his father's murder. The assassination set off a wave of terror by the Mazorca.

MICHELET, JULES (1798–1874): French nationalist historian. Best known for his *Histoire de France* (1833–67).

MONTESQUIEU, CHARLES-LOUIS (1689–1755): French political philosopher. Major work, *L'Esprit de lois* (The spirit of the laws; 1750).

MONVOISIN, AUGUST RAIMOND QUINSAC (1790–1870): French romantic painter and Orientalist. Painted works inspired by South America, where he lived for an extended period in the 1840s and 1850s.

MURAT, JOACHIM (1767–1815): French cavalry officer who became marshal of France and king of Naples under Napoleon Bonaparte. Was deposed and later executed.

ORIBE, MANUEL (1772–1857): Uruguayan general and president of the Republic, 1835–38. Fought with Artigas in the Uruguayan independence and supported Rivera. Went to Buenos Aires when the Brazilians took over

Montevideo and returned to Uruguay as one of the Treinta y Tres Orientales (Famous thirty-three), with Lavalleja. Joined the Argentines under Alvear and fought at Ituzaingó. Minister of war under Rivera. Lost a power struggle to Rivera and fled to Argentina, where Rosas recognized him as the legitimate president. Rivera then declared war on Argentina. Fought in Rosas's forces under López and was later made commander in chief. Defeated Rivera in 1842 and began the siege of Montevideo, which he retook in 1851.

ORO, DOMINGO DE (1800–1879): Held several diplomatic posts with Rivadavia, Mansilla, Alvear, and Díaz-Vélez. Fought with the San Juan forces against Quiroga. Emigrated to Chile where he published pamphlets against Rosas. Returned to Buenos Aires after Rosas's fall.

ORO, FRAY JUSTO SANTA MARÍA DE (1772–1836): Cleric and politician from San Juan, he was exiled from 1818 to 1828. He later became bishop of San Juan.

ORTIZ, JOSÉ SANTOS (1785–1835): Governor of San Luis in 1821. Joined Quiroga in his fight against Paz. In 1834 he accompanied Quiroga on his mission to Santiago del Estero and was murdered along with Quiroga on their way back.

PAUNERO, WENCESLAO (1805–71): Military commander. Began his career against Brazil. Fought with Paz against Quiroga and with Lamadrid. Went into exile in Bolivia following the defeat of Paz's army. Accompanied Mitre and Sarmiento to join Urquiza and fought at Caseros.

PAZ, JOSÉ MARÍA (1791–1854): Argentine general who fought under Belgrano in the Wars of Independence, losing an arm. Joined the fight against Brazil as army commander in 1827. Declared himself a unitarist against Rosas and Buenos Aires. Paz defeated Rosas at Córdoba and Quiroga at La Tablada and Oncativo. Established the League of the Interior but was captured by López's Federalist forces. Paz escaped in 1840 and fought against Rosas in Corrientes where he defeated General Echagüe. Directed the defense of Montevideo against Oribe (1843).

PEREIRA, SIMÓN (1801–52): Argentine manufacturer. Supplied the army, amassing a fortune. Rosas paid him with land which later became quite valuable.

PÉREZ, SANTOS (?–1837): Caudillo from Córdoba. Executed in 1837 for Quiroga's murder.

PRINGLES, JUAN PASCUAL (1795–1831): Independence fighter assassinated by Quiroga's men. Fought on the Unitarist side with Paz at the battles of Oncativo and La Tablada.

QUIROGA, JUAN FACUNDO (1788–1835): Member of a landowning family in La Rioja. Began his military and political rise in 1820. Opposed the Unitarist policies of Rivadavia. Won decisive battles and became the most powerful caudillo of the interior provinces. Murdered at Barranca-Yaco.

RAUCH, FREDERICK (1790–1829): Soldier and Indian fighter. Prussian colonel who fought with Napoleon. Accused by Rosas of being a unitarist.

RAWSON, GUILLERMO (1821–90): Physician. San Juan provincial legislator, he opposed Sarmiento and organized a failed rebellion against Governor Benavides.

RAYNAL, GUILLAUME-THOMAS (1713–96): French writer and prorevolutionary propagandist. Wrote a six-volume history of the European colonies in India and America.

REINAFÉ, FRANCISCO ISIDORO (1796–1840), GUILLERMO (1799–1837), JOSÉ ANTONIO (1798–1835), and JOSÉ VICENTE (1782–1837): Brothers from Córdoba who were caudillos and politicians implicated in the murder of Quiroga. José Vicente and Guillermo were tried and hanged in Buenos Aires for this crime.

RIVADAVIA, BERNARDINO (1780–1845): Argentine politician and Unitarist. First president of the Republic. Fought against the English and was secretary of the first triumvirate (1811). Known for his ecclesiastical reforms. Tried to organize Argentina along the lines of early nineteenth-century liberal ideology. Resigned when unable to end the war with Brazil (1827) and faced with opposition from all fronts. He then retired to Spain and lived the rest of his life as an expatriate.

RIVERA, FRUCTUOSO (1788–1854): Uruguayan general, independence fighter, and president of Uruguay (1830–34 and 1839–43). Took part in the first and second sieges of Montevideo (1811–12). Elected president of Uruguay in 1830, turning the government over to Oribe at the end of his four-year term. Immediately, clashes arose from political differences, the party supporting Oribe being known as the Blancos and the opposition as the Colorados. Rosas supported Oribe. Rivera became president again in 1839; Rosas supported Oribe as the legitimate president. Rivera declared war against Rosas. Rivera was defeated in 1845 and exiled to Brazil. In 1853 he was named to a triumvirate to form a new government, but died before he could undertake his assignment.

RONDEAU, JOSÉ (1773–1844): Argentine general in the independence movement. Fought against the English and was sent to London as a prisoner. From there went to Spain where he fought against Napoleon. Returned to Montevideo in 1810 and joined the May revolution. Supreme director of the United Provinces of Rio de la Plata. Served as Dorrego's war minister and as provisional governor of Uruguay (1828–30).

ROSAS, JUAN MANUEL DE (1793–1877): Argentine military and political leader. Caudillo, landowner, military officer, and dictatorial governor of Buenos Aires (1835–52). Began his career as a successful landowner whose first official action was to protect the southern frontier from Indian attacks under the directorate. Joined Rodríguez's army to fight with Dorrego against the opposition to the Buenos Aires government. Returned to his frontier *estancia* and became a Federalist violently opposed to Rivadavia and the Unitarists. Joined with López to defeat Lavalle after Dorrego's fall. Rosas became governor of Buenos Aires in 1829 and held that post with dictatorial powers until 1852, when his forces were defeated at the Battle of

Caseros. He was taken by the British to England, where he lived until his death.

ROSAS, MANUELITA (1817–98): Daughter of Juan Manuel de Rosas. After her mother's death, she acted as official hostess for her father. Accompanied him in exile to England.

SAN MARTÍN, JOSÉ DE (1778–1850): With Bolívar, one of the two greatest figures of the South American independence movement. Served in the Spanish army against Napoleon before returning to Buenos Aires in 1812. Created the Army of the Andes and liberated Chile and Peru. Sent reinforcements to Sucre and Bolívar, helping win victory at Pichincha. Steadfastly refused to involve his army in civil wars or other disputes not directly involved with independence. Renounced his title as protector after a meeting in Guayaquil with Bolívar.

SAY, JEAN BATISTE (1767–1832): French economist known for Say's Law of Markets, which states that supply creates its own demand. This law obviates the need for governmental regulation of the economy.

SCOTT, SIR WALTER (1771–1832): Scottish writer, poet, historian, and novelist known for historical novels. *Ivanhoe* (1819) is perhaps his most famous work.

SISMONDI, JEAN-CHARLES-LEONARD SIMONDE DE (1773–1842): Swiss economist and historian. At first an advocate of laissez-faire and a follower of Adam Smith, he later wrote of the risks involved in this theory.

SMITH, ADAM (1723–90): Scottish philosopher and economist known for the first major work on laissez-faire economics, *An Inquiry into the Nature and Causes of the Wealth of Nations* (1776).

SOLER, MIGUEL ESTANISLAO (1783–1849): General of the Army of the Andes and political figure. Began his career fighting the British and later held several posts in the independence, becoming a general in San Martín's army. Became active in Buenos Aires politics. Was one of three competing governors in 1820 but was defeated by López and Alvear. Was a general in the war against Brazil and later emigrated to Montevideo.

TALLIEN, JEAN-LAMBERT (1767–1820): French revolutionary and secretary of the Paris commune. Enemy of Robespierre and leader of the moderates, the Thermidorians.

TAMBERLAINE, OR TAMERLANE (1336–1405): Real name Timur. Central Asian conqueror who sought to restore the empire of Genghis Khan. His empire stretched from India to Turkey.

TEJEDOR, CARLOS (1817–1903): Jurist, statesman, and writer. Prominent anti-Rosas intellectual. Joined the Unitarist army of Lavalle and went into exile in Brazil and later Chile, where he was a close friend of Sarmiento. Returned to Buenos Aires after the fall of Rosas and became active in politics. Tejedor codified the penal code under Mitre and was minister of foreign affairs under Sarmiento.

THIERRY, JACQUES-NICOLAS (1795–1856): French figure well known as a romantic historian, liberal, and ardent supporter of the revolution of 1830.

TOCQUEVILLE, ALEXIS DE (1805–59): French historian and political theorist. Studied American democracy and the French Revolution. One of the foremost proponents of nineteenth-century liberalism. Major works: *De la Démocratie en Amerique* (Democracy in America; 1835–40) and *L'Ancien Régime et la Révolution* (The old regime and the Revolution; 1856).

TORQUEMADA, TÓMAS DE (1420–98): Spanish inquisitor general, and confessor and counselor to the Catholic kings Ferdinand and Isabel. Major figure in the Spanish Inquisition, under whose authority all Jews were expelled from Spain.

VARELAS, LOS: Prominent and talented family of writers, journalists, lawyers, and public figures. The first generation consists of three brothers: FLORENCIO (1807–48), writer and anti-Rosas journalist; JUAN CRUZ (1794–1839), one of Argentina's first national poets; RUFINO (1815–40), journalist. All three were Unitarists and eloquently anti-Rosas. The second generation consisted of Florencio's five sons, who collaborated on the family newspaper *La Tribuna*.

VÉLEZ SARSFIELD, DALMACIO (1800–1875): Cordoban jurist, statesman, author of the Argentine civil code. A Unitarist who supported Rivadavia, he ended his public career after Rivadavia's fall. He was consulted by Rosas as an expert on church-state relations. Later allied himself with Tejedor over the question of Buenos Aires autonomy. Was minister of finance under Mitre (1862–63) and minister of the interior under Sarmiento (1868–72).

VIAMONTE, JUAN JOSÉ (1774–1843): Military and political leader of the independence, governor of Buenos Aires several times on an interim basis. Was governor for one month in 1821, again for three months just before Rosas in 1829, and finally after Rosas refused reelection in 1832.

VIDELA CASTILLO, JOSÉ (1792–1832?): General who fought in Paz's army. Named governor of Mendoza in 1830. Defeated by Quiroga at Chacón in 1831.

VIGODET, GASPAR DE (?–1823): Last representative of Spanish power in the Río de la Plata area. As governor of Montevideo, surrendered the city in 1814.

VILLAFAÑE, JOSÉ BENITO (?–1831): Governor of La Rioja and ally of Quiroga.

VILLANUEVA, GENOVEVA (1814–90): Heroine of Mendoza province. She refused to wear the obligatory red ribbon signaling Federalist loyalty.

Translator's Notes

Author's Note

1. Sarmiento wrongly attributes this quotation to Hippolyte Fortoul; according to the critic Paul Verdevoye, it is most likely a misquoted phrase of Diderot ("On ne tue pas de coups de fusil aux idées"), used as the epigraph to a 1832 article by Charles Didier that Sarmiento would have read in the journal *Revue Encyclopédique*. For more information, see Sylvia Molloy, *At Face Value: Autobiographical Writing in Spanish America* (Cambridge: Cambridge University Press, 1991), pp. 30–32; Diana Sorensen Goodrich, *Facundo and the Construction of Argentine Culture* (Austin: University of Texas Press, 1996), pp. 83–85; and in Spanish, Nora Dottori and Silvia Zanetti's note 5 (p. 4) to the Biblioteca Ayacucho edition (Caracas, 1977) of *Facundo*. Sarmiento first gives the French quotation and then his Spanish translation. The English rendering of the Spanish is "Men can have their throats cut, but ideas cannot."

2. The *mazorqueros* were members of the paramilitary Mazorca, a highly disciplined group controlled by the Argentine dictator Juan Manuel de Rosas. As Sarmiento explains in later chapters of *Facundo,* the Mazorca executed victims by cutting their throats, or by beheading them with swords while riding by on horseback.

Introduction

1. "I ask from the historian a love of humanity and of liberty; his impartial justice should not be unfeeling. On the contrary, he must wish, he must hope, he must suffer or be made happy by that which he narrates." All translations by Kathleen Ross unless otherwise noted. Abel François Villemain's *Cours de littérature français* was published in 1828–29.

2. The reference here is to José Gaspar Rodríguez Francia, dictator of Paraguay between 1814 and 1840.

3. Sagunto and Numancia, Spanish towns located in Valencia and Soria, respectively, are famous for resisting terrible sieges during Spain's Roman era. The inhabitants of Numancia decided to perish rather than surrender, inspiring Miguel de Cervantes's play *Numancia*.

4. François Charette de la Contrie (1763–96) was a leader of the royalist counterrevolutionary forces in the Wars of the Vendée (1793–96). He commanded groups of *chouans*, peasant fighters who joined the royalist cause, as described in Balzac's novel *Les Chouans*.

5. The *montoneras* were troops of peasant militias on horseback.

6. The Prix Montyon is a prestigious medal awarded by the French Académie des Sciences.

Chapter I. Physical Aspect of the Argentine Republic

1. "The expanse of the Pampas is so huge, that to the north it is bordered by forests of palms, and to the south by eternal snows." According to Nora Dottori and Silvia Zanetti in their annotations of *Facundo* (Caracas: Biblioteca Ayacucho, 1977), p. 35n1, this text comes not from Sir Francis Bond Head (1793–1875), but from Humboldt's *Tableaux de la nature* (Paris, 1808), vol. 1, p. 21.

2. The South American *tigre*, misnamed by the conquering Spanish in the sixteenth century, is not a tiger at all, but a jaguar.

3. Arroyo del Medio is the natural border separating Buenos Aires and Santa Fe provinces.

4. The "interior" of the country refers to the interior provinces of Argentina, in contrast to the city of Buenos Aires on the coast, as Sarmiento has already made clear in this chapter. The "interior" is a term Sarmiento will use repeatedly throughout *Facundo*, as he sets up the dichotomy between city and province, civilization and barbarism.

5. In other words, Argentina; Sarmiento is writing from exile in Chile.

6. "The full moon in the East rose over the bluish bed of the flat banks of the Euphrates." Constantin-François Volney (1757–1820) was a noted French scholar who wrote on his travels in Egypt and Syria.

7. A *chicote* is a short whip.

8. "Dame, general, un chiripá." Sarmiento mixes Spanish with the *guaraní* term *chiripá*, an article of clothing typically worn by gauchos, consisting of a rough cloth drawn between the legs and held at the waist by a leather belt.

9. A *zambo* is a person of mixed Indian and African blood.

Chapter II. Argentine Originality and Characters

1. "Like the ocean, the steppe fills the soul with a feeling of infinity." Alexander von Humboldt published his *Voyage aux régions équinoxiales du Noveau Continent* in Paris in 1816.

2. The *pelota* (literally "ball"), improvised from a tough hide or saddle blanket, serves as a vehicle for pulling someone across a narrow river. *Batear,* according to Roberto Yahni in his edition of *Facundo* (Madrid: Cátedra, 1997), means "to baptize. In this case, to sprinkle brine over the meat" (p. 77n5).

3. This is the second ten-line stanza, or *décima,* of Esteban Echeverría's 1837 *La cautiva* (part 1, *El desierto*):

> Gira en vano, reconcentra
> su inmensidad, y no encuentra
> la vista en su vivo anhelo
> do fijar su fugaz vuelo,
> como el pájaro en la mar.
> Doquier, campo y heredades,
> del ave y bruto guaridas;
> doquier cielo y soledades
> de Dios sólo conocidas,
> que El sólo puede sondear.

4. The Spanish text reads:

> De las entrañas de América
> dos raudales se desatan:
> el Paraná, faz de perlas,
> y el Uruguay, faz de nácar.
>
> Los dos entre bosques corren,
> o entre floridas barrancas,
> como dos grandes espejos
> entre marcos de esmeraldas.
>
> Salúdanlos en su paso
> la melancólica pava,
> el picaflor y el jilguero,
> el zorzal y la torcaza.
>
> Como ante reyes se inclinan
> ante ellos seibos y palmas,
> y le arrojan flor de aire,
> aroma y flor de naranja;
>
> luego, en el Guazú se encuentran,
> y reuniendo sus aguas,
> mezclando nácar y perlas
> se derraman en el Plata.

Luis Domínguez (1819–98) was an Argentine poet and political figure exiled during the Rosas regime. He is best known for his poem *El ombú* (1843), which expresses romantic and nationalist sentiments similar to those of this poem.

5. A *vihuela* is a six-stringed, guitarlike instrument, somewhat larger than the four-stringed *guitarra*.

6. Mestizos are people of mixed white and indigenous blood.

7. *Cajetilla* is the slang Sarmiento uses.

8. The *majo* epitomizes the good looks and elegant style of the Spanish popular classes. The *compadrito* was a character typical of the Buenos Aires lower classes in the nineteenth and early twentieth centuries, celebrated in literature and in tango lyrics. The *compadrito,* as described by Jorge Luis Borges in his *Evaristo Carriego,* was a type of poor, single man known for his passionate temperament, ability with words, and attention to detail in dress. *Jaleo* and *cielito* are types of popular music, accompanied by singing and dancing. The South American *cielito* dates from colonial times; it has a repeated refrain of *cielo, cielito, cielo,* whence the name.

9. The *rastreador* is a tracker, *rastro* meaning "track."

10. The *baqueano* (or *baquiano*), a word of Haitian origin, is an expert, particularly one with knowledge of paths and roads. It also denotes the person who is a guide to paths and roads.

11. An *estancia* is a large cattle ranch.

12. Banda Oriental was a name for the Spanish territory to the east of the Uruguay River, comprised of the present-day Republic of Uruguay and several Brazilian provinces.

13. Sarmiento uses the English words *outlaw* and *squatter* here.

14. The "vices" are items such as tobacco, yerba mate, and liquor, obtained at the *pulpería* or country store, described further in chapter III.

15. According to Mary Mann's translation of *Facundo,* a *churriador* is a sheep-stealer (*Facundo: Or, Civilization and Barbarism,* trans. Mary Mann, introduction by Ilan Stavans [New York: Penguin Books, 1998], p. 42).

16. *De tapera en galpón,* that is, from poor one-family farms (*tapera*) to large ranches (*estancias*) with storehouses (*galpón*).

Chapter III. Association

1. "The Gaucho lives in deprivation, but freedom is his luxury. Proud of an unbounded independence, his sentiments, wild like his life, are nevertheless noble and good." The English general Francis Bond Head published his work *Rough Notes during Some Rapid Journeys across the Pampas and the Andes* in 1826.

2. "El Chacho" was General Angel Vicente Peñaloza (1796–1863). Sarmiento wrote a book about him (*Vida del Chacho,* 1863) after being accused of conspiring in his assassination.

3. Victor Hugo, cited by Sarmiento in Spanish. *Le Rhin: Lettres à un ami* (The Rhine: Letters to a friend) was published in 1842, following an 1840 trip through the Rhine Valley.

4. "*Guerra a cuchillo!*" literally means "War by knifeplay."

5. A *desgracia*, that is, a killing, as mentioned in chapter II.

6. Tomás de Zumalacárregui (1788–1835) was a Spanish Carlist general and antiliberalist. Francisco Javier Mina (1789–1817) was a Spanish revolutionist who fought against the French invasion. He later fled to Mexico, supported the movement for independence, and was ultimately tried and executed.

7. The *comandante de campaña:* a military authority named by the government, whose function was the recruitment of troops, often by force, into the army.

Chapter IV. The Revolution of 1810

1. "When the battle begins, the Tartar gives a terrible cry, advances, wounds, disappears, and returns like lightning." In his article "Los epígrafes y la elaboración del *Facundo*," the scholar Emilio Carilla identifies the purported source of this text as Hugo's *Le Rhin,* quoted by Sarmiento in chapter III. While Carilla goes on to say that neither quote actually comes from *Le Rhin,* he does not identify their true source (*Academia Argentina de Letras* 54 [1989]: 156–57).

2. That is, Rosas, as will be immediately made clear.

3. Sarmiento places the term *manea,* which I have translated as "hobble," in italics. "Straitjacket" is *enchalecar* in the original, literally, to enclose in a *chaleco* or leather vest. A *chaleco de fuerza* is a straitjacket.

4. Martín Yanzón, governor of San Juan, 1834–36.

Chapter V. Life of Juan Facundo Quiroga

1. "Moreover, these traits belong to the original character of humankind. The natural man, who has not yet learned to contain or disguise his passions, shows them in all their energy, giving himself over to all their impetuousness." Alix (Alexandre-Louis Félix, 1795–1868) published his three-volume *Précis de l'histoire de l'Empire Ottoman* in Paris in 1822–24.

2. *Travesía:* the distance or passage between two places. In nineteenth-century Argentina, the term came to mean certain provincial areas totally lacking in water or vegetation. *Chifles:* the horns of cattle, fitted with a wooden base at the wide end and a plugged hole at the point, used as a canteen for water.

3. The Argentine expression *cebado,* which I have translated as "ravening," also means fed or fattened, as livestock or cattle, and primed, as a gun.

4. The Llanos, literally "the Plains," are an area of La Rioja, as Sarmiento will explain in detail in chapter VI.

5. Monvoisin: French painter who visited Chile in 1842–43, on the invitation of the Chilean government. He painted there a portrait of the sultan of Egypt, Mehemet Ali.

6. Chacón was the place where Quiroga won a battle in 1831. José Benito Villafañe was a provincial governor and ally of Quiroga. His death will be treated further in chapter XI.

7. Arribeños was a regiment created in 1806 in response to the English invasion of Buenos Aires.

8. The Granaderos Cavalry was an army and cavalry organized by San Martín in 1816 and 1812, respectively.

9. Chacabuco and Maipú were sites of important battles in the Wars of Independence.

10. Note that this is my rendering of Sarmiento's Spanish translation of the epigraph, different from my translation directly from the French in note 1.

Chapter VI. La Rioja

1. Sarmiento cites this text in English, with the author's name misspelled. It is taken from the Right Reverend Michael Russell's *Palestine or the Holy Land* (New York: Harper and Brothers, 1832). The original quote ends "even mosses disappear, and a red burning hue succeeds to the whiteness of the rocks" (p. 31).

2. The Llanos, as noted earlier, are plains.

3. The Lautaro Lodge was an organization created in Buenos Aires in 1812 by a group that included San Martín, with the objective of American independence.

4. Matt. 24:2: "But he answered them, 'You see all these, do you not? Truly, I say to you, there will not be left here one stone upon another, that will not be thrown down'" (Revised Standard Version).

5. The reference is to April 13, 1835, when Rosas assumed power for the second time as governor of Buenos Aires province. The various titles and epithets of campaign commander, Hero of the Desert, governor of Buenos Aires, and Restorer are all ways in which Sarmiento makes reference to Rosas.

6. "Tithes" here refers to the tax each landowner paid the province in cattle. The custom was for the government to auction off these animals to the highest bidder in order to obtain cash revenue.

7. Another reference to Rosas.

8. Matt. 11:21: "Woe to you, Chorazin! woe to you, Bethsaida! for if the mighty works done in you had been done in Tyre and Sidon, they would have repented long ago in sackcloth and ashes. But I tell you, it should be more tolerable on the day of judgment for Tyre and Sidon than for you."

Chapter VII. Social Life (1825)

1. "The society of the Middle Ages was composed of the debris of a thousand other societies. All forms of liberty and servitude came together: the monarchical liberty of the king, the individual liberty of the priest, the privileged liberty of the cities, the representative liberty of the nation, Roman slavery, barbarian servitude, the servitude of escheatage." François-Auguste-René Chateaubriand (1768–1848), influential French romantic writer, wrote the well-known novels *Atala* and *René*.

2. These are the names of the men who were shot in 1810 when they resisted

the Buenos Aires revolutionary junta. *Clamor* means clamor, protest, a cry for vengeance.

3. The Girondists were a moderate political party of revolutionary France.

4. *Pelucones:* literally, "long-haired"; in other words, the Conservative party.

5. Natives of Buenos Aires are called *porteños,* that is, port-city dwellers.

Chapter VIII. Tests of Strength

1. A literal translation of Sarmiento's quote would read: "How long is the day! because tomorrow I want to gallop ten leagues over a field sown with corpses." The source of the quote reads: "Will it never be day? I will trot tomorrow a mile, and my way shall be pav'd with English faces" (*Henry V* III.vii).

2. Tyrtaeus of Sparta was a Greek poet of the late seventh century B.C.E., famous as a writer of patriotic elegiac poetry spurring Spartan soldiers to war.

3. "In the execution of judgment on criminals, so as to have the effect of inspiring terror and fear in the captives with their mighty presence."

4. "Hykso" refers to the shepherd kings of Egypt in the Second Intermediate Period (1759–1539 B.C.E.).

5. The word Sarmiento uses that I translate "hides" is *toldo,* a portable shelter used by indigenous peoples in the Pampas and Patagonia region.

Chapter IX. Society at War

1. "There enters a fourth element: the barbarians, the new hordes, who thrust themselves onto the old society with a complete freshness of manners, soul, and spirit, who have done nothing yet, who are ready to receive everything with all the aptitude of a most docile, naive ignorance." Jean-Louis Eugène Lerminier (1803–57) was a prominent liberal philosopher of law, university professor, and a journalist who published widely in the *Revue des Deux Mondes* and other journals.

2. The "Fort" refers to the government palace, the Casa Rosada.

3. This refers to the title given to Juan Manuel de Rosas.

4. Sarmiento possibly refers here to Louis Blanc (1811–82), French social theorist, who published his *Histoire de dix ans,* a history of France from 1830 to 1840, in 1841.

5. The French *Revue des Deux Mondes.* The article Sarmiento refers to was published in 1832, according to Dottori and Zanetti (p. 146, n. 12), and authored by Théodore Lacordaire.

6. Ituzaingó was a famous battle where General Paz fought against Brazil.

7. Sarmiento uses the word *boleado,* referring to the bringing down of horse and rider (or cattle) by entangling their legs with bolas, as described in chapter III. General Paz had indeed been captured in this manner by López's men in 1831; the word *boleado* implies an insult to his horsemanship, and by extension his masculinity, in the parlance of the gaucho. Sarmiento, of course, repeats the insult ironically.

8. *La Gaceta Mercantil* was the official newspaper of Rosas's government. It was published between 1823 and 1852.

9. That is, the Battles of La Tablada of June 22 and 25, 1829.

Chapter X. Society at War

1. "What are you looking for? If you wanted to see a collection of frightful evil and horrors, you have found it." Although Emilio Carilla ("Los epígrafes y la elaboración del *Facundo*," *Academia Argentina de Letras* 54 [1989]: 131–69) implies that he has identified the source of this quotation, he does not give it. I have been unable to confirm Shakespeare as the source.

2. The "Friar" was José Félix Aldao.

Chapter XI. Society at War

1. "A horse, a horse! my kingdom for a horse!" (*Richard III* V.iv).

2. This refers to the Battle of Cancha Rayada, where San Martín was defeated in 1820.

3. "Mediterranean" here means surrounded by dry land.

4. *Boleada,* or tangled up with the bolas.

Chapter XII. Society at War

1. "The inhabitants of Tucumán end their work days with pastoral gatherings, where in the shade of beautiful trees they improvise, to the sound of a rustic guitar, alternating songs of the kind that Virgil and Theocritus elaborated. Everything, down to the Greek first names, reminds the astonished traveler of ancient Arcadia." Conrad Malte-Brun (1775–1826) was a geographer and writer who settled in France after being exiled from his native Denmark in 1800. Most of his best-known work was written in French and published in France, including the *Précis de géographie universelle* (Universal geography), begun in 1810. According to Emilio Carilla ("Los epígrafes y la elaboración del *Facundo*," *Academia Argentina de Letras* 54 [1989]: 147), this quote, taken from the *Précis,* is actually a translation of a passage from the 1778 *Lazarillo de ciegos caminantes* (*El lazarillo:* A guide for inexperienced travelers), authored by Carrió de la Vandera (alias Concolorcorvo).

2. Captain Joseph Andrews published *Journey from Buenos Aires, through the Provinces of Cordova, Tucuman, and Salta, to Potosi, Undertaken on Behalf of the Chilian and Peruvian Mining Assn., 1825–26,* in 1827.

Chapter XIII. Barranca-Yaco!!!

1. Quoted by Sarmiento in Spanish, with the title in English. Cadwallader Colden (1688–1776), born in Ireland to Scottish parents, immigrated to Philadelphia in 1710 and settled in New York in 1718. He held the office of lieutenant governor of New York and published treatises in various fields, including medicine, botany, and philosophy. *The History of the Five Indian Nations Depending on the Province of New York in America* was originally published in London in 1727, but later enlarged, reprinted, and widely read. Emilio Carilla ("Los epígrafes del *Facundo*," *Academia Argentina de Letras* 54 [1989]: 147–49) notes Sarmiento's error in giving the title of the work as *History of Six Nations*. He also states his inability to find the exact quote cited in *Facundo* in Colden's work, and suggests that Sarmiento offers a synthesis of various paragraphs, perhaps translating into Spanish his own reading of the text in French translation. This, according to Carilla, resulted in Sarmiento's translation of what should logically be "Albany" as "Albania."

2. The "great river" referred to is the Río Negro.

3. The "sum of public power" will be further explained in chapter XIV.

4. The *lomos negros* were the moderate Federalists, who sought some understanding with the moderate Unitarists during Balcarce's government. The expression literally means "black backs."

5. The correct date is December 18, 1834.

Chapter XIV. Unitarist Government

1. Cited by Sarmiento in Spanish. Alphonse Marie Louis Prat de Lamartine (1790–1869), French poet, essayist, and diplomat, was a major figure in the development of poetry and romanticism in his country. Given Sarmiento's theme of comparing Argentina with the East, the source of this quote may be *Voyage en Orient* (A pilgrimage to the Holy Land; 1835), where Lamartine recorded impressions of his travels in the Near East. Lamartine was elected to public office in the 1830s; his 1831 *Politique rationnelle* (On rational policy) sets out his ideas of government.

2. The correct date is February 16, 1835.

3. As noted earlier, *cajetillas* is derogatory slang for "city slickers."

4. According to Roberto Yahni (*Facundo: Civilización y barbarie*, 3rd ed. [Madrid: Cátedra, 1997], p. 315n2), the Sociedad Popular comprised the Mazorca, Rosas's police and shock troops, and "a group of people from traditional society, followers of Rosas."

5. This phrase echoes the Gospels (Matt. 12:30 and Luke 11:23): "He who is not with me is against me."

6. The "highly placed official" was Baldomero García, plenipotentiary minister to Chile under Rosas's government at the time *Facundo* was written.

7. That is, Rosas's deceased wife.

8. In Spanish, *rosas y sangre,* with obvious reference to Sarmiento's topic of the Rosas dictatorship.

9. The Cabochiens, a popular Parisian faction, was indeed composed of members of the butchers' and skinners' guilds. In 1413 they violently seized power in Paris, and were later overthrown by the Armagnacs.

10. "Goths" (*godos*) refers to pro-Spanish Argentines during the Wars of Independence.

Chapter XV. Present and Future

1. "After having been a conqueror, after deploying himself completely, he gives out, he has used up his time, he himself is conquered; that day he leaves the face of the earth, since he has become useless to humanity." Victor Cousin (1792–1867), one of the preeminent French philosophers of his era, borrowed from Locke, Hegel, and others to form a school of eclectic thought on the stages of consciousness and spirituality. His principle publications include *Fragments philosophiques* (1826), *Du vrai, du beau, et du bien* (Of the true, the beautiful, and the good; 1836), and *Cours d'histoire de la philosophie moderne* (Course on the history of modern philosophy; 1841–46), along with later works on literature and history.

2. The Thermidorians were a moderate French faction whose 1794 coup defeated Robespierre.

3. The Colegio de Ciencias Morales existed between 1823 and 1830. Its purpose was to prepare young men from the city and the provinces for university study.

4. The Salón Literario of Buenos Aires, which began in 1837 and was suspended in early 1838, brought together notable intellectual figures to discuss cultural, economic, and political issues in weekly meetings.

5. This group was the Asociación de Mayo. The Carbonaria was a secret society formed in Italy in the early nineteenth century to advocate liberal ideals and political unification. Its members were called, collectively, the *carbonari.*

6. According to Roberto Yahni (*Facundo: Civilización y barbarie,* 3rd ed. [Madrid: Cátedra, 1997], p. 346n2), the Palabras Simbólicas, or "Symbolic Words," were written by Esteban Echeverría in 1838 as the basis for his later work, *Dogma socialista* (1846).

7. Sarmiento here refers to the French École Polytechnique, founded in 1794 during the French Revolution. He calls it, in Spanish, "la Escuela Politécnica."

8. The French blockade of Buenos Aires (1838–40) was ended when Baron Mackau was sent to formulate and sign a peace treaty with Rosas.

9. May 25 is the anniversary of the revolution.

10. Pedro de Angelis (1784–1859), a Neapolitan by birth, emigrated to Buenos Aires at the invitation of Rivadavia. He later came to be totally identified with Rosas's dictatorship—thus the scorn of Sarmiento's comment here. De Angelis published several volumes of documents relating to Argentina's history in his *Colección de obras y documentos relativos a la historia de las Provincias del Río de la Plata* (1835–37).

Index

Designer:	Nola Burger
Compositor:	G&S Typesetting, Inc.
Text:	10/13 Galliard
Display:	Galliard
Printer and binder:	Maple-Vail Manufacturing Group